Palgrave Studies in Cross-disciplinary Business Research, In Association with EuroMed Academy of Business

Reflecting the growing appetite for cross-disciplinary business research, this series aims to explore the prospects of bringing different business disciplines together in order to guide the exploration and exploitation of scholarly and executive knowledge. Each book in the series will examine a current and pressing theme and consist of a range of perspectives such as management, entrepreneurship, strategy and marketing in order to enhance and move our thinking forward on a particular topic.

Contextually the series reflects the increasing need for businesses to move past silo thinking and implement cross-functional and cross-disciplinary strategies. It acts to highlight and utilize the emergence of cross-disciplinary business knowledge and its strategic implications across economic sectors, geographic regions and organizational types.

Published in conjunction with the EuroMed Academy of Business, books will be published annually and incorporate new scientific research works developed specifically for the book or based on the best papers from their conferences. Over the last decade EuroMed have developed a cross- disciplinary academic community which comprises more than 30,000 students and scholars from all over the world.

Each submission is subject to a proposal review and a double blind peer review. For further information on Palgrave's peer review policy please visit this website: https://www.palgrave.com/gp/book-authors/your-career/early-career- researcher-hub/peer-review-process For information on how to submit a proposal for inclusion in this series please contact Liz Barlow: liz.barlow@palgrave.com.

For information on the book proposal process please visit this website: https://www.palgrave.com/gp/book-authors/publishing-guidelines/submit-a-proposal

Demetris Vrontis • Alkis Thrassou
Leonidas Efthymiou • Yaakov Weber
S. M. Riad Shams • Evangelos Tsoukatos
Editors

Business for Sustainability, Volume I

Strategic Avenues and Managerial Approaches

palgrave
macmillan

Editors
Demetris Vrontis
Department of Management, School of Business
University of Nicosia
Nicosia, Cyprus

Department of Management Studies, Adnan Kassar School of Business
Lebanese American University
Beirut, Lebanon

Leonidas Efthymiou
Department of Management, School of Business
University of Nicosia
Nicosia, Cyprus

S. M. Riad Shams
Newcastle Business School
Northumbria University
Newcastle upon Tyne, UK

Alkis Thrassou
GNOSIS Mediterranean Institute for Management Science, School of Business
University of Nicosia
Nicosia, Cyprus

Yaakov Weber
School of Business Administration, Research Unit
College of Management
Rishon LeZion, Israel

Evangelos Tsoukatos
Nicosia, Cyprus

ISSN 2523-8167 ISSN 2523-8175 (electronic)
Palgrave Studies in Cross-disciplinary Business Research, In Association with EuroMed Academy of Business
ISBN 978-3-031-37360-2 ISBN 978-3-031-37361-9 (eBook)
https://doi.org/10.1007/978-3-031-37361-9

This Palgrave Macmillan imprint is published by the registered company Springer Nature Switzerland AG.
The registered company address is: Gewerbestrasse 11, 6330 Cham, Switzerland

Paper in this product is recyclable.

Contents

Notes on Contributors

Elena Bruno is Associate Professor in Banking at the University of Pisa (Italy). She gained her doctorate in Business Administration from the University of Pisa. Her research interests focus on the areas of bank competition and performance; credit risk analysis; bank corporate governance, regulation, and supervision. Her research has been presented at national and international conferences and published in books and journals.

Sheshadri Chatterjee is a post-doctoral research scholar at Indian Institute of Technology Kharagpur, India. He has completed PhD from Indian Institute of Technology Delhi, India. He has work experience in different multinational organizations such as Microsoft Corporation, Hewlett Packard Company, IBM, and so on. Sheshadri has published research articles in several reputed journals such as *Government Information Quarterly*, *Information Technology & People*, *Journal of Digital Policy, Regulation and Governance*, and so on. Sheshadri is also a certified project management professional, PMP from Project Management Institute (PMI), USA, and completed PRINCE2, OGC, UK, and ITIL v3 UK.

Dimos Chatzinikolaou is a PhD candidate in the Democritus University of Thrace, Department of Economics, in the fields of competitiveness, business ecosystems, and industrial policy. He also contributes (from this capacity) to the same department as a research assistant in the courses and workshops coordinated by Dr Charis Vlados and assists as a non-editing teacher at the University of Nicosia. His specialization concerns business ecosystems, entrepreneurship, economic policy, and energy systems, based on more than 60 scientific papers published in peer-reviewed journals and conference proceedings. He is currently a researcher under contract in the European project ENIRISST (Intelligent Research Infrastructure for Shipping, Supply Chain, Transport and Logistics).

Ranjan Chaudhuri is a professor of Marketing at IIM Ranchi, Jharkhand, India. He was a Fulbright Fellow in the USA in 2012. Dr Chaudhuri also served as an associate professor at NITIE, Mumbai, Vinod Gupta School of Management, Indian Institute of Technology, Kharagpur, and at the Department of Management Studies, Indian Institute of Technology Delhi. Dr Chaudhuri has over eighteen years of industrial, teaching, and research experience. Dr Chaudhuri's teaching and research interests are in the areas of Business-to-Business Marketing, Global Marketing, and Retail Management.

Laura Corazza received a PhD degree in Business and Management from the University of Turin, Turin, Italy, in 2014. Currently, she is Researcher and Adjunct Professor at the Department of Management, University of Turin, and has also qualified as Associate Professor. She is the editor of the University of Turin's annual Sustainability Report and Editor-in-Chief of the Journal of Public Affairs. Her research has been published in books and peer-reviewed journals, including *The British Accounting Review, Accounting, Auditing and Accountability Journal, Journal of Business Research, IEEE Transaction on Engineering Management, Sustainability Accounting, Management and Policy Journal, Knowledge Management Research and Practice, Journal of Applied Accounting Research, Corporate Social Responsibility and Environmental Management,* and *Business Society and the Environment.* Her research interests include stakeholder engagement, sustainability accounting, and accountability in private, public, and social enterprise organizations.

Dario Cottafava, PhD in "Innovation for the Circular Economy", is currently PostDoc Researcher in "Accounting of socio-economic impacts in megaprojects" at the University of Turin. He is a multidisciplinary scholar, and his research focuses on the intersection of Circular Economy,

Open Data, and Sustainability. His works have been published in journals that include the *Journal of Business Research*, *Sustainability Accounting, Management and Policy Journal*, and *Environment, Development and Sustainability*.

Kate Daly is a head of Commissioning working within the Adults and Health Integrated Commissioning Team for Leeds City Council and has over 20 years of professional experience working in sustainability, project management, procurement, and commissioning fields for both the private and public sectors. She leads partnerships and commissioning arrangements for people experiencing health and homelessness issues, unpaid carers, older people in community services, and people with dementia. She has recently completed an MBA in Leadership and Management from Leeds Beckett University.

Nicola Davola graduated from Bocconi University in Economics and Management, Mastered in Auditing at Luiss Guido Carli University of Rome, and is currently a PhD student of Sport Management at IUSM of Rome. His main research interest is football and economics and applying management skills to the soccer sector. Nowadays, his particular focus is on gender gaps applied to female football.

Marlen Demetriou is Associate Professor at the School of Management, University of Nicosia. Her research interests are Business Ethics, Corporate Social Responsibility, and Cause Related Marketing. She has published different articles on CSR and Cause Related Marketing in International peer-reviewed and refereed journals and has presented her research at more than 65 international conferences. She is an active member of a number of charity organizations in Cyprus and an executive board member at the Cyprus Anti-Cancer Society. In 2006, she initiated a social partnership between the University of Nicosia and the Anti-Cancer Society in an effort to financially support the society in a continuous and well-coordinated effort with the active participation of students, faculty, and staff of the university.

Panagiotis E. Dimitropoulos is a faculty member of the Department of Sport Organization and Management, University of Peloponnese. He has a PhD in Economics from Hellenic Open University and an MA in

Banking and Finance from Bangor University. He has taught sport financial management and investments for several years at undergraduate and graduate levels. His research interests include sport finance and corporate accounting and financial analysis. He has published in international academic journals such as *European Sport Management Quarterly*, *International Journal of Sport Finance*, *International Journal of Sport Management and Marketing*, *British Accounting Review*, *Corporate Governance: An International Review*, *Journal of Economic Behavior and Organization*, *R&D Management*, and others.

Leonidas Efthymiou is Associate Professor in Organisation, Tourism and Hospitality Studies at the University of Nicosia, and adjunct faculty at Unicaf University. He previously worked at Intercollege, Pearson Education and the University of Leicester. He has also taught online for universities in Europe, Africa, and the United States. He also travels frequently to Africa, in his capacity as Instructional Designer. He has coedited and published several books, articles, media reports, policy papers, and encyclopaedia articles. His research output lies at the intersection of employment, digitization, and education. Leonidas received a number of awards, including the best PhD Thesis award, by the Academy of Management in 2011, Boston Massachusetts. He trained at the universities of Leicester (PhD, MSc), Derby (BA), and the Higher Hotel Institute Cyprus (Dip. Hons).

Aleksandra Figurek is a graduate of the Faculty of Economics of the University of Banja Luka (Republic of Srpska, B&H), finishing top of her class of 600+ students. She later obtained a Master's degree from the same university and a PhD thesis from the University of Novi Sad in Serbia. She developed her knowledge at various institutions in many European countries and was awarded for her achievements by the Government of the Republic of Srpska. Dr Figurek reached the rank of Associate Professor at the University of the Republic of Srpska and has been involved in several research projects, publishing also in scientific journals and books. She speaks Serbian, German, and English and is currently studying for her second PhD at the School of Business of the University of Nicosia, while also being a researcher for GNOSIS Mediterranean Institute for Management Science.

Silvia Gordano has a PhD in Business and Management, Department of Management, University of Turin. Her PhD thesis looks at mergers and acquisitions in the sustainable era. Her research interests cover topics at the intersection between corporate social responsibility and corporate reorganization.

Giuseppina Iacoviello is Associate Professor in Business Administration at the University of Pisa (Italy). She gained her doctorate in Finance and Banking from the University of Pisa and is Co-Coordinator of Subject Area Group of Business Administration in the CALOHex project (Measuring and Comparing Achievements of Learning Outcomes in Higher Education in Europe, KA3-Erasmus). She is also a member of International Institute of Informatics and Systemics and a reviewer for national and international journals. Her research interests include Financial Accounting, Information System, Strategic Planning and Control System, and Bank Performance.

Konstantinos Koronios is a postdoctoral researcher at the Department of Sports Organization and Management, University of Peloponnese. His research interests include Marketing, Business Administration, and Business Strategy. His field of expertise is Sport Marketing and Sponsorship. He holds the position of Communication Manager of the "Managing Sport" SIG of the European Academy of Management (EURAM).

Niki Kyriakidou is a senior academic in HRM and Organisational Behaviour and the Chartered Manager Degree Apprenticeship Programme Director at Leeds Business School. Niki leads the Equity, Diversity and Wellbeing Research Cluster at the Business School and the European and Mediterranean Business Institute (EMBRI) international HRM unit. Niki has extensive experience in European-funded research programmes, collaborating effectively with international academic, professional, and government institutions. She networks across Europe in various symposia and is also a senior fellow of the UK Higher Education Academy and the CIPD (Chartered Institute of Personnel and Development). Niki specializes in cross-cultural projects regarding strategic leadership, EDI (Equality, Diversity, Inclusion), workplace well-being, and employee engagement.

Mavillonio Maria Saveria is a PhD student in Economics at the University of Pisa, where she earned a Master's Degree (Hons) in Financial Markets and Finance, in October 2019. She started her PhD program in November 2021 and her main research interest is the combination of statistical and econometric techniques with modern ML algorithms in the context of macroeconomics. Moreover, she won a fellowship at the Sant' Anna School of Advanced Studies, Pisa, on the application of statistical analysis to health care data.

Avros Morphitis is Lecturer in Marketing and the Director of the Department of Continuing Education (DCE) at the American University of Cyprus (AUCY). He holds a BA degree in Business Innovation and Enterprise from Oxford Brookes University, an LLM in International trade and commercial law from Oxford Brookes University, and a PhD in Sustainability Marketing and Corporate Social Responsibility from Leeds Beckett University. He has considerable industrial experience, both in sales and marketing. He was actively working with international beverage brands in a brand manager position and as a regional sales supervisor. He was also working as a research assistant in a business consultancy firm with a considerable clientele list. His research interests include Sustainability Marketing, Branding, and the use of Digital Marketing and Social Media as communication and promotional tools.

Lior Naamati-Schneider, PhD, is Head of the health program, at the Management department at Hadassah Academic College and a senior lecturer and researcher in healthcare management, medical education, and healthcare policy and marketing. She has multi-disciplinary training in management, service organizations, and healthcare system and holds a PhD (2013) in Marketing and Managing Health Organizations from the School of Public Health, Hadassah Jerusalem, MSc in business administration, combined marketing (MBA) and science track, the School of Business Administration, the Hebrew University of Jerusalem, BSc Medical Sciences, the Department of Medical Sciences, the Hebrew University—Hadassah School of Medicine, Ein Kerem, Jerusalem, and a teaching certificate, with over 25 years of curriculum and lesson plan development in the fields of Public Health, Health Systems in Israel, Patient–Therapist Relationship, Quality in the Health System, Marketing Management and Business Administration.

Ioanna Papasolomou is a professor in the Department of Marketing (School of Business Administration) at the University of Nicosia in Cyprus. She is a certified Chartered Marketer at the UK Chartered Institute of Marketing. Professor Papasolomou obtained her MBA, MPhil, and PhD from the University of Keele (United Kingdom). She has acted as a conference host for international conferences and contributed papers to academic journals such as the *Journal of Marketing Management, Marketing Intelligence and Planning, Journal of Brand Management, Journal of Product and Brand Management, Journal of Business Research*, and the *Journal of Marketing Communications*. She has written chapters and case studies for academic books. She is also a member of the editorial or reviewer boards for several academic journals, such as the *Journal of Marketing Communications, International Journal of Corporate Communications, International Journal of Social Responsibility*, and *Euro Mediterranean Journal in Business*.

Fiorella Pia Salvatore, PhD, is a researcher in Business Economics at the Department of Economics, University of Foggia. Her research interests include several topics in accounting, public organization, healthcare organization and management, and managerial issues of public health. She analyses health managerial data and the performance of the healthcare sector. She develops quantitative and qualitative analysis in different types of studies and also deepens the managerial aspects of telemedicine systems. She is the author of several works published in scientific journals such as the *British Food Journal, BMC Health Services Research, International Journal of Organizational Analysis, International Journal of Business Research and Management*, and so on. She is a member of academic associations of national and international repute, a member of several editorial boards, a reviewer of journals of international rank, and a guest editor of special issues.

Elena I. Semenova, Doctor of Economics, Professor, specialist in the management and marketing in agribusiness, editor of the scientific journal *Economics of Agriculture of Russia*, author of 8 textbooks for higher education. She is the head of the branch of the Federal State Budgetary Scientific Institution "Federal Research Center of Agrarian Economy and Social Development of Rural Areas—All Russian Research Institute of

Agricultural Economics". She completed an internship at the University of Edinburgh. For more than 20 years, she worked as dean and then vice-rector at the Russian State Agrarian Correspondence University. She has a scientific school, and has trained 6 doctors of economic sciences and 25 candidates of economic sciences.

S. M. Riad Shams is a senior lecturer in marketing and PhD Programme Leader at the Newcastle Business School, Northumbria University. He has extensive academic and industry experience. Riad has co-authored a core textbook, *Marketing Management: Past, Present and Future* (which is currently in its 4th edition) for postgraduate and advanced undergraduate teaching. He delivered an invited keynote at the SIDREA International Conference in January 2020, which was sponsored by the Sapienza University of Rome. He has published seventeen books and contributed articles to top-tier marketing and business journals. Riad obtained second place in the Cambridge-Kent-Czinkota Competition for Excellence in International Business Research—2019, and entered into the Kent Business School's Honours Board. He received the Emerald Literati Award (Outstanding Paper) in 2019, the Emerald Literati Award (Outstanding Reviewer) in 2018, and the EuroMed Research Award in 2014. As per Google Scholar, Riad is the fifth most-cited author in social business research and sixth most-cited author in sustainable marketing research.

Caroline S. L. Tan is an associate professor of Marketing at the Graduate School of Business Sciences, University of Tsukuba, Japan. Her main research interests include consumer and fan psychology and behaviour, social media marketing, and sustainability. Her work has appeared in journals such as *Young Consumers* and *Journal of Vacation Marketing*. She has also authored case studies that are available on *SAGE Business Cases*, *Ivey Publishing*, *The Case Centre*, and *Bloomsbury Fashion Central* (under Bloomsbury Publishing).

Alkis Thrassou is a professor at the University of Nicosia (Cyprus, EU) and holds a PhD from the University of Leeds (UK). He is the Director of Gnosis Mediterranean Institute for Management Science, the Chief Editor of Palgrave Intersections of Business and the Sciences, the Managing Editor of Palgrave Studies in Cross-disciplinary Business Research, an Associate Editor of EuroMed Journal of Business, and a

Senior Research Fellow of the EuroMed Academy of Business. He has edited and published in numerous internationally esteemed scientific journals and books, and his works have been cited in thousands of scientific publications. He further retains strong ties with the industry, acting also as a consultant and holding the prominent professional qualifications of Chartered Marketer (FCIM), Chartered Construction Manager (FCIOB), and Chartered Management Consultancy Surveyor (MRICS).

Daniel Torchia has a PhD in Business and Management from the Alliance Manchester Business School, University of Manchester, UK. Currently, he is a PostDoc Research Fellow at the Department of Management, University of Turin. He is interested in researching organizations from a critical point of view to promote more humane forms of management. He has published research in both organizational and accounting journals, including *Culture and Organization* and *The British Accounting Review*.

Evangelos Tsoukatos is an associate professor of Management at the Helleninc Mediterranean University and adjunct faculty at the University of Nicosia, Cyprus, and the Hellenic Open University. He holds a PhD in Management Science from the Lancaster University Management School (LUMS), UK, a BSc in Mathematics from the "Aristotelion" University of Thessaloniki, Greece, a Postgraduate Diploma and MSc in Operational Research from LUMS, UK. Dr Tsoukatos holds the position of Vice President—Operations and Development at the EuroMed Research Business Institute. He has authored and edited books and journal special issues and has heavily published internationally in scholarly journals and presented at academic conferences. For his published research, he has gained wide recognition from his peers. He is Associate Editor of the *EuroMed Journal of Business* (EMJB) and an editorial board member in a number of international scholarly journals.

Naziyet Uzunboylu received her BA in Events Management from Manchester Metropolitan University and an MBA in Marketing from the University of Nicosia (Cyprus). She worked as a senior event manager in The Academic Events Group (TAEG) and Social Activities Coordinator at Cyprus International University. Currently, she is a PhD student at the School of Business of the University of Nicosia. She is actively publishing articles and chapters in prominent peer-reviewed journals, conference proceedings, and books, in the wider field of marketing and management; while her PhD topic relates to social media marketing, user-generated content, and strategic branding.

Francesca Vicentini is Associate Professor of Strategy at the "Foro Italico" University of Rome. She was a visiting scholar at prestigious international universities. Her main research interests are focused on the management of project companies, business models, and more recently on circular economy. She is the author of several articles in top management journals.

Charis Vlados obtained his PhD ("mention très honorable") for his thesis on the types and forms of evolutionary integration of the firms operating in Greece into globalization that took place within the framework of the Research and Studies Center on Multinational Enterprises (CEREM) of the University "Paris X-Nanterre." He is an assistant professor (academic tenure) in International Economics and Entrepreneurship in the Department of Economics of the Democritus University of Thrace. Charis Vlados has authored 16 books, having more than 100 participations in peer-reviewed international journals and conference proceedings.

Demetris Vrontis is the Vice-Rector for Faculty and Research and a Professor of Strategic Marketing Management at the University of Nicosia, Cyprus. He is the president of the EuroMed Academy of Business and the Managing Director of Gnosis Mediterranean Institute for Management Science, which serve as important and influential regional hubs in the area of Business and Management. He is the Founder and Editor-in-Chief of the *EuroMed Journal of Business*, Associate Editor of the *International Marketing Review*, Associate Editor of the *Journal of Business Research*, Consulting Editor of the *Journal of International Management*, and Associate Editor of the *Journal of Strategic Marketing*. He has published widely in over 300 refereed journal articles, 50 books, and 80 chapters in books, and has presented papers at over 80 conferences around the globe. He is a certified Chartered Marketer and a Chartered Business Consultant.

Yaakov Weber is Professor Emeritus and teaches courses on Strategic Management, Mergers and Acquisitions Management, Strategic Alliances, Corporate Strategy, Cross-Cultural Management, and Global Strategic Management. He lectured at various universities in the United States (for example NYU), Western and Eastern Europe, and China, in graduate schools of business administration as well as executive programs, in private and public organizations as well as Industrial Associations for CEOs and directors He is also participating and conducting international PhD seminars in PhD committees as well as is a referee in international PhD exams. Prof. Weber's studies were published in top leading international academic journals, such as *Strategic Management Journal*, *Journal of Management*, *Management Science*, *Journal of Business Research*, *California Management Review*, and *Human Relations*, among others. His papers have received more than 8500 citations in leading journals and books. Several papers were selected by various academic collections and were described as representing "the most significant new material" and, "most important works published in Sociology" (in 1996). Other papers are "2nd most cited in last 5 years" (2010–2015) and "most read" (2011–2015), or "most downloaded" in leading journals. He served as associate editor and in the editorial boards of several journals and acted as a referee for numerous leading journals. He served as Guest Editor for special issues in leading journals, such as *California Management Review*, *Human Resource Management*, *Journal of World Business* among others. Recently, Prof. Weber won the Outstanding Author Contribution Award. His recent book, which was invited by *Financial Times: A Comprehensive Guide for Mergers and Acquisitions*, was published in 2014. He is also co-editor of a three-book series at Emerald, Routledge, and Palgrave Macmillan. Prof. Weber is Co-Founder and Co-President of the EuroMed Business Research Institute (www.emrbi.org), the EuroMed Academy of Business, and the EuroMed Research Centre. Prof. Weber has been a senior consultant to CEOs, top executives, and directors in leading domestic and international companies such as Coca-Cola, Dead-Sea Works, Society of Israel Plastics & Rubber Manufacturers, the largest International Engineering company in Israel, Health-care Organizations, the USA-Israel Chamber of Commerce, large and small organizations in the chemical industry, high-tech industry and many others in various industries as well as the largest international consulting firm in Israel. His recent large project of international consulting was an international merger in Moscow, Russia. Prof. Weber conducted numerous workshops for top executives in many countries. Recently he conducted workshops for the senior executives of one of the four largest investment companies in China.

List of Figures

List of Diagrams

List of Tables

1

An Overview of Business for Sustainability: Strategic Avenues and Managerial Approaches

Demetris Vrontis, Alkis Thrassou, Naziyet Uzunboylu, and Leonidas Efthymiou

1 Introduction

Business sustainability has become popular for firms in almost every sector and industry (Randhawa et al., 2021; Leonidou et al., 2020; Marjamaa et al., 2021). Businesses' alignment with the principles of sustainability allows them to operate in a manner that balances economic, environmental, and social considerations. At the same time, businesses ought to consider and satisfy stakeholders' needs, requirements, and expectations. For instance, governments expect compliance with environmental protection (Quarshie et al., 2021; Muhmad & Muhamad, 2021); the society and regulatory bodies put pressure for societal responsibility (Tapaninaho &

D. Vrontis
Department of Management, School of Business, University of Nicosia, Nicosia, Cyprus

Department of Management Studies, Adnan Kassar School of Business, Lebanese American University, Beirut, Lebanon
e-mail: vrontis.d@unic.ac.cy

D. Vrontis et al. (eds.), *Business for Sustainability, Volume I*, Palgrave Studies in Cross-disciplinary Business Research, In Association with EuroMed Academy of Business, https://doi.org/10.1007/978-3-031-37361-9_1

Heikkinen, 2022) and economic wellbeing (Minatogawa et al., 2022; Luederitz et al., 2021); employees prefer to work for 'employers of choice' with proper working conditions and career advancement (Eikelenboom & de Jong, 2021), suppliers and vendors prefer to collaborate with companies that act legally and ethically while reducing their environmental impact (Ferrell et al., 2013), and consumers tend to make choices based on environmental sensitivities (Csutora et al., 2022). While everyone has something to expect, firms now ought to establish collaborations with partners that adopt a philosophy of sustainable development.

Within this dynamic and ever-changing environment, business sustainability is increasingly associated with change (Chatterjee et al., 2022a, 2022b), improvement, innovation (Arici & Uysal, 2022), or adjustment of an entity to its surroundings and supporting environment (He & Ortiz, 2021). The ability to innovate in the domain of sustainability represents a necessary business capability (Hanaysha et al., 2022; Wong & Ngai, 2021), whether related to small incremental steps (Gao et al., 2022) or to radical, disruptive innovations (Bouncken et al., 2021). Within this framework, the current chapter draws on the latest trends, improvements, developments, and state-of-the-art accounts, to discuss strategic avenues of and managerial approaches to business sustainability.

A. Thrassou
GNOSIS Mediterranean Institute for Management Science, School of Business, University of Nicosia, Nicosia, Cyprus
e-mail: thrassou.a@unic.ac.cy

N. Uzunboylu
University of Nicosia, Nicosia, Cyprus
e-mail: uzunboylu.n@unic.ac.cy

L. Efthymiou (✉)
Department of Management, School of Business, University of Nicosia, Nicosia, Cyprus
e-mail: efthymiou.l@unic.ac.cy

1.1 Context and Theoretical Foundations

The importance of green consumers in emerging economies calls for strategies in shifting consumer attitudes and behavior (Alagarsamy et al., 2021) towards the purchase (Chatterjee et al., 2022), consumption (Nascimento & Loureiro, 2022), and disposal of eco-friendly goods or services (Norris et al., 2020). This dynamic calls for a shift from generic or traditional consumer behavior towards green consumer behavior (Alagarsamy et al., 2021; Papadopoulou et al., 2022).

On the other hand, the growing complexity of different products and services (Rajesh, 2022), fluctuating demands in markets (Randhawa et al., 2021), and shorter product life cycles (Kusi-Sarpong et al., 2022) urges organizations to develop new or improved capabilities (Hanaysha et al., 2022; Wong & Ngai, 2021) and be innovative (Arici & Uysal, 2022) in order to secure sustainable competitive advantages. The business literature further highlights that businesses emphasizing on the introduction of innovative products and services (Hanaysha et al., 2022), as well as promotion through digital marketing technologies (Thrassou et al., 2022; Mihalache & Volberda, 2021; Efthymiou et al., 2022a), can achieve distinctive advantages. According to certain scholars (e.g., Suto & Takehara, 2022; Hanaysha et al., 2022; Esmaelnezhad et al., 2023), product innovation enables firms to adapt and respond to changing market needs and develop brand image. Hanaysha et al. (2022) demonstrated that firms can develop their innovation capabilities in diverse aspects, such as processes, products, and services. When a firm proves its ability to innovate (Randhawa et al., 2021) and come up with new products or services (Arici & Uysal, 2022) to please market targets (Tapaninaho & Heikkinen, 2022), it tends to obtain greater profitability and nurture its businesses competencies (Tres et al., 2021).

Sustainable consumption and production take strength from each other (Alagarsamy et al., 2021; Rustam et al., 2020; Romano et al., 2021). Sustainable production is based on green marketing approaches (Nascimento & Loureiro, 2022). Green marketing approaches aim at protecting the environment (Alagarsamy et al., 2021; Romano et al., 2021) when producing goods and services to meet consumer needs and wants (Rustam et al., 2020). Hence, consumers can find eco-friendly products in the market easily (Gupta et al., 2021).

Furthermore, earlier research (e.g., Leonidou et al., 2020; Chatterjee et al., 2022a) stressed on the significance of various innovation types in driving business sustainability and competitiveness. Hanaysha et al. (2022) stated that firms with innovative processes concentrate on activities and products that ensure greater energy efficiency and minimal resource consumption (Molina-Castillo et al., 2021). Moreover, dynamic (Bocken & Geradts, 2020) and innovation capabilities (Thrassou et al., 2021) have been regarded as key determinants of business sustainability. It is further stated that sustainable businesses benefit from lower risks and costs of doing business (Wong & Ngai, 2021). They have higher interest among talent (Suto & Takehara, 2022) and develop a successful brand reputation (Rosati et al., 2022). Also, they are more likely to gain competitive advantage (Rincon-Roldan & Lopez-Cabrales, 2022).

1.2 Toward a Green Marketing

The increasing worry of households and individuals due to increased environmental issues and problems (Gennari, 2022) transform consumption patterns (Alagarsamy et al., 2021). Additionally, organizations' production systems (Gupta et al., 2021; Kusi-Sarpong et al., 2022) have become one of the most important change movements towards sustainable development. In todays' dynamic markets, businesses have to regularly analyze and assess their internal as well as external environment (Marjamaa et al., 2021; Tapaninaho & Heikkinen, 2022) towards learning customers' expectations (Guo et al., 2022). Then, they will be able to utilize available resources efficiently in an attempt to face emerging challenges (Silveira et al., 2022) and strive for sustainable competitive advantage (Trollman & Colwill, 2021).

It is crucial to comprehend consumer green behavior since it is the bedrock of green marketing (Alagarsamy et al., 2021) as well as the basis upon which businesses decide on the green marketing strategies and tactics to pursue (Arici & Uysal, 2022). Furthermore, they would be able to decide which product to produce and how to produce it (Trapp & Kanbach, 2021); the promotion, pricing, and distribution strategies (Tres et al., 2021) as well as the people, and physical evidence strategy, and tactics (Shakeel et al., 2020). Companies that act responsibly benefit their credibility (Alonso-Martinez et al., 2021), altruistic attribution (Alagarsamy et al., 2021), and how they are perceived, (Gennari, 2022) which in turn improve their image and consumer loyalty (Ferlito & Faraci, 2021). As a result of corporate environmental scandals, including the ExxonMobil global warming scandal, Volkswagen emissions scandal, and House of Fraser sale of real fur (as fake fur had a negative impact on their customer loyalty, brand value, and profitability (Goni et al., 2021)), corporations have begun to recognize the benefits of green marketing to their businesses (Romano et al., 2021; Nascimento & Loureiro, 2022).

1.3 Orchestrating Sustainability

Managers often act as the link between 'employees' and the 'organization' (Eikelenboom & de Jong, 2021). As such, they play a crucial role in providing meaning (Corrales-Estrada et al., 2021). The tension between financial (Muhmad & Muhamad, 2021) and environmentally sustainable decisions (Kluza et al., 2021) is therefore affected by the cognitive frame of the leader (Suriyankietkaew, 2022), which often results in the leader creating a business case for sustainability (Boeske & Murray, 2022). Various scholars highlight the importance of strategic leadership (Eikelenboom & de Jong, 2021) and management (Klein & Spychalska-Wojtkiewicz, 2022) towards business sustainability. Theories of strategic leadership that work in the dynamic twenty-first century environment need to tactically consider multiple internal and external factors, as well as care for all employees (Batiz-Lazo et al., 2022).

Organizations are being forced by the dynamic changes to rethink their business-as-usual leadership (Suriyankietkaew, 2022) towards new normal management practices (Klein & Spychalska-Wojtkiewicz, 2022) for corporate sustainability to survive and thrive for future success (Bhattacharya et al., 2022). Business sustainability thus becomes a key leadership and management agenda. Recent research (e.g., Gao et al., 2022; Suriyankietkaew, 2022) suggests that the entrepreneurs who operate businesses with focus on sustainability and care for socio-economic and environmental aspects above and beyond minimum regulatory requirements, can outperform those without and can even further create profitable opportunities and competitive gains. Studies also support a growing future trend towards a green ideology (Arici & Uysal, 2022; Trapp & Kanbach, 2021) and socio-environmental sustainability to improve social, economic, and environmental performance (Tseng et al., 2020). Indeed, a crucial quest for present-day leaders and entrepreneurs examines what can be done to achieve superior performance outcomes (Alonso-Martinez et al., 2021; Suriyankietkaew, 2022) and business sustainability in the long run (Silveira et al., 2022).

Worldwide, the literature stresses an importance of strategic (Esmaelnezhad et al., 2023), organizational-level leadership (Luederitz et al., 2021) as it becomes a critical factor that drives business sustainability. Modern entrepreneurial leaders and managers thus need to develop organizational leadership abilities (Suriyankietkaew, 2022; Boeske & Murray, 2022) and strategic foresights (Arici & Uysal, 2022) to move away from a sole focus on economic performance (Boeske & Murray, 2022) and profit-maximization to just survive (Luederitz et al., 2021) to thrive for long-term balance and business sustainability (Chatterjee et al., 2022a).

Sustainability of Employment

At the intersection of employment and business, sustainability encompasses benefits such as better working conditions (Suto & Takehara, 2022), flexible scheduling (Batiz-Lazo et al., 2022), maternity, family benefits (Rincon-Roldan & Lopez-Cabrales, 2022), learning, and employee development opportunities (Bhattacharya et al., 2022). In the light of sustainability, companies are encouraged to reconsider employee retention (Kulshrestha, 2022) and engagement strategies (Rincon-Roldan & Lopez-Cabrales, 2022) by adopting better human resource management practices. Rincon-Roldan and Lopez-Cabrales (2022) have noted that engaged employees benefit the organization through more productivity and commitment, resulting in better financial performance that leads to sustainability activities. Further, employee engagement is now being recognized as an important parameter for measuring organizational performance (Gupta et al., 2021), as it has been accepted as an important determinant of shareholder value in a firm (Tapaninaho & Heikkinen, 2022). It has also been revealed that the top ten engagement drivers for business sustainability include top management's concern for employee well-being (Suto & Takehara, 2022), policies for participative management (Rincon-Roldan & Lopez-Cabrales, 2022), and the creation of opportunities for employees for growth and development (Bhattacharya et al., 2022) besides the firm's reputation for fulfilling its corporate social responsibility. Employees have to be actively engaged in the responsibility of integrating sustainability in all the operations of a firm (Kulshrestha, 2022; Rincon-Roldan & Lopez-Cabrales, 2022), which would help the firm to satisfy stakeholders like shareholders, customers, and communities, in general, and thus create value for the firm (Tapaninaho & Heikkinen, 2022; Gupta et al., 2021).

Such employment practices have an impact on broader society as well (Molina-Castillo et al., 2021). Businesses often give back to society, besides employment, through fundraising, scholarships, and investments in community development projects (Suto & Takehara, 2022; Molina-Castillo et al., 2021). Further, it has been observed that potential employees are increasingly likely to apply for and accept jobs from companies they view as socially and environmentally sustainable (Bhattacharya et al., 2022). Sustainability, therefore, can help to create a talent advantage for companies.

1.4 Dynamic Capabilities on Business Sustainability

Organizations must have certain abilities to perceive the changing markets and develop sustainable relationships with customers (Eikelenboom & de Jong, 2021). To do so, organizations must possess 'sustainable' dynamic capabilities to easily interact with customers (Bocken & Geradts, 2020). Dynamic capability (DC)—*sensing, seizing, and reconfiguring*—is considered a higher-order capability to explain sustainability (Buzzao & Rizzi, 2021; Chatterjee et al., 2022a) and competitive advantage in volatile, changing markets (Heider et al., 2021). DCs are crucial for companies pursuing sustainable business model innovation (SBMI) (Oliveira-Dias et al., 2022; Gao et al., 2022). Within the context of SBMI, *sensing* involves companies being aware of emerging sustainability issues (Bocken & Geradts, 2020) and understanding and appraising these as potential business opportunities (Chatterjee et al., 2022c). For example, SBMI sensing may entail companies identifying and taking action upon constraints created by the natural environment, such as resource depletion that could cause abrupt discontinuities and threaten firms' resources (Kluza et al., 2021). *Seizing* is about mobilizing resources to address emerging (sustainability) opportunities (Alonso-Martinez et al., 2021) and capture value from doing so (Gennari, 2022) by translating these into SBMI opportunities (Norris et al., 2020). Finally, *reconfiguring* is about the deliberate continued renewal of the organization's capabilities (Buzzao & Rizzi, 2021) towards becoming a sustainable business. It is also about implementing new sustainable business model concepts (Bocken & Geradts, 2020). In sum, while sensing, seizing, and reconfiguring capabilities are essential for BMI, they are also seen as vital for SBMI.

1.5 Innovation Capabilities

Sustainability is often seen to require the adoption of an integrated view of innovation (Hanaysha et al., 2022), which brings together economic, environmental, and social concerns (Tseng et al., 2021) as a basis for system changes. There is widespread consensus that radical innovations are needed (Arici & Uysal, 2022; Alagarsamy et al., 2021) to decrease the environmental and social impacts of production and consumption (Hanaysha et al., 2022) and to deal effectively with the challenges of a sustainable business model (SBM) (He & Ortiz, 2021; Ferlito & Faraci, 2021). These innovations are primarily meant to integrate environmental (Gao et al., 2022) and social interests with economic interests (Kluza et al., 2021) and bring about change that goes beyond the singular criteria of competitiveness and economic success (Wong & Ngai, 2021).

Product innovation, for example, has largely been regarded as one of the foremost organizational capabilities (Corrales-Estrada et al., 2021) and it was conceptualized in the literature as a firm's ability (Bouncken et al., 2021) to offer a new or improved product (Esmaelnezhad et al., 2023) that can meet the needs of the market target (Gupta et al., 2021). Esmaelnezhad et al. (2023) demonstrated that successful businesses regularly analyze their capabilities and customers' perceptions towards their products and services, and they place a strong emphasis on periodically introducing new products to satisfy market needs and ensure social welfare.

Service innovation is another important organizational strategy that has received noteworthy attention in the literature. Service innovation was defined as an organization's ability to provide new (Arici & Uysal, 2022) or upgraded services (Hanaysha et al., 2022) and adopt innovative approaches for serving its customers in the best way to maintain them in the long term (Heider et al., 2021). Firms can capitalize on various digital and mobile technologies (Trapp & Kanbach, 2021; Efthymiou et al., 2022b) for serving and reaching customers. Thus, innovations in service delivery provide customers with superior values (Tapaninaho & Heikkinen, 2022) and improve their satisfaction (Norris et al., 2020).

Furthermore, process innovation has been established as an important strategy for achieving business sustainability objectives. Firms focus on process innovation in order to ensure the speed of service delivery (Hanaysha et al., 2022) and provide customers with added values (Gennari, 2022) through implementing efficient systems and applications. Moreover, the legal framework for overseeing the businesses' impact on the environment (Zhao et al., 2021) and minimizing the emissions of CO_2 (Quarshie et al., 2021; Romano et al., 2021) has forced several firms to improve process innovation (Kluza et al., 2021).

Overall, it has been revealed that innovation capabilities have a significant positive impact on business sustainability (He & Ortiz, 2021). When firms focus on green innovation (Arici & Uysal, 2022) and look for new means to meet the expectations (Leonidou et al., 2020; Marjamaa et al., 2021) and different claims of several stakeholders (Guo et al., 2022), they can maintain their business in the long-term (Silveira et al., 2022), fulfill social needs (Marjamaa et al., 2021), and act responsibly towards environmental protection (Quarshie et al., 2021; Kluza et al., 2021; Rustam et al., 2020).

In sum, as it has been suggested by Alonso-Martinez et al. (2021) and Corrales-Estrada et al. (2021), sustainability should be in the DNA of companies. It should be embedded in their goals, missions, operations, structure, and values (Gennari, 2022; Norris et al., 2020; Rajesh, 2022). When the core activity of a company is highly integrated with its socially responsible activities, consumers take a favorable attitude toward the organization. Similarly, poor sustainability practices can lead to corporate reputational damage (Rosati et al., 2022). Such reputational damage impacts organizational attempts to engender customer (Chatterjee et al., 2022b; Alagarsamy et al., 2021) and stakeholder loyalty (Leonidou et al., 2020; Marjamaa et al., 2021). Therefore, the 'green' aspect of sustainability has been shown to improve company or brand reputations and customer loyalty.

Furthermore, business is an engine of change through its capacity for sustainability development and innovation. Reducing the environmental burden of these complex systems will involve companies in stimulating and redirecting the focus of innovation (Arici & Uysal, 2022; Bouncken et al., 2021). This places a demand on the capacities of the actors who contribute to existing systems to collaborate (Boeske & Murray, 2022; Suriyankietkaew, 2022). It also invokes questions about the capabilities and competences needed (Corrales-Estrada et al., 2021; Gao et al., 2022) to affect innovation (Bocken & Geradts, 2020; Ferlito & Faraci, 2021) and change toward environmental sustainability and how they can be developed (Goni et al., 2021; Kluza et al., 2021; Rustam et al., 2020).

1.6 Book Content and Structure

In the spirit of the foregoing analysis, the current book explores strategic avenues and managerial approaches for business sustainability. The book presents twelve (12) chapters, which seek to enhance our understanding of current and future issues in the field of sustainability while presenting sector-wide examples and best practices. The works purposely cover an array of theoretical, industry, and geographic contexts, which aim at bridging theory and practice.

In Chap. 2 ('Exploring consumer boycott intention toward corporate sustainable business practices'), the authors examine consumer perception towards corporate communications regarding sustainable business practices. They also explore how the perception of sustainable business communications is translated into their behavioral intention, depicted through the intention to boycott. Furthermore, the study explores the mediating effect of socially responsible consumption behavior and examines if perceived hypocrisy changes the strength of the indirect and direct relationships.

From China, Chap. 3 ('Sustainability of youth development in drylands: A systematic approach') explores partnerships that are integrated and well-coordinated to assist young people who work in agriculture. More specifically, the chapter explains the importance of creating the conditions for rural youth to actively engage in the agricultural value chain in drylands.

In Chap. 4, 'Exploring the intersection of change, innovation and sustainability in Indian family businesses', the authors explore the underdeveloped links between family firms, innovation, and sustainability. Drawing on the findings of in-depth interviews in Indian family businesses, the chapter presents innovation and change as a standard feature of a firm's culture rather than a reaction to events. Sustainability and sustainable growth stem out of a firm's capacity to treat innovation as dynamic and constant, as opposed to being static and instant.

Moreover, Chap. 5 examines the impact of sustainable partnership responses to prevent homelessness and discharges from other institutions. It focuses on one of the largest local councils in the UK (Leeds City Council) to explore how homelessness is a key strategic priority for the council and how it is addressed to prevent significant social impacts for the individual and the city. Drawing on the findings of thirteen semi-structured interviews, the authors report that despite increasing demands on organizations and partnerships, the potential for the partnerships to achieve effective place-based governance is not fully maximized. This could be achieved through self-review to target resources, empower the workforce, and integrate strategic goals into their performance management to enable partnerships to learn, develop, and celebrate success together.

Then, Chap. 6 looks at the banking and accounting sectors. The analysis combines environmental, social, and governance rating (ESGr), Credit Risk (CR), and Financial Performance in an empirical analysis to understand the correlation between the three. The findings suggest that ESGr has a positive impact on mitigation of CR. Also, the study suggests that quality of green credit (measured by GAR) and financial performance can be significantly improved. This result is achieved using the regression technique, by testing if the GAR increase can reduce the non-performing loans (NPLs ratio) and improve the solvency ratio.

Within the environmental dimension of corporate social responsibility (CSR), which is considered as the most significant feature of CSR, Chap. 7 explores Corporate Environmental Performance (CEP). CEP is examined as an aspect of firms' investment that is being closely monitored by stakeholders; and a prominent determinant of firms' financial performance and creditworthiness. The authors examine the impact of corporate environmental performance (capturing three dimensions, namely emission reduction, environmental innovation, and resource use efficiency) on firms' creditworthiness, measured through bonds' credit ratings.

Furthermore, drawing on the findings of a survey, Chap. 8 presents a business plan for female football teams. The analysis considers both social and economic factors while emphasizing the importance of diversity as a global business imperative. The intersection of sustainability, diversity, and inclusion enables the development of strategic plans for long-term success. The study finds that the wider interpretation of 'pink quota' increases firms' capability of benefiting from diversity and increases performance, while improving external image.

Chapter 9 provides a content analysis of sustainability disclosures of the largest 20 European construction companies by revenues, taken from 'The CE100 list of European contractors'. The 2030 Agenda by the United Nations has introduced 17 Sustainable Development Goals (SDGs) to provide a blueprint for societies to reach peace and prosperity (Efthymiou et al., 2023). In particular, SDG 9 (industry, innovation, and infrastructure) promotes the concept of 'resilient infrastructure' to drive the transition towards sustainable industrialization. Discussions around the construction industry are not only relevant for its global size, but especially for the large-scale effects on society and the environment that construction activities have, from smaller endeavors, to mega or giga-projects.

Within the framework of change management, Chap. 10 examines the adaptive behavior of Greek firms in the light of ongoing crisis. First, the analysis presents secondary research data concerning the productivity of typical Greek and the rest of European firms. Then, the analysis conducts field research to discern dimensions contributing to empirically interpreting these deficiencies. The chapter concludes that, in addition to challenging external conditions caused by the emerging phase of the new globalization, the structural weaknesses of Greek firms are attributed to evolutionary physiology. These firms, in their majority, reproduce a rationale of monad-centered hybridization due to the functional limitations of the typical family business.

In Chap. 11, titled 'Sustainability for Healthcare Organisations and Systems: Cultivating Strategy and Governance Processes for a Better Future', the analysis unfolds in a setting where healthcare systems worldwide face enormous and complex challenges. Within this framework, the authors map change processes in hospitals based on a literature review of the topic and in-depth interviews with medical staff. Deepening and expanding knowledge of this topic may help decision-makers in the field to make system-wide decisions regarding managing the system, adopt efficient managerial tools, avoid resistance to the change guiding it, and make it more efficient, hence sustainable. Such approaches allow laying the foundations for change and structural improvement of the healthcare organization as a whole.

Last but not least, Chap. 12 offers insights into Social Partnerships between non-profit organizations and multinational retail corporations at times of severe economic, health, and societal crisis. In doing so, the analysis explores the potential utilization of digital technology at the intersection of Cause Related Marketing and Philanthropy. The study is longitudinal, spanning over a period of seven years. During this time, technology played an important role, since it enabled social partnerships to remain successful and stakeholders to remain committed to charitable giving. Also, digitization opened up new dimensions and measurable results to cause-related marketing.

Finally, based on the interest of each audience, readers may select specific cases, or read the book from cover to cover, or simply, utilize the index to navigate through the content. The chapters offer a useful range of practices, mechanisms, and strategies that promote sustainable business while minimizing the negative impact of operations on the environment and society.

References

Alagarsamy, S., Mehrolia, S., & Mathew, S. (2021). How green consumption value affects green consumer behaviour: The mediating role of consumer attitudes towards sustainable food logistics practices. *Vision, 25*(1), 65–76.

Alonso-Martinez, D., De Marchi, V., & Di Maria, E. (2021). The sustainability performances of sustainable business models. *Journal of Cleaner Production, 323*, 1–11.

Arici, H. E., & Uysal, M. (2022). Leadership, green innovation, and green creativity: A systematic review. *The Service Industries Journal, 42*(5–6), 280–320.

Batiz-Lazo, B., Efthymiou, L., & Davies, K. (2022). The spread of artificial intelligence and its impact on employment: Evidence from the banking and accounting sectors. In: A. Thrassou, D. Vrontis, L. Efthymiou, Y. Weber, S. M. R. Shams, & E. Tsoukatos (Eds.), *Business advancement through technology: The changing landscape of industry and employment.* Palgrave Studies in Cross-disciplinary Business Research, In Association with EuroMed Academy of Business. Palgrave Macmillan.

Bhattacharya, C. B., Sen, S., Edinger-Schons, L. M., & Neureiter, M. (2022). Corporate purpose and employee sustainability Behaviors. *Journal of Business Ethics*, 1–19.

Bocken, N. M. P., & Geradts, T. H. J. (2020). Barriers and drivers to sustainable business model innovation: Organization design and dynamic capabilities. *Long Range Planning, 53*, 1–23.

Boeske, J., & Murray, P. A. (2022). The intellectual domains of sustainability leadership in SMEs. *Sustainability, 14*(4), 1978.

Bouncken, R., Kraus, S., & Rolg-Tierno, N. (2021). Knowledge- and innovation- based business models for future growth: Digitalized business models and portfolio considerations. *Review of Managerial Science, 15*(1), 1–14.

Buzzao, G., & Rizzi, F. (2021). On the conceptualization and measurement of dynamic capabilities for sustainability: Building theory through a systematic literature review. *Business Strategy and the Environment, 30*, 135–175.

Chatterjee, S., Chaudhuri, R., Vrontis, D., & Chaudhuri, S. (2022a). The impact of dynamic capability on business sustainability of organizations. *FIIB Business Review, 11*(4), 455–467.

Chatterjee, S., Chaudhuri, R., Vrontis, D. & Thrassou, A. (2022b). The influence of online customer reviews on customers' purchase intentions: a cross-cultural study from India and the UK. *International Journal of Organizational Analysis, 30*(6), 1595–1623.

Chatterjee, S., Chaudhuri, R., Vrontis, D. & Thrassou, A. (2022c). Impact of organizational dynamic capability on international expansion and the moderating role of environmental dynamism. *International Journal of Organizational Analysis,* ahead-of-print.

Corrales-Estrada, A. M., Gomez-Santos, L. L., Bernal-Torres, C. A., & Rodriguez-Lopez, J. E. (2021). Sustainability and resilience organizational capabilities to enhance business continuity management: A literature review. *Sustainability, 13*(15), 8196.

Csutora, M., Harangozo, G., & Szigeti, C. (2022). Factors behind the consumer acceptance of sustainable business models in pandemic times. *Sustainability, 14,* 1–18.

Efthymiou, L., Dekoulou, E., Orphanidou, Y., Sdoukopoulos, E., Perra, V. M., Boile, M., & Bras, I. (2022b). Crisis, adaptation and sustainability: Digital system interoperability in the Cruise Industry. In D. Vrontis, A. Thrassou, Y. Weber, S. M. R. Shams, E. Tsoukatos, & L. Efthymiou (Eds.), *Business under crisis, volume III: Avenues for innovation, entrepreneurship and sustainability.* Palgrave Studies in Cross-disciplinary Business Research, In Association with EuroMed Academy of Business. Palgrave Macmillan. https://doi.org/10.1007/978-3-030-76583-5_1.

Efthymiou, L., Morphitis, A., Drousiotis, P., & Orphanidou, Y. (2022a). *Sustainability initiatives in cypriot hotels and the way forward through digital marketing communication.* Conference Proceedings: CMC2022, 26th Corporate and Marketing Communications Conference.

Efthymiou, L., Kulshrestha, A., Kulshrestha, S. (2023). A Study on Sustainability and ESG in the Service Sector in India: Benefits, Challenges, and Future Implications. *Administrative Sciences, 13,* 165. https://doi.org/10.3390/admsci13070165

Eikelenboom, M., & de Jong, G. (2021). The impact of managers and network interactions on the integration of circularity in business strategy. *Organization & Environment,* 1–29.

Esmaelnezhad, D., Taghizadeh-Yazdi, M., Mahdiraji, H. A., & Vrontis, D. (2023). International strategic alliances for collaborative product innovation: An agent-based scenario analysis in biopharmaceutical industry. *Journal of Business Research, 158,* 113663.

Ferlito, R., & Faraci, R. (2021). Business model innovation for sustainability: A new framework. *Innovation and Management Review, 19*(3), 222–236.

Ferrell, O. C., Rogers, M. M., Ferrell, L., & Sawayda, J. (2013). A framework for understanding ethical supply chain decision making. *Journal of Marketing Channels, 20*(3–4), 260–287. https://doi.org/10.1080/1046669X.2013.803428

Gao, S., Ma, X., & Zhao, X. (2022). Entrepreneurship, digital capabilities, and sustainable business model innovation: A case study. *Mobile Information Systems*, 1–13.

Gennari, F. (2022). Sustainable business model innovation: From value uncaptured to value opportunities. *Symphonya Emerging Issues in Management, 2*, 27–46.

Goni, F. A., Chofreh, A. G., Orakani, Z. E., Klemes, J. J., Davoudi, M., & Mardani, A. (2021). Sustainable business model: A review and framework development. *Clean Technologies and Environmental Policy, 23*, 889–897.

Guo, L., Cao, Q., & Y. & Tseng, M-L. (2022). Developing sustainable business model innovation through stakeholder management and dynamic capability: A longitudinal case study. *Journal of Cleaner Production, 372*, 1–14.

Gupta, H., Kumar, A., & Wasan, P. (2021). Industry 4.0, cleaner production and circular economy: An integrative framework for evaluating ethical and sustainable business performance of manufacturing organizations. *Journal of Cleaner Production, 295*, 126253.

Hanaysha, J. R., Al-Shaikh, M. E., Joghee, S., & Alzoubi, H. M. (2022). Impact of innovation capabilities on business sustainability in small and medium enterprises. *Fortune Institute of International Business, Article Reuse Guidelines, 11*(1), 67–78.

He, J., & Ortiz, J. (2021). Sustainable business modeling: The need for innovative design thinking. *Journal of Cleaner Production, 298*, 126751.

Heider, A., Gerken, M., van Dinther, N., & Hülsbeck, M. (2021). Business model innovation through dynamic capabilities in small and medium enterprises—Evidence from the German Mittelstand. *Journal of Business Research, 130*, 635–645.

Klein, M., & Spychalska-Wojtkiewicz, M. (2022). The role of Design Management in the Creation of sustainable business models. *Energies, 15*, 1–17.

Kluza, K., Ziolo, M., & Spoz, A. (2021). Innovation and environmental, social and governance factors influencing sustainable business models- meta-analysis. *Journal of Cleaner Production, 303*, 1–11.

Kulshrestha, S. (2022). The role of technology enabled HRM systems in developing hybrid workplaces: A case study of the information technology sector in India. In: A. Thrassou, D. Vrontis, L. Efthymiou, Y. Weber, S. M. R. Shams, & E. Tsoukatos (Eds.), *Business advancement through technology: The changing landscape of industry and employment*. Palgrave Studies in Cross-disciplinary Business Research, In Association with EuroMed Academy of Business. Palgrave Macmillan.

Kusi-Sarpong, S., Mubarik, M. S., Khan, S. A., Brown, S., & Mubarak, M. F. (2022). Intellectual capital, blockchain-driven supply chain and sustain-able production: Role of supply chain mapping. *Technological Forecasting and Social Change, 175*.

Leonidou, E., Christofi, M., Vrontis, D., & Thrassou, A. (2020). An integrative framework of stakeholder engagement for innovation management and entrepreneurship development. *Journal of Business Research, 119*, 245–258.

Luederitz, C., Caniglia, G., Colbert, B., & Burch, S. (2021). How do small businesses pursue sustainability? The role of collective Agency for Integrating Planned and Emergent Strategy Making. *Business Strategy and the Environment, 30*, 3376–3393.

Marjamaa, M., Salminen, H., Kujala, J., Tapaninaho, R., & Heikkinen, A. (2021). A sustainable circular economy: Exploring stakeholder interests in Finland. *South Asian Journal of Business and Management Cases, 10*(1), 50–62.

Mihalache, O. R., & Volberda, H. W. (2021). Business model innovation in transforming economies: A co-evolutionary perspective for a global and digital world. *Management and Organisation Review, 17*, 202–225.

Minatogawa, V., Franco, M., Rampasso, I. S., Holgado, M., Garrido, D., Pinto, H., & Quadros, R. (2022). Towards systematic sustainable business model innovation: What can we learn from business model innovation. *Sustainability, 14*(5), 2939.

Molina-Castillo, F.-J., Sinkovics, N., & Sinkovics, R. R. (2021). Sustainable business model innovation: Review. *Analysis and Impact on Society. Sustainability, 13*(16), 8906.

Muhmad, S. N., & Muhamad, R. (2021). Sustainable business practices and financial performance during pre and post-SDG adoption periods: A systematic review. *Journal of Sustainable Finance & Investment, 11*(4), 291–309.

Nascimento, J., & Loureiro, S. M. C. (2022). The PSICHE framework for sustainable consumption and future research directions. *EuroMed Journal of Business, ahead-of-print No. ahead-of-print.*

Norris, S., Hagenbeck, J., & Schaltegger, S. (2020). Linking sustainable business models and supply chains- toward an integrated value creation framework. *Business Strategy and the Environment, 30*(8), 3425–4296.

Oliveira-Dias, D., Kneipp, J. M., Bichueti, R. S., & Gomes, C. M. (2022). Fostering business model innovation for sustainability: A dynamic capabilities perspective. *Management Decision, 60*(13), 105–129.

Papadopoulou, M., Papasolomou, I., & Thrassou, A. (2022). Exploring the level of sustainability awareness among consumers within the fast-fashion clothing industry: A dual business and consumer perspective. *Competitiveness Review: An International Business Journal, 32*(3), 350–375.

Quarshie, A., Salmi, A., & Wu, Z. (2021). From equivocality to reflexivity in biodiversity protection. *Organization & Environment, 34*(4), 530–558.

Rajesh, R. (2022). Sustainability performance predictions in supply chains: Grey and rough set theoretical approaches. *Annals of Operations Research, 310*, 171–200.

Randhawa, K., Wilden, R., & Gudergan, S. (2021). How to innovate toward an ambidextrous business model? The role of dynamic capabilities and market orientation. *Journal of Business Research, 130*, 618–634.

Rincon-Roldan, F., & Lopez-Cabrales, A. (2022). The impact of employment relationships on firm sustainability. *Employee Relations, 44*(2), 386–406.

Romano, G., Masserini, L., & Lombardi, G. V. (2021). Environmental performance of waste management: Impacts of corruption and public maladministration in Italy. *Journal of Cleaner Production, 288*, 125521.

Rosati, F., Rodrigues, V. P., Cosenz, F., & Li-Ying, J. (2022). Business model innovation for the sustainable development goals. *Business Strategy and the Environment*, 1–14.

Rustam, A., Wang, Y., & Zameer, H. (2020). Environmental awareness, firm sustainability exposure and green consumption behaviors. *Journal of Cleaner Production, 268*, 1–12.

Shakeel, J., Mardani, A., Chofreh, A. G., Goni, F. A., & Klemes, J. J. (2020). Anatomy of sustainable business model innovation. *Journal of Cleaner Production*, 1–14.

Silveira, L. L., De Benedicto, S. C., da Silva, L. H. V., & Bittencourt, J. J. (2022). Strategic business sustainability: Study of critical success factors. *Brazilian Journal of Management, 15*, 760–780.

Suriyankietkaew, S. (2022). Effects of key leadership determinants on business sustainability in entrepreneurial enterprises. *Journal of Entrepreneurship in Emerging Economies, ahead-of-print No. ahead-of-print.*

Suto, M., & Takehara, H. (2022). Employee-oriented corporate social responsibility, innovation, and firm value. *Corporate Social Responsibility and Environmental Management, 29*(4), 765–778.

Tapaninaho, R., & Heikkinen, A. (2022). Value creation in circular economy business for sustainability: A stakeholder relationship perspective. *Business Strategy and the Environment, 31*(6), 2728–2740.

Thrassou, A., Chebbi, H., & Uzunboylu, N. (2021). Postmodern approaches to business management and innovative notions for contextual adaptation—a review. *EuroMed Journal of Business, 16*(3), 261–273.

Thrassou, A., Vrontis, D., Efthymiou, L., & Uzunboylu, N. (2022). An overview of business advancement through technology: The changing landscape of work and employment. In: A. Thrassou, D. Vrontis, L. Efthymiou, Y. Weber, S. M. R. Shams, & E. Tsoukatos (Eds.), *Business advancement through technology: The changing landscape of work and employment.* Palgrave Studies in Cross-disciplinary Business Research, In Association with EuroMed Academy of Business. Palgrave Macmillan.

Trapp, C. T. C., & Kanbach, D. K. (2021). Green entrepreneurship and business models: Deriving green technology business model archetypes. *Journal of Cleaner Production, 297*, 126694.

Tres, N., Zanin, A., Kruger, A. D., Magro, D., & C.B. (2021). Sustainability practices adopted by industrial companies. *Brazilian Journal of Management, 14*, 1140–1159.

Trollman, H., & Colwill, J. (2021). The imperative of embedding sustainability in business: A model for transformational sustainable development. *Sustainable Development, 29*(5), 974–986.

Tseng, M. L., Chang, C. H., Lin, C. W. R., Wu, K. J., Chen, Q., Xia, L., & Xue, B. (2020). Future trends and guidance for the triple bottom line and sustainability: A data-driven bibliometric analysis. Environmental science and pollution research. *Environmental Science and Pollution Research, 27*, 33543–33567.

Wong, D. T. W., & Ngai, E. W. T. (2021). Economic, organizational, and environmental capabilities for business sustainability competence: Findings from case studies in the fashion business. *Journal of Business Research, 126*, 440–471.

Zhao, J., Wei, Z., & Yang, D. (2021). Organizational search, dynamic capability, and business model innovation. *IEEE Transactions on Engineering Management, 68*, 785–796.

2

Exploring Consumer Boycott Intention towards Corporate Sustainable Business Practices

Caroline S. L. Tan and Ioanna Papasolomou

1 Introduction

The chapter examines consumer perceptions toward corporate communications regarding sustainable business practices, namely the organization's efforts in sustainability, diversity, and inclusion. It builds on the empirical evidence produced by a research study that explored the constructs of consumer-brand identification and how the perception of sustainable business communications is translated into their behavioral intention depicted through the intention to boycott. The study explores the mediating effect of socially responsible consumption behavior and examines whether perceived hypocrisy changes the strength of indirect

C. S. L. Tan (✉)
The University of Tsukuba, Tokyo, Japan
e-mail: tan@mbaib.gsbs.tsukuba.ac.jp

I. Papasolomou
University of Nicosia, Nicosia, Cyprus
e-mail: papasolomou.i@unic.ac.cy

D. Vrontis et al. (eds.), *Business for Sustainability, Volume I*, Palgrave Studies in Cross-disciplinary Business Research, In Association with EuroMed Academy of Business, https://doi.org/10.1007/978-3-031-37361-9_2

and direct relationships. For the data collection, a web panel was utilized based on a survey instrument that consisted of scale items taken and adapted from various studies. Data was collected from 416 Japanese millennials, with a mean age of 34.9 (SD = 4.51). The results showed that socially responsible consumption behavior partially mediates the relationship between consumer-brand identification and intention to boycott in the context of consumer reaction toward corporate sustainable business practices communications. On the other hand, perceived hypocrisy did not affect the indirect and direct relationships. The study highlights the need for corporations to manage their communications regarding their sustainable business practices to ensure consumer support and engagement.

The chapter is organized in the following manner: the next section offers a review of the literature. Then, the analysis presents the research design and methods of the study, prior to presenting the findings. The analysis is then summarized by a concluding discussion.

2 Theoretical Background

Over the last 50 years, there has been impressive growth among academics and practitioners towards the subject of corporate branding and corporate identity constructs (Abratt & Kleyn, 2012; Balmer & Chen, 2017; Du Preez et al., 2017). The influence of corporate branding and corporate identity is widespread, impacting both the external and internal environments of the organization (Melewar & Karaosmanoglu, 2006). Similarly, corporate sustainability is increasingly becoming not only a corporate value but also an integrative part of the business strategy in many companies. According to Signitzer and Prexl (2008), corporate sustainability is an umbrella term for various other concepts related to the role of business in society, such as corporate social responsibility (CSR) and corporate citizenship, corporate social performance (Woods, 1991); social accountability/triple bottom line (Dyllick & Hockerts, 2002); people, planet, profit (PPP) (Elkington, 1997); corporate governance; the stakeholder approach (Freeman, 1984); and lastly CSC (corporate sustainability communication), one of the key concepts explored in this chapter. Instead of the term (CSC), some authors use the terms corporate social responsibility communication or CSR-communication. Other related terms are corporate environmental communication and social-ecological communication. For this chapter, the authors propose the term corporate sustainable business practices communications to refer to corporate communications about sustainability issues related to business practices since sustainability, by definition, includes societal, environmental, and business aspects.

According to Signitzer and Prexl (2008), CSC builds on the corporate social reports and environmental communication programs of the 1970s and 1980s. In the early 1970s, several corporations published social reports to project socially responsible behaviour. However, many of the reports were (mis)used, and often took the form of advertising ploys lacking honesty and transparency, aimed at 'greenwash' (Greer & Kenny, 1998), by highlighting the positive side of the story, consequently harming the story's credibility and believability. Consequently, by the end of the 1970s, many businesses stopped publishing social information (Fichter, 1998).

We argue that any (mis)use of corporate sustainable business practices communications, to achieve short-term benefits such as a boost in sales, is counterproductive to the long-term interests of the organization. Instead, corporations that adopt the concepts of corporate sustainability and corporate sustainable business practices communications (with its broad array of interconnected components such as stakeholder communications, integrated marketing communications campaigns, media relations, packaging and labelling, digital and social media marketing, and sustainability reporting) may generate valuable benefits and create long-term value that fosters corporate longevity since the emphasis is placed on how a given organization operates in the ecological, social, and economic environments. Signitzer and Prexl (2008) argue that corporate sustainable business practices communications should be regarded as the integration of sustainability issues into existing program areas such as advertising and marketing communications.

An increasing number of businesses have committed to working towards corporate sustainability and CSR (von Rosen, 2003, p. 40); for example, a survey of the German stock market institute (Deutsches

Aktieninstitut) showed that 40.5% of the German companies listed on the stock exchange have embedded the concept of sustainability into their mission statements. But it is not just businesses that are increasingly committed to sustainability. The COVID-19 pandemic brought changes in consumption patterns in many sectors such as tourism (Franco, 2022; Thrassou et al., 2022) and motivated consumers towards responsible consumption (Šimanskienė et al., 2022). Consumer preferences and consumption patterns tend to follow the environmental changes that are taking place in the marketing environment. Bounfantino (2022) in his article builds on the findings that emerged from a Harris Poll research commissioned by Google Cloud, which revealed that US shoppers are thinking about consumer goods brands (apparel, electronics, and beauty products, to food and beverage) in new ways: 82% of consumers claimed that they buy from brands that reflect their personal values; over 50% said they would spend more for a product from a company that emphasizes sustainability; 66% of shoppers seek out eco-friendly brands; 55% are willing to pay more for sustainable products; 52% of consumers are interested in supporting sustainable brands and they want to know how companies are managing their resources, specifically whether they are sourcing responsibly. More importantly, 39% of shoppers stated that they would permanently boycott their favourite brand and 24% would break ties at least temporarily; 28% would share their concerns with friends and family and another 15% shared content on social media; 72% of them share the view that companies and brands overstate their sustainability efforts. In a different global survey of 1491 executives across 16 countries conducted by The Harris Poll for Google Cloud, 58% of executives admitted that their organization has overstated its sustainability efforts and roughly two-thirds (66%) questioned how genuine some of their organization's sustainability initiatives are (Keeble, 2022).

You and Hon (2021) suggest that there is a need for corporate/brand practitioners to build a favourable reputation through effective communication that externalizes organizational values among consumers and includes companies' commitment to the communities in which they operate. This, in turn, will promote consumers' positive word-of-mouth intentions. Auger et al. (2003) suggest that CSR's ability to produce positive consumer attitudes and purchase behaviour has been extensively investigated primarily through experimental studies. However, Pomering and Dolnicar (2009) stipulate that while in theory CSR is effective in stimulating favourable consumer attitudes and behaviour, in practice there is often low consumer awareness of the various social issues in which firms engage with their CSR programs and thus, there is a need for educating them. Mohr et al. (2001) further stipulate that consumers tend to have difficulty in retrieving and storing CSR information about the firms they buy from. Dawkins (2004, p. 4) pinpoints that the problem is in fact at an earlier stage of the process, the corporate communication stage. He claims that businesses are rarely successful in the effective communication of their CSR programs, thus consumer awareness levels of CSR initiatives tend to be low, but consumers are in fact interested in enhancing their knowledge and understanding about CSR initiatives. CSR/sustainability-related marketing communications present an opportunity to shape organizational image and brand beliefs. Marketing communications should, however, be integrated with corporate communications to create a strong corporate reputation and drive consumer behaviour towards the brand. According to Bittner-Fesseler and Weicht (2020), corporate communication performs a dual role when it comes to sustainability: (1) helping companies inform about their sustainability performance and (2) supporting a company's sustainability efforts.

Today businesses and brands are incredibly competitive. For both businesses and brands, connection is crucial—connection with internal and external stakeholders. Corporate communications and marketing communications are the opposite sides of the same coin. Companies often ignore this very important issue, either confusing the two or not giving enough weight to one, consequently missing the opportunity to connect and engage with their target audiences, both internal and external. The corporate communications' role is to enable a business to present itself and its values to the world as well as to internal and external audiences, telling them what the corporation stands for and what are its values. On the other hand, the role of marketing communications is to disseminate brand information in a creative and interactive manner to subsequently engage customers and other audiences and build long-term relationships with them.

Thus, corporate sustainable business practices communications fulfil multiple roles, such as building relations with customers to enhance the sales of sustainable products, increasing sensitivity amongst employees towards the idea of sustainability, communicating corporate and brand values linked to sustainability, or creating favourable publicity for sustainable brands. What is critical to their effectiveness though is that they are perceived as genuine attempts and are not manipulative in any way.

The following section presents the literature on the key constructs used in the study, namely consumer-brand identification, socially responsible consumer behaviour, and boycott. This is followed by the conceptual model and method employed in this study. Next, the results are discussed and this chapter closes with the discussion and conclusion.

3 Consumer-Brand Identification

Brands embody and communicate identities that consumers desire (Bhattacharya & Sen, 2003; Fournier, 2009). As brands carry meanings, they help consumers attain and communicate their identities (Fournier, 2009). Therefore, consumer-brand identification refers to the extent that an individual has incorporated a brand into the self-concept (Fournier, 2009). It can also be defined as a psychological state of perceiving, feeling, and valuing their belongingness with the brand (Lam et al., 2013) and the state of oneness with a brand (Stokburger-Sauer et al., 2012).

Brand self-similarity positively influences consumer-brand identification (Stokburger-Sauer et al., 2012), where the higher consumer perceives a similarity between the brand and one's sense of self, the more the consumer will identify with the brand (Bhattacharya & Sen, 2003). The more consumers identify with the brand, the stronger the relationship is forged between the brand and consumer, which leads to brand attachment and loyalty (Bhattacharya & Sen, 2003). As such, consumer brand-identification also hinders brand switching (Lam et al., 2013). Hence, companies strive to establish a strong consumer-brand identification with the consumer.

Companies that engage in CSR are more likely to increase consumer identification with the company and brand (Murray & Vogel, 1997).

With higher consumer-brand identification, companies can build stronger and lasting relationships with consumers, resulting in brand loyalty and brand equity. CSR impacts consumer attitude, where consumers demonstrate a positive attitude and increased purchase intention toward companies that support social causes that benefit the community and the world (Murray & Vogel, 1997).

4 Socially Responsible Consumption Behaviour

The concept of socially responsible consumption was initially attached to environmental consumption (Brooker, 1976) but has since extended to include social change (Mohr et al., 2001). Mohr et al. (2001) defined socially responsible consumption behaviour (SRCB) as the decisions and actions that a consumer takes from product acquisition to consumption and disposal that is based on both tenets of minimizing or eliminating destructive effects and maximizing long-term positive social impact. Generally, consumer responsibility can be categorized into three areas: natural environment, social environment, and individual well-being (Schlaile et al., 2016). As such, socially responsible consumers find themselves committed to various social, ethical, and environmental issues where they demonstrate their support through their purchase decisions and choices. Alternatively, consumers also opt to refrain from buying specific products if they deem the products have harmful social and environmental effects and violate their values. The demand and expectations from socially responsible consumers contribute to propel businesses to pay attention to being socially responsible in their business practices (Webb et al., 2008).

With socially responsible consumption, the criteria of social and environmental responsibility are included in consumer decision-making (Villa Castaño et al., 2016). Research has been extensively conducted on whether and which values, attitudes, obligations, and ethics guide sustainable purchases (Barnett et al., 2005). Studies have postulated that socially responsible consumers demonstrate positive traits through actions, learning, and ethical practices that they have repeated through life and innate personality traits, which suggest that such traits (i.e. virtuous and personality traits) are predictors of socially responsible consumption (Paek & Nelson, 2009; Song & Kim, 2018). Consumers are driven to consume responsibly due to factors such as self-interest and altruism (Berger, 2017). Personal values have also been shown to be a determinant of socially responsible consumption (Mohr & Schlich, 2015). Prendergast and Tsang (2019) used the Theory of Planned Behaviour (TPB) to examine socially responsible consumption and found that attitude towards the behaviour, subjective norms, and perceived behavioural control are significant predictors of socially responsible consumption.

Consumers learn about the socially responsible practices of businesses through various sources, including corporate communications regarding business conduct and corporate social responsibility (CSR) initiatives. CSR initiatives enhance the image of the business that results in increased loyalty (Sen & Bhattacharya, 2001), higher credibility (Gruber et al., 2017), stronger corporate identity and identification (Chong, 2009), and competitive advantage (Vilanova et al., 2009). As attitude has been identified as a predictor of socially responsible consumption behaviour, weak and insufficient communication regarding a company's CSR practices will create an attitude–behaviour gap, which leads to a weak association between socially responsible consumption attitude and actual purchase behaviour (Pomering & Dolnicar, 2009). This further solidifies the vital role of corporate communications as consumers seek for transparency in determining that companies are engaged in the social causes that matter to the consumers (Kim et al., 2017). As consumers enjoy more clarity and transparency in the information that they obtain regarding the CSR activities, not only do they respond positively to these activities but also engage more in socially responsible consumption (Öberseder et al., 2011).

5 Boycott

Consumers utilize their purchasing power through everyday activities to exert their sociopolitical stance on a plethora of issues such as environment, worker, and animal welfare (Newman & Bartels, 2011; Schudson,

2006). They reflect on the sociopolitical impact of their purchases, which leads to either intentional purchase to show support and reward the companies (known as 'buycott') or punish the companies through making a conscious choice to abstain from making future purchases, referred to as boycott (Neilson, 2010; Yuksel, 2013). Both buycott and boycott are the most common forms of political consumerism where acts of buying or abstaining are intentional as reactions to political, social, or ethical issues (Newman & Bartels, 2011).

Boycotts have been used to punish companies that are perceived to be bad through a conflict-oriented approach (Neilson, 2010; Schudson, 2006). Additionally, it demonstrates consumer discontent and disapproval toward products or company behaviour (Zack, 1991). Boycott is seen as a form of anti-consumption as consumers refrain from making purchases (Yuksel, 2013). Historically, boycott was used as a non-violent way to influence governmental and organizational decisions (Scruggs et al., 2011). Through time, boycott became known as lifestyle politics wherein consumers voice their stance on sociopolitical issues through purchase and consumption decisions (Bennett, 1998: Copeland & Boulianne, 2020). Today, the target of political consumerism is usually corporations and not the government (Micheletti, 2003). The act of boycott is carried out not to just punish but also to force companies to change their behaviours via discrediting the company and calling out to other consumers to cease buying from the company (Romani et al., 2013).

Various studies have examined the factors that drive consumers to engage in boycotts, ranging from self-expression (Hoffmann & Müller, 2009) to influence from social groups such as family, friends, and even public figures (Garrett, 1987) and social pressure (Klein et al., 2003). One of the reasons consumers participate in boycotts is that they perceive the private benefits as greater than the private costs associated with joining boycotts (Albrecht et al., 2013; Klein et al., 2004) while other studies have shown contradictory findings where consumers' boycott is not based on a cost-benefit perspective (Tyran & Engelmann, 2005).

Existing literature have also explored individual-level determinants extensively from angles of demographic, ideological, and attitudinal (Endres & Panagopoulos, 2017; Newman & Bartels, 2011; Stolle & Micheletti, 2013). For instance, those with low trust in the government yet higher political interest tend to participate in political consumerism (Newman & Bartels, 2011). Demographic wise studies have shown that political consumers are those who are more educated, with higher income, and more likely than not to be white (Carfagna et al., 2014; Newman & Bartels, 2011), while gender and age established mixed results (Newman & Bartels, 2011). Moral outrage stemming from injustice and immorality drives consumers to express their outrage and emotions through boycotts (Heijnen & van der Made, 2012; Lindenmeier et al., 2012). This occurs as consumers perceive a conflict between their moral standards and that of the company's conduct, which leads to indignation and causes consumers to demand justice (Lindenmeier et al., 2012). Personality traits, perception, and attitudes have been identified as antecedents of engaging in acts of boycott (Klein et al., 2003; Neilson, 2010). Those who display higher levels of altruism, for instance, are more likely to boycott (Neilson, 2010) as well as individuals with higher media use, political distrust, and liberal ideology (Copeland & Boulianne, 2020).

The impact of boycotts on companies have been mixed and inconclusive (Klein et al., 2004; Neureiter & Bhattacharya, 2021). In polarized situations, while boycotts reduce sales, they also drive an increase in sales since the opposing side would rally around the brand and resort to boycotting or purchasing to show support (Neureiter & Bhattacharya, 2021). However, studies have established that companies face losses in revenues and decrease in stock prices (Farah & Newman, 2010), while at the same time suffering reputational loss as well as have a negative impact on brand perception that results in negative attitudes and low purchase intention (Klein et al., 2004).

6 Study

6.1 Conceptual Model

A theoretical model (Fig. 2.1) was constructed to test several hypothesized relationships from the constructs discussed in the previous sections where:

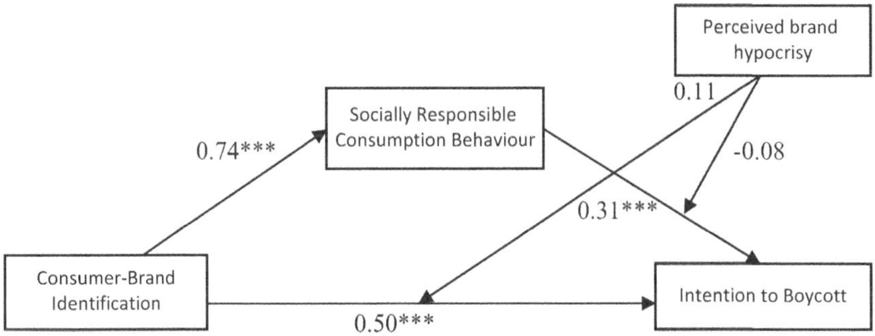

Fig. 2.1 Results of direct and indirect tests. (Note: $^{***}p < 0.001$)

H1a: Consumer-brand identification is positively related to SRCB
H1b: Consumer-brand identification is negatively related to intention to boycott
H2: SRCB is negatively related to intention to boycott
H3: SRCB mediates the relationship between consumer-brand identification and intention to boycott.

7 The Moderated Mediating Role of Perceived Brand Hypocrisy

Hypocrisy is perceived when talk and actual action is incongruent (Greenbaum et al., 2015). Hypocrisy affects not just the moral integrity of the company (Christensen et al., 2020) but also their image (Carlos & Lewis, 2018). When consumers perceive companies as behaving hypocritically, they tend to reject the message and resort to avoiding or boycotting the company and its products or services (Klein et al., 2004). This is more prevalent amongst socially responsible consumers as they strongly rally around companies that they perceive to be authentic in their approach regarding sociopolitical and environmental issues. On the other hand, if they deem a company to show inconsistency, they will reduce their support or even avoid making purchases altogether. Hence:

H4: Perceived brand hypocrisy moderates the relationships between SRCB and intention to boycott, and consumer-brand identification and intention to boycott, with higher perceived brand hypocrisy leading to stronger intention to boycott.

8 Methods

8.1 Sampling and Study Procedure

A survey was conducted using a Japanese web panel research company using a survey instrument that was designed based on scale items taken and adapted from various studies. Potential respondents were contacted via email, inviting them to participate in a survey regarding corporate communications. They were provided the assurance of anonymity and confidentiality. They were also informed that the findings of the study will be solely used for academic research and that participation was voluntary. Those who opt-in to participating moved on to the main part of the survey.

Respondents were provided with a vignette that they were asked to read prior to answering the questions. The vignette contained news regarding CSR activities undertaken by company X that contained both environmental and sociopolitical initiatives. Respondents were asked to replace company X with the company of their choice. In the vignette, the CSR initiatives took the forms of resource conservation, recycling efforts, and the improving of labour policies with a focus on diversity and inclusion. Respondents were required to indicate their agreement with the statements that were being presented in the survey. Data were collected from 527 Japanese millennials. After data cleaning, a total of 416 responses were deemed usable, with a mean age of 34.9 (SD = 4.51), where 60.1% were female and 39.9% were male.

8.2 Measures

All measurement items were derived from literature and have been tested in various studies. Consumer-brand identification is measured using three items taken from Bhattacharya and Elsbach (2002) and Kucharska et al. (2020). To measure socially responsible consumption behaviour, four items were used from Mohr and Webb (2005). The measurement for intention to boycott consisted of three items taken from Chang (1998) and Martin et al. (2004). Finally, perceived brand hypocrisy is measured using four items taken from Wagner et al. (2009). All the items were measured using a six-point Likert scale from 1 = Strongly Disagree to 6 = Strongly Agree.

9 Results

9.1 Model Fit

IBM SPSS Statistics 28.0 and AMOS 28.0 were used to perform data analysis. Sample adequacy was shown with the Kaiser-Meyer-Olkin (KMO) value of 0.850. Based on the confirmatory factor analysis (CFA), which demonstrated an acceptable model fit, $\chi 2/\mathrm{df} = 2.765$, SRMR = 0.0315, GFI = 0.947, AGFI = 0.911, NFI = 0.961, TLI = 0.964, CFI = 0.975, and RMSEA = 0.065. All constructs demonstrated high reliability, with Cronbach's alpha (α) ranging from 0.882 (consumer-brand identification) to 0.910 (intention to boycott). The composite reliability (CR) values ranged from 0.865 to 0.910, while the average variance extracted (AVE) values were 0.617 to 0.772, establishing convergence validity (Table 2.1). Discriminant validity was also exhibited, demonstrated by the square root of the AVE being greater than the correlation of the latent construct.

Table 2.1 Mean, SD, Cronbach's alpha, CR and AVE

	Mean	SD	α	CR	AVE
CBI	4.058	1.175	0.882	0.870	0.691
SRCB	3.762	1.101	0.865	0.865	0.617
INBT	3.936	1.163	0.910	0.910	0.772
PH	4.016	1.184	0.901	0.903	0.757

CBI Consumer-brand identification, *SRCB* Socially responsible consumption behaviour, *INBT* Intention to boycott, *PH* Perceived hypocrisy

9.2 Direct Effect Tests

The structural model was using the bootstrap procedure of 10,000 samples. The fit statistics reflected that the structural model was acceptable: $\chi 2/df = 3.263$, SRMR = 0.0269, GFI = 0.959, AGFI = 0.917, NFI = 0.97, TLI = 0.965, CFI = 0.979, and RMSEA = 0.074. H1a predicted a positive relationship between consumer-brand identification and SRCB, which is supported ($b = 0.742$, $p < 0.001$). This demonstrated that when there is strong consumer-brand identification, it increases the consumer's SRCB. However, H1b, which hypothesized a negative relationship between consumer-brand identification and intention to boycott is not supported ($b = 0.501$, $p < 0.001$) where stronger consumer-brand identification did not reduce the intention to boycott. Finally, the results also established that SRCB did not decrease the intention to boycott ($b = 0.31$, $p < 0.001$), thus H2 is not supported. The results are summarized in Table 2.2.

9.3 Indirect Effect Tests

To examine the mediation effect of SRCB, mediation analysis using SPSS PROCESS v4.0 (Model 4) with the bootstrap procedure at 10,000 samples with bias-corrected 95% confidence levels was conducted. The results demonstrate that SRCB partially mediates the relationship between brand identity and intention to boycott (indirect = 0.206, SE = 0.041, 95% CI [0.128, 0.291], supporting H3. As for the moderated mediation effect of perceived brand hypocrisy, SPSS PROCESS v4.0 (Model 15) with the bootstrap procedure at 10,000 samples with bias-corrected 95%

Table 2.2 Direct and indirect effects test results

Hypothesis	Path	beta	SE	CR	*p*	Result
H1a	CBI → SRCB	0.742	0.051	12.463	***	Supported
H1b	CBI → INBT	0.501	0.072	6.981	***	Not supported
H2	SRCB → INBT	0.31	0.084	4.314	***	Not supported

		Indirect	SE	BootLLCI	BootULCI	
H3	CBI → SRCB → INBT	0.206	0.041	0.128	0.291	Supported
H4	SRCB x PH, CBI x PH	-0.0477	0.0305	-0.1037	0.0168	Not supported

Note: χ^2/df = 3.263, SRMR = 0.0269, GFI = 0.959, AGFI = 0.917, NFI = 0.97, TLI = 0.965, CFI = 0.979, RMSEA = 0.074

CBI Consumer-brand identification, *SRCB* Socially responsible consumption behavior, *INBT* Intention to boycott, *PH* Perceived hypocrisy, *SE* Standard errors; CR = Critical ratios, *Boot LLCI* bootstrapping lower limit confidence, *BootULCI* bootstrapping upper limit confidence

***$p < 0.001$

confidence levels was used. The results demonstrated that perceived brand hypocrisy did not display any moderated mediation (indirect = -0.0477, SE = 0.0305, 95% CI [-0.1037, 0.0168]). Thus, H4 was not supported (see Table 2.2). The findings are illustrated in Fig. 2.1.

10 Discussion and Conclusion

The results showed that there is a positive relationship between consumer-brand identification and SRCB where the stronger the consumer identifies with the brand, the more they tend to engage in SRCB. This reflects that consumers tend to participate in similar socially responsible activities when the brand is actively engaging in similar things. Therefore, companies need to ensure that not only do they actively participate in and drive socially responsible initiatives, but they also need to communicate their actions in a transparent and clear manner to consumers to increase consumer engagement in SRCB (Kim et al., 2017; Öberseder et al., 2011).

SRCB is found to partially mediate the relationship between consumer-brand identification and intention to boycott in the context of consumer reaction toward corporate sustainable business practices communications. On the other hand, perceived brand hypocrisy did not affect the indirect and direct relationships. This demonstrates that SRCB plays a crucial role in reducing the intention to boycott, further stressing the need for companies to incorporate and encourage SRCB in its business practices as well as its brand values that need to be communicated effectively through their corporate sustainable business practices communications. As corporations continue to strive to focus on impactful sustainable business practices, this study contributes to help shed light on how consumers view corporate communications regarding sustainable practices which will help corporations develop robust communications strategies. This is particularly timely as political consumerism is gaining more traction and prominence as consumers demand corporations to be involved in sociopolitical issues, including sustainability.

References

Abratt, R., & Kleyn, N. (2012). Corporate identity, corporate branding and corporate reputations: Reconciliation and integration. *European Journal of Marketing, 46*(7/8), 1048–1063. https://doi.org/10.1108/0309056121123019

Albrecht, C.-M., Campbell, C., Heinrich, D., & Lammel, M. (2013). Exploring why consumers engage in boycotts: Toward a unified model. *Journal of Public Affairs, 13*(2), 180–189.

Auger, P., Burke, P. F., Devinney, T. M., & Louviere, J. J. (2003). What will consumers pay for social product features? *Journal of Business Ethics, 42*(3), 281–304.

Balmer, J. M. T., & Chen, W. (2017). Corporate heritage brands, augmented role identity and customer satisfaction. *European Journal of Marketing, 51*(9/10), 1510–1521. https://doi.org/10.1108/EJM-07-2017-0449

Barnett, C., Cafaro, P., & Newholm, T. (2005). Philosophy and ethical consumption. In R. Harrison, T. Newholm, & D. Shaw (Eds.), *The ethical consumer* (pp. 11–24). Sage Publifications.

Bennett, W. L. (1998). The uncivic culture: Communication, identity, and the rise of lifestyle politics. *PS: Political Science and Politics, 31*(4), 741–761.

Berger, J. (2017). Are luxury brand labels and "green" labels costly signals of social status? An extended replication. *PLoS One, 12*(2), 1–17.

Bhattacharya, C. B., & Elsbach, K. D. (2002). Us versus them: The roles of organizational identification and disidentification in social marketing initiatives. *Journal of Public Policy & Marketing, 21*(1), 26–36.

Bhattacharya, C. B., & Sen, S. (2003). Consumer–company identification: A framework for understanding consumers' relationships with companies. *Journal of Marketing, 67*(2), 76–88.

Bittner-Fesseler, A., & Weicht, J. F. (2020). Beyond sustainability communication: Sustainability-integrated corporate communications. *Journal of Strategic Innovation and Sustainability, 15*(1), 93–101.

Bounfantino, G. (2022). New Research shows consumers more interested in brand's values than ever. *Consumer Goods Technology*. Retrieved November 12, 2022, from https://consumergoods.com/new-research-shows-consumers-more-interested-brands-values-ever

Brooker, G. (1976). The self-actualizing socially conscious consumer. *Journal of Consumer Research, 3*, 107–112.

Carfagna, L. B., Dubois, E. A., Fitzmaurice, C., Ouimette, M. Y., Schor, J. B., Willis, M., & Laidley, T. (2014). An emerging eco-habitus: The reconfiguration of high cultural capital practices among ethical consumers. *Journal of Consumer Culture, 14*(2), 158–178.

Carlos, W. C., & Lewis, B. W. (2018). Strategic silence: Withholding certification status as hypocrisy avoidance tax. *Administrative Science Quarterly, 63*(1), 130–169.

Chang, M. K. (1998). Predicting unethical behaviour: A comparison of the theory of reasoned action and the theory of planned behaviour. *Journal of Business Ethics, 17*, 1825–1834.

Chong, M. (2009). Employee participation in CSR and corporate identity: Insights from a disaster-response program in the Asia-Pacific. *Corporate Reputation Review, 12*(2), 106–119.

Christensen, L. T., Morsing, M., & Thyssen, O. (2020). Timely hypocrisy? Hypocrisy temporalities in CSR communication. *Journal of Business Research, 114*, 327–335.

Copeland, L., & Boulianne, S. (2020). Political consumerism: A meta analysis. *International Political Science Review, 43*(1), 3–18.

Dawkins, J. (2004). *The public's views of corporate responsibility 2003*. White Paper Series, MORI. Retrieved May 31, 2006, from http://mori.com

Du Preez, R. D., Bendixen, M., & Abratt, R. (2017). The behavioural consequences of internal brand management among frontline employees. *Journal of Product & Brand Management, 26*(3), 251–261. https://doi.org/10.1108/JPBM-09-2016-1325

Dyllick, T., & Hockerts, K. (2002). Beyond the business case for corporate sustainability. *Business Strategy and the Environment, 11*, 130–141.

Elkington, J. (1997). *Cannibals with forks: The triple bottom line of the 21st century business*. Capstone.

Endres, K., & Panagopoulos, C. (2017). Boycotts, buycotts, and political consumerism in America. *Research and Politics, 4*(4), 1–9.

Farah, M. F., & Newman, A. J. (2010). Exploring consumer boycott intelligence using a socio-cognitive approach. *Journal of Business Research, 63*, 347–355.

Fichter, K. (1998). Umweltkommunikation und Wettbewerbsfähigkeit: Wettbewerbstheorien im Lichteempirischer Ergebnisse zur Umweltberich terstattung von Unternehmen [Environmental communication and competitiveness: Competition theories in the light of empirical results on corporate environmental reporting]. Marburg, Germany: Metropolis Verlag.

Fournier, S. M. (2009). Lessons learned about consumers' relationships with their brands. In D. J. MacInnis, C. W. Park, & J. R. Priester (Eds.), *Handbook of brand relationships* (pp. 5–23). M.E. Sharpe.

Franco, M. (2022). Changes in consumption patterns of tourists after the COVID-19 pandemic. In D. Vrontis, A. Thrassou, Y. Weber, S. M. R. Shams, E. Tsoukatos, & L. Efthymiou (Eds.), *Business under crisis volume I*. Palgrave Studies in Cross-disciplinary Business Research, In Association with EuroMed Academy of Business. Palgrave Macmillan. https://doi.org/10.1007/978-3-030-76567-5_5.

Freeman, R. (1984). *Strategic management: A stakeholder approach*. Pitman.

Garrett, D. E. (1987). The effectiveness of marketing policy boycotts: Environmental opposition to marketing. *The Journal of Marketing, 51*(2), 46–57.

Greer, J. and Bruno, K. (1998). Greenwash: The Reality Behind Corporate Environmentalism. Maryland, USA: Rowman & Littlefield Publishers.

Greenbaum, R. L., Mawritz, M. B., & Piccolo, R. F. (2015). When leaders fail to "walk the talk": Supervisor undermining and perceptions of leader hypocrisy. *Journal of Management, 41*(3), 929–956.

Gruber, V., Kaliauer, M., & Schegelmilch, B. (2017). Improving the effectiveness and credibility of corporate social responsibility messaging: An Austrian model identifies influential CSR content and communication channels. *Journal of Advertising Research, 57*(4), 397–409.

Heijnen, P., & van der Made, A. (2012). A signalling theory of consumer boycotts. *Journal of Environmental Economics and Management, 63*, 404–418.

Hoffmann, S., & Müller, S. (2009). Consumer boycotts due to factory relocation. *Journal of Business Research, 62*(2), 239–247.

Keeble, J. (2022). *Report: What it will take for CEOs to fund a sustainable transformation*. Retrieved November 12, 2022, from https://cloud.google.com/blog/topics/sustainability/new-survey-reveals-executives-views-about-sustainability

Kim, J., Lee, J., & Kim, S. (2017). The efficacy of cause related marketing within a social network: The effects of congruency, corporate credibility, familiarity of cause brands, and perceived altruistic motive. *Journal of Marketing Communications, 23*(5), 429–455.

Klein, J. G., Smith, N. C., & John, A. (2003). Exploring motivations for participation in a consumer boycott. In S. Broniarczyk & K. Nakamoto (Eds.), *Advances in consumer research* (Vol. 29, pp. 363–369). Association for Consumer Research.

Klein, J. G., Smith, N. C., & John, A. (2004). Why we boycott: Consumer motivations for boycott participation. *Journal of Marketing, 68*(3), 92–109.

Kucharska, W., Confente, I., & Brunetti, F. (2020). The power of personal brand authenticity and identification: Top celebrity players' contribution to loyalty toward football. *Journal of Product & Brand Management, 29*(6), 815–830.

Lam, S.K., Ahearne, M., Mullins, R., Hayati, B., & Schillewaert, N. (2013). Exploring the dynamics of antecedents to consumer-brand identification with a new brand. *Journal of the Academy of Marketing Science, 41*(2), 234–252. https://doi.org/10.1007/s11747-012-0301-x.

Lindenmeier, J., Schleer, C., & Pricl, D. (2012). Consumer outrage: Emotional reactions to unethical corporate behaviour. *Journal of Business Research, 65*, 1364–1373.

Martin, B. A. S., Lang, B., & Wong, S. (2004). Conclusion explicitness in advertising. *Journal of Advertising, 32*(Winter), 57–65.

Melewar, T. C., & Karaosmanoglu, E. (2006). Corporate branding, identity and communications: A contemporary perspective. *Journal of Brand Management, 14*(1/2), 1–4. https://doi.org/10.1057/palgrave.bm.2550061

Micheletti, M. (2003). *Political virtue and shopping: Individuals, consumerism, and collective action*. Palgrave Macmillan.

Mohr, L. A., & Webb, D. J. (2005). The effects of corporate social responsibility and Price on consumer responses. *Journal of Consumer Affairs, 39*(Spring), 127–147.

Mohr, L. A., Webb, D. J., & Harris, K. E. (2001). Do consumers expect companies to be socially responsible? The impact of corporate social responsibility on buying behaviour. *Journal of Consumer Affairs, 35*(1), 45–72.

Mohr, M., & Schlich, M. (2015). Socio-demographic basic factors of German customers as predictors for sustainable consumerism regarding foodstuffs and meat products. *International of Journal Consumer Studies, 40*, 158–167.

Murray, K. B., & Vogel, C. M. (1997). Using a hierarchy-of-effects approach to gauge the effectiveness of corporate social responsibility to generate goodwill toward the firm: Financial versus nonfinancial impacts. *Journal of Business Research, 38*(2), 141–159.

Neilson, L. A. (2010). Boycott or buycott? Understanding political consumerism. *Journal of Consumer Behaviour, 9*(3), 214–227.

Neureiter, M., & Bhattacharya, C. B. (2021). Why do boycotts sometimes increase sales? Consumer activism in the age of political polarization. *Business Horizons, 64*(5), 611–620.

Newman, B. J., & Bartels, B. L. (2011). Politics at the checkout line: Explaining political consumerism in the United States. *Political Research Quarterly, 64*(4), 803–817.

Öberseder, M., Schlegelmilch, B. B., & Gruber, V. (2011). "Why don't consumers care about CSR?": A qualitative study exploring the role of CSR in consumption decisions. *Journal of Business Ethics, 104*(4), 449–460.

Paek, H.-J., & Nelson, M. R. (2009). To buy or not to buy: Determinants of socially responsible consumer behaviour and consumer reactions to cause-related and boycotting ads. *Journal of Current Issues & Research in Advertising, 31*(2), 75–90.

Pomering, A., & Dolnicar, S. (2009). Assessing the prerequisite of suc- cessful CSR implementation: Are consumers aware of CSR initiatives? *Journal of Business Ethics, 85*(2), 285–301. https://doi.org/10.1007/s10551-008-9729-9

Prendergast, G. P., & Tsang, A. S. L. (2019). Explaining socially responsible consumption. *Journal of Consumer Marketing, 36*(1), 146–154.

Romani, S., Grappi, S., & Bagozzi, R. P. (2013). Explaining consumer reactions to corporate social responsibility: The role of gratitude and altruistic values. *Journal of Business Ethics, 114*, 193–206.

Schlaile, M., Klein, K., & Böck, W. (2016). From bounded morality to consumer social responsibility: A transdisciplinary approach to socially responsible consumption and its obstacles. *Journal of Business Ethics, 149*, 1–28.

Schudson, M. (2006). The troubling equivalence of citizen and consumer. *The Annals of the American Academy of Political and Social Science, 608*(1), 193–204.

Scruggs, L., Hertel, S., Best, S., & Jeffords, C. (2011). Information, choices and political consumption: Human rights in the checkout lane. *Human Rights Quarterly, 33*(4), 11092–11121.

Sen, S., & Bhattacharya, C. B. (2001). Does doing good always lead to doing better? Consumer reactions to corporate social responsibility. *Journal of Marketing Research, 38*(2), 225–243.

Signitzer, B., & Prexl, A. (2008). Corporate communications sustainability: Aspects of theory and professionalization. *Journal of Public Relations Research.*

Šimanskienė, L., Paužuolienė, J., Fiore, M., & Župerkienė, E. (2022). Responsible consumption: Society habits in time of crisis. In D. Vrontis, A. Thrassou, Y. Weber, S. M. R. Shams, E. Tsoukatos, L. Efthymiou (Eds.), *Business under crisis, Volume III.* Palgrave Studies in Cross-disciplinary Business Research, In Association with EuroMed Academy of Business. Palgrave Macmillan. https://doi.org/10.1007/978-3-030-76583-5_12.

Song, S. Y., & Kim, Y.-K. (2018). Theory of virtue ethics: Do consumers' good traits predict their socially responsible consumption? *Journal of Business Ethics, 152,* 1159–1175.

Stokburger-Sauer, N., Ratneshwar, S., & Sen, S. (2012). Drivers of consumer-brand identification. *International Journal of Research in Marketing, 29,* 406–418.

Stolle, D., & Micheletti, M. (2013). *Political consumerism: Global responsibility in action.* Cambridge University Press.

Thrassou, A., Efthymiou, L., Vrontis, D., Weber, Y., Shams, S. M. R., & Tsoukatos, E. (2022). Editorial introduction: Crisis in context. In D. Vrontis, A. Thrassou, Y. Weber, S. M. R. Shams, E. Tsoukatos, L. Efthymiou (Eds.), *Business under crisis volume I.* Palgrave Studies in Cross-disciplinary Business Research, In Association with EuroMed Academy of Business. Palgrave Macmillan. https://doi.org/10.1007/978-3-030-76567-5_1.

Tyran, J.-R., & Engelmann, D. (2005). To buy or not to buy? An experimental study of consumer boycotts in retail markets. *Economica, 72*(285), 1–16.

Vilanova, M., Lozano, J. M., & Arenas, D. (2009). Exploring the nature of the relationship between CSR and competitiveness. *Journal of Business Ethics, 87*(1), 57–69.

von Rosen, R. (2003). Nachhaltigkeit und shareholder value aus Sicht börsennotierter Unternehmen. [Sustainability and shareholder value from the perspective of listed companies]. Frankfurt, Germany: Deutsches Aktieninstitut.

Villa Castaño, L. E., Perdomo-Ortiz, J., Dueñas Ocampo, S., & Durán León, W. F. (2016). Socially responsible consumption: An application in Colombia. *Business Ethics, the Environment & Responsibility, 25*(4), 460–481.

Wagner, T., Lutz, R. J., & Weitz, B. A. (2009). Corporate hypocrisy: Overcoming the threat of inconsistent corporate social responsibility perceptions. *Journal of Marketing, 73*(6), 77–91.

Webb, J. D., Mohr, L. A., & Harris, K. H. (2008). A re-examination of socially responsible consumption and its measurement. *Journal of Business Research, 61*, 91–98.

Woods, D. (1991). Social issues in management: Theory and research in corporate social performance. *Journal of Management, 17*(2), 384–406.

You, L., and Hon, L.C. (2021). Testing the effects of reputation, value congruence and brand identity on word-ofmouth intentions. *Journal of Communication Management, 25*(2), 160–181. https://doi.org/10.1108/JCOM-10-2020-0119.

Yuksel, U. (2013). Non-participation in anti-consumption: Consumer reluctance to boycott. *Journal of Macromarketing, 33*(3), 204–216.

Zack, J. (1991). The hullabaloo over boycott ballyhoo. *Business and Social Review, 78*(Summer), 9–15.

3

Sustainability of Youth Development in Drylands: A Systematic Approach

Aleksandra Figurek, Elena I. Semenova, and Alkis Thrassou

1 Introduction

Dryland climate change persists to pose significant and developing threats to rural livelihoods and young people's chances of finding quality, climate-resilient employment (Wiggins et al., 2021; Levine et al., 2021; Gony et al., 2021). According to estimates, 798.8 million people in Africa

A. Figurek (✉)
GNOSIS Mediterranean Institute for Management Science, University of Nicosia, Nicosia, Cyprus

School of Business, University of Nicosia, Nicosia, Cyprus
e-mail: figurek.a@live.unic.ac.cy

E. I. Semenova
Federal Research Center of Agrarian Economy and Social Development of Rural Areas, All Russian Research Institute of Agricultural Economics, Moscow, Russia

Russian State Correspondence Agricultural University, Moscow, Russia

D. Vrontis et al. (eds.), *Business for Sustainability, Volume I*, Palgrave Studies in Cross-disciplinary Business Research, In Association with EuroMed Academy of Business, https://doi.org/10.1007/978-3-031-37361-9_3

(59.6% of the population) and 282 million people (21% of the population) had moderate to severe food insecurity in 2020. These numbers climbed by about 30% from 2015 to the present (FAO, 2021). Land degradation in drylands is being caused by human activities, including inappropriate land use and climate change, which has a severe negative impact on agricultural and livestock output (Stavi et al., 2021).

Due to the absence of educational and job prospects in their hometowns as a result of these developments, many rural young people must leave their homes in order to pursue their futures (Farrugia, 2016). Because of the devastating effects of climate change on drylands, human movement is significantly impacted in Africa (Šedová et al., 2021). As a result of a sudden or gradual shift in the climate, individuals or groups of individuals known as "climate migrants" are compelled to leave their usual residence for prolonged periods of time or permanently (IOM, 2021). If those who have been first displaced do not go back to where they were initially displaced, migration may also arise from that original displacement. This is certainly relevant in relation to how youth ambitions, involvement with the land, and employment in rural areas are influenced by education, migration, and technology; all of which are relevant to FTA (FAO, 2018).

About 27% of China's population lives in the drylands of northern China (DNC), which make up 41% of China's geographical area (Wu et al., 2014; Li et al., 2016). Due to its enormous size and numerous difficulties with water shortage, ecological deficit, and poverty, the DNC is one of the main regions in connection to sustainable development. The realisation of a harmonious cohabitation between man and environment, the application of the ecological construction idea of experience, and the building of a new structure of human civic society all depend greatly on sustainable development both theoretically and practically (Guo et al., 2022). In order to transform the society, restructure the markets, concentrate on information and technology breakthroughs, and enhance social systems, sustainable development became a part of several international

---

A. Thrassou
GNOSIS Mediterranean Institute for Management Science,
School of Business, University of Nicosia, Nicosia, Cyprus
e-mail: thrassou.a@unic.ac.cy

and regional programmes (Thrassou, Vrontis, et al., 2022). Sustainability is an effort to reconcile people's life quality with environmental, economic, and societal goals (Vasileiou & Morris, 2006). Sustainable development also entails deliberate initiatives to link science with realistic decision-making and execution.

The relative importance of agriculture in national economies, the current level of intensification in agricultural production, the limitations and opportunities posed by the availability of agricultural resources, as well as the needs of individuals in communities, are just a few of the many considerations that must be made when developing sustainable approaches. Across a range of situations, the configuration of agriculture and the tools for promoting sustainability processes will unavoidably alter. To assist the young people who work in agriculture, increase productivity and production, and reduce agriculture's environmental impact, sustainable agriculture will necessitate ongoing adjustment, innovation, and improvement in strategies, policies, and technology. The primary goals of sustainable agriculture are: (a) enhancing the health of farmers and consumers (through organic farming and food security); (b) preserving the stability of the environment (through biological pest control and fertilisation techniques); (c) working to ensure long-term advantages for farmers; and (d) taking into account the needs of both the present and future generations (Leyva et al., 2021).

The sustainability of this industry is essential since it produces the majority of the world's food, textiles, papers, and building materials (Pashaei Kamali et al., 2017). Young people need to continue living in rural regions and working in agriculture, especially in difficult terrain like drylands, for the sustainability of agriculture and food production (Reddy et al., 2021). Sustainability in agricultural development is defined by the FAO as "the management and conservation of the natural resource base, and the orientation of technological and institutional change in such a manner as to ensure the attainment and continued satisfaction of human needs for present and future generations." This type of development protects genetic resources for plants, animals, and the environment while also being technically sound, commercially feasible, and socially acceptable (FAO, 2019). The term "drylands" refers to regions with a high degree of climatic unpredictability, poor soil fertility, sparse and transient populations, geographic isolation from development infrastructure, weak institutions, low human capital, a wealth of indigenous knowledge, and ethnic and cultural diversity.

The purpose of the chapter is to provide a methodological approach for youth sustainability in dryland areas in order to achieve a balance between social, economic, and environmental objectives. In order to offer a thorough foundation for the sustainability of food and agricultural systems, participants and their involvement in the agri-food supply-chain in drylands are of utmost importance while respecting the objectives of sustainable development.

2 Methodology

The systematic approach will be used because of the chapter's methodological and applied character. The objective of the methodological concepts through a systematic approach is to discover crucial components for youth sustainability in drylands. The development of a conceptual framework, which is reflected in the analysis, improvement of current systems, and creation of an entirely novel one, requires systematic study (Cavallo, 1982). By using system analysis and methodological procedures, it is feasible to tear down the system into its component parts in order to investigate how they interact.

Decision-makers can be assisted by system analytical research to find solutions to their immediate, medium-term, and long-term problems. Anticipatory action and planning are required in the context of climate mobilities to allow forward-looking, solution-oriented approaches (Thalheimer et al., 2022). These can aid in promoting sustainability and resilience in communities in drylands that are impacted by climate change. With regard to both natural (such as atmospheric, biological, and hydrologic) and human systems (such as economic, social, and infrastructural), system thinking recognises the strong ties and interdependencies between various types of systems and their constituent elements (Berry et al., 2018).

System analytical methodologies, which are intrinsically interdisciplinary and multidisciplinary, are ideally suited to understanding climate mobility in many contexts, emphasising that the climate mobility nexus is deeply anchored in larger challenges of sustainable development and other population dynamics (Hoffmann, 2022). Studying the effects of climate change in drylands on youth mobility, as well as its implications and associated difficulties for origin and destination communities, requires such a broad approach. For instance, the intricately intertwined social, economic, and political systems in a community that are impacted by environmental and nonenvironmental elements shape decisions about (non)migration. Translocal migration networks (Greiner & Sakdapolrak, 2013) connect origin and destination regions and make up a separate social system that works closely with other systems.

To solve complex problems and interrelated difficulties, system analytical techniques prioritise integrative thinking (Hynes et al., 2020). Systems can react to inputs in unpredictable ways; this structure also holds true for the effects of climate change on living societies (Gaupp et al., 2021). These are referred to as social consequences (such as limitations of liability) above which the systems can no longer adjust to changes in environmental circumstances, potentially increasing migration (Bentley et al., 2014). It is vital to include players amongst varied partners—from research and policy—in order to produce a greater integration of different viewpoints in the system and its tighter cooperation.

Governmental assistance, international initiatives and finances, and the creation of youth groups can all help to slow the exodus of young

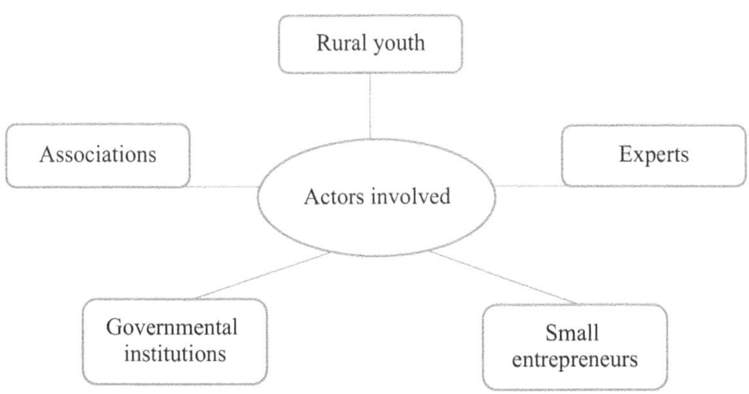

Fig. 3.1 Actors as system components

people from drylands (Fig. 3.1). Young farmers can obtain land, financing, and technical expertise through initiatives and projects for young people, according to Ghanem (2015). Youth cannot make use of the available funding if they are not provided with proper information. As they are undereducated and poorly organised into organisations or economic interest groups, they are frequently unable to participate in supporting programs (Bouzidi et al., 2015). The key players in any global scenario involving dryland investment were identified by United Nations Environment Management System (2011) as follows:

- Government: the sectoral ministries of the state, such as the Ministries of Agriculture, Transport, and Environment, parastatals, and governance at all levels;
- Private: commercial: large-scale farming enterprises, corporations, and companies;
- Family: family farms, herders and livelihoods, small-scale businesses, and the informal sector;
- Public: national and international organisations outside the state pursuing particular agendas, such as nongovernmental organisations;
- Donors: Bilateral and multilateral financial backers of programs and initiatives for international development.

The first step in encouraging young people in drylands to stay in rural regions might be for the state and other actors to provide capacity building for them. Youth education in agricultural drylands is necessary for sustainable dryland systems that enable youth to create respectable and long-lasting livelihoods in rural communities based on agriculture. In order to empower individuals and make them accountable for providing possibilities, research and development are being done on a mentorship model that might be used as the next step between public authorities and rural youth.

The institutions that control agricultural production—deciding what is produced, who produces it, with what kinds of technology and techniques, and to what degree—are crucial levers for controlling the kind and distribution of the goods and services that may be generated from agriculture. The advantages derived from such services range across many geographical dimensions, from individual farmers to landscape/watershed or local levels, to national and global levels, and they may be immediate, near-term, or long-term in nature.

These must be founded on equitable, accessible, and inclusive knowledge creation, transfer, and implementation systems that engage a variety of stakeholders, including those from the communities most directly impacted by the effects of climate change (Piguet et al., 2018). The key to effectively integrating academics from other areas as well as from varied geographical and economic origins is to establish more equitable funding schemes and research collaborations as well as to invest in science and education. Additionally, multistakeholder collaborations and participatory methods may help enable evidence-based decision-making that is pertinent to local settings and involves participants from academics, the public, and commercial sectors (Lemos, 2015).

3 Sustainable Development Goals (SDG)

It is anticipated that climate change would have significant socioeconomic repercussions and pose a significant challenge to achieving equitable and sustainable development in drylands. Climate change, unexpected severe weather, biodiversity loss, soil erosion, land degradation, and water pollution have all had an impact on agriculture and the food chain. All definitions of agricultural vulnerability, regardless of variations, essentially incorporate exposure, sensitivity, and adaptation capability (Rao et al., 2019). The type and extent of a system's vulnerability to climatic fluctuations are defined here as vulnerability. In the literature on rural distress, vulnerability is frequently mentioned (Gallai et al., 2009; Khan et al., 2021).

The ability to adapt is essential for adjusting risk exposure, risk absorption, and the capacity to recover from exposure-related losses. The tendency or predisposition to suffer damage is another definition of adaptive capability. Therefore, it is crucial to decrease sensitivity and increase the adaptive capability of local populations in order to reduce vulnerability stress. The capacity to adapt varies between settings and systems and is tightly correlated with aspects related to infrastructure, institutions, communities, social, political, economic, educational, health, technological, and cognitive factors (Chauhan et al., 2020).

As part of the Sustainability Assessment of Food and Agriculture (SAFA) systems, organisations involved in the global agri-food supply chain will be assessed in order to provide a comprehensive framework for the sustainability of food and agricultural systems (FAO, 2014). For example, by limiting warming to 1.5 °C, various regions can significantly lower hazards, which would significantly lessen the pressure on impacted populations to migrate (Thalheimer et al., 2021).

The Sustainable Development Goals (SDGs) announced by the United Nations in 2015 and the difficulties encountered by rainfed agriculture are intertwined. SDGs 1 (no poverty), 2 (zero hunger), 13 (action on climate change), and 15 (life on land) are incorporated into this area (Raghavan et al., 2018). The SDGs and the potential contributions that citizen science can make to their fulfilment have drawn more and more attention in the last five years from the subject of scientific research (Parkinson et al., 2022).

CGIAR focuses on agricultural research for development, and its work helps the world struggle against issues including hunger, poverty, serious nutrient deficiencies, and environmental degradation. According to the CGIAR Strategy and Results Framework 2016–2030, it will directly contribute to the realisation of the Sustainable Development Goals (SDGs) set out by the United Nations: reducing and adjusting to the risks and shocks of climate change, enhancing the institutional and policy framework that promotes inclusion of youth, as well as developing the ability of national partners and beneficiaries (Fig. 3.2).

Achievements in many different fields might be threatened by climate change. These accomplishments include, among others, those related to the Sustainable Development Goals (SDGs) on ending poverty (SDG1), achieving food security (SDG2), promoting health (SDG3), promoting gender equality (SDG5), ensuring access to clean water and sanitation (SDG6), reducing inequality (SDG10), improving working conditions (SDG8), and promoting peace, justice, and strong institutions (16).

The identification and maintenance of a balance between the social, economic, and environmental goals of agriculture as well as between agriculture and other economic sectors is seen as an ongoing process toward

Fig. 3.2 Contribution to the SDG. (Source: CGIAR database access 30.01.2023)

promoting sustainability in food and agriculture (Diagram 3.1). The procedure is a reflection of how society's values and body of knowledge have changed over time, which has a significant influence on how sustainability objectives are actually created. This suggests a significant, complex, and dynamic system of interactions with several access points. There are hard and soft boundaries that human and natural systems must operate within for the process as a whole to be sustainable. Within this complex system, specific constraints and natural and socio-economic boundaries will define what falls into the sustainable operating space.

4 Agricultural Production by the Youth in Drylands

The majority of people who reside in rural regions of many developing nations, particularly those in Sub-Saharan Africa (SSA), struggle with poverty and food insecurity (AGRA, 2020; Bello et al., 2021; FAO, 2014). According to statistics, more than 34% of South Africa's workforce is jobless (Statistics South Africa, 2021). This is true despite the introduction and execution of a number of policies and programmes, including the Expanded Public Works Program, the Growth, Employment

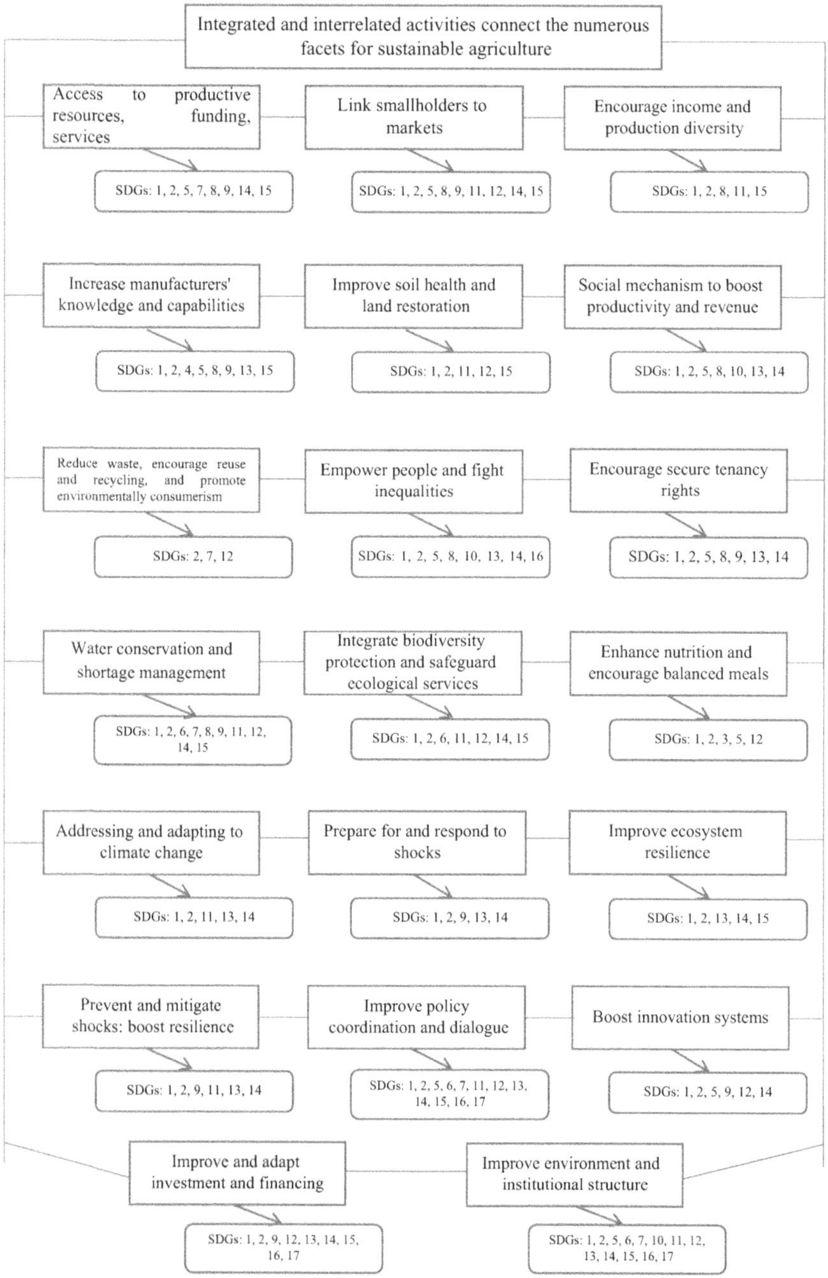

Diagram 3.1 Integrated activities related to sustainable agriculture, authors work according to FAO

and Redistribution Policy, the National Development Plan Vision 2030, and the Employment Tax Incentives Bill (also known as the Youth Wage Subsidy). These programmes were put in place to boost economic development and address a number of socioeconomic issues, such as unemployment, inequality, and poverty. However, these issues are still a constant, particularly for the underprivileged and young people.

There is a need for more disaggregated data regarding various youth—in terms of age, gender, and so on—in order to better understand the heterogeneity of young people and be able to build suitable and successful policies and programmes for promoting sustainable livelihoods (Bennell, 2017; Grant & Furstenberg, 2007; Senders et al., 2014). Even in the long run, it is uncertain that enough jobs will be created to accommodate all of the active job searchers due to the pandemic's effects and the economy's persistently weak growth rate. Due to this, government officials, academics, and politicians have recognised self-employment as a viable option to help reduce unemployment, particularly among young people.

According to the theory of bounded rationality (TRB), social validation (how people support or disapprove of a certain activity/choice) and perceptions (how people around you see a specific situation/activity/choice) influence the response to a choice/action (Fishbein & Ajzen, 2011; Montano & Kasprzyk, 2015). Youth are persons who primarily take their inspiration and goals from the accomplishments, views, and practical experiences of people around them, therefore how they view agricultural-related economic activities and what other people think about agriculture affects how they make decisions.

The principal economic activity in rural regions is agriculture, which has the ability to provide rural youth with employment opportunities. The youth, however, view agriculture as a part-time job rather than a career or means of support. Studies show that people view agriculture as a low status, labour-intensive, and undesirable occupation (Geza et al., 2021; Irungu et al., 2015). Because they view non-agricultural occupations and off-farm work as more stable, giving comparatively more pay, and demanding less physical effort, youth choose them (Bello et al., 2021; Rietveld et al., 2020)

Eight broad categories can be used to organise the youth's biggest problems (Endris et al., 2022): (1) regional norms and customs, (2) finances, (3) technical capacity and education, (4) market and infrastructure, (5) economic, (6) administration and policy-related issues, (7) environmental issues, and (8) others. For the growth of rural people as well as the regeneration of the sector, it is essential to create the conditions for young people in rural areas to actively engage in the agricultural value chain. This is due to the fact that participating in these activities might have benefits that go beyond just them. The backward and forward interconnections will have a variety of positive implications for the larger community, including the creation of job opportunities and the improvement of skills. The increasing demand for raw materials (farm products) and technical skills necessary for companies throughout the agricultural value chain are only a couple of the possible investment possibilities that might be sparked by backward linkages. Value-adding operations will make food more easily accessible to rural customers thanks to the forward connections. A favourable environment for agricultural operations will be created by these connections taken together.

Arslan et al. (2021) and Bello et al. (2021) also made note of the fact that youth inherently possess special cognitive abilities and admirable qualities (like creativity, innovative thinking, and adaptability) that are essential for the transformation, growth, and sustainability of the agricultural sector in drylands. In order to reduce rural youth unemployment and improve the inadequate succession plan in smallholder agriculture, it is crucial to identify the agricultural activities that rural youth would be interested in participating in as well as the variables that enable and restrict their involvement.

Dryland systems are diverse, and the development issues they provide differ. Mitigating vulnerability or risk and boosting resilience are the main challenges facing dryland livelihood systems. It is important to locate and seize possibilities for production intensification in situations where the environment drives output in response to market and human opportunities. The likelihood of such livelihood systems is centred on linking to economic growth, equality, and environmental sustainability as well as agricultural production.

There is a need for technical ad-hoc training on livestock (fodder, breeding, vaccinations), the sustainable use of crop production inputs (seeds, fertilisers, plant protection products), and so on to support livelihoods in drylands. Youth should also be educated on how to better organise their production in rural areas. On their family farms, young people are also not frequently involved in decision-making, which demotivates them from implementing their ideas in rural regions. Rural youth in drylands would be able to assess their production potential and make a better assessment of variables indicating the success or failure of production activities by obtaining more organisation in the fulfilment of production activities. Control over work processes and a database of previous company results need to serve as the foundation for good decision-making assistance.

In pastoral and agropastoral areas, general recommendations to increase youth involvement in agriculture may include: (1) developing infrastructure and regulatory interventions, as well as specific training in agricultural practises aimed at and engaging youth, (2) expanding access to youth-friendly credit and saving, (3) encouraging agripreneurship training and business startups, and (4) ensuring the availability of locally tailored and gender-responsive rural finance (Endris et al., 2022).

Controlling or managing the farm may be made easier by keeping track of production processes, specific farm operations, and costs associated with those activities. The subsequent decisions made in the field are crucial for the planning and control of production operations and should be treated with great care and in light of well-planned future actions. The financial statements' economic data, which portrays the farm's financial situation, is crucial for the farm's future management.

Depending on the type of farm, records on farms provide better projections of future activities. These reports have to highlight a genuine representation of the farm company, pinpoint key production phases and the requirement to implement specific changes through improved production activity organisation, which would have the impact of enhancing the financial outcome.

A barrier to the development of agriculture in drylands is the lack of accurate data on the production and operations of agricultural holdings and the undereducation of agricultural producers. In the future, it will be necessary to work on the creation of a system that would gather the required data and create an information base for creating quality measures of agricultural policy in drylands, as well as educate the young agricultural producers.

5 Ensuring the Sustainability of Young People in Dryland Agriculture

Sustainability has been viewed as requiring innovation as a key component. However, because it creates a competitive edge in the agri-food industry and adds value to the food supply chain, innovation has turned into a financial opportunity for managers. With measurable benefits on profitability or sustainability, innovation may help food firms with a variety of problems or obstacles. Numerous innovations have been put into place along the agri-food supply chain to reduce costs, implement new technologies, improve food quality, develop new products, adhere to the best manufacturing or hygiene practices, guarantee cleaner production, optimise processes, implement lean manufacturing, highly valorise food by-products, recycle food waste, recover energy, and so on.

In another line of reasoning, Bigliardi and Galanakis (2020) analysed innovation classification in the food business. They identified a few food sector innovation models, focusing on food innovation examples motivated by sustainability (e.g., food waste recovery, packaging materials, or modern sanitation). Effective investment and gaining local and regional economic and environmental advantages will depend on involving young people in all their diversity—women, men, and individuals with different (dis)abilities and other qualities. Particularly, there are enormous unmet demands and potential to invest in more locally relevant, climate-smart education, technical and vocational training, and pathways for young people in the drylands into respectable employment. This is particularly true for young people from pastoralist communities, whose access to educational and training programmes has, up until now, been incredibly limited.

Young people themselves might be influenced to choose new career options, both inside and outside of agriculture and pastoralism, that is, their impression of the "opportunity spaces" available (Dupar & Lovel, 2021). Importantly, decision-makers and practitioners in the field of development may recognise and capitalise on the many opportunities that are present to promote economic growth in the drylands. This includes attracting investment for some of the priorities, like renewable energy production (including solar, geothermal, and wind power) and new and green technologies, which would all increase the actual "opportunity spaces" or job prospects for young people. It also includes the tourism, processing, and service industries, as well as new livelihood opportunities in urban centres.

To overcome the lack of experience, young farmers require access to the correct knowledge (Diagram 3.2). Advantages comprise integrated training techniques that meet their requirements rather than the number of technical education or extension services that may be insufficient. While contemporary information and communication technologies (ICTs) (such as mobile phones, laptops, and the Internet) are appealing to young people, there are numerous features to their usage, such as illiteracy, cost, and restricted Internet coverage. Initiatives or activities that aim to encourage youth interests and comparative advantages, such as farm fellowships for further agricultural education or business development and management combined with financing for young people are from big importance. Crises are often the driving force of change, be it technological, social, economic or other (Vrontis et al., 2022; Thrassou, Efthymiou, et al., 2022).

The development of rural groups may be beneficial to young people because they provide economies of scale for purchasing food production, access to land as well as other resources, a platform to sell products and share knowledge, and a stronger voice for policy engagement. Partnerships are integrated and structured in order to engage with young people entering agriculture. These collaborations must be open and consistent from the municipal to the regional planning agencies, organisations, private sector, and donor agencies.

Development organisations and actors operating in the drylands should consciously seek out young people, especially those with

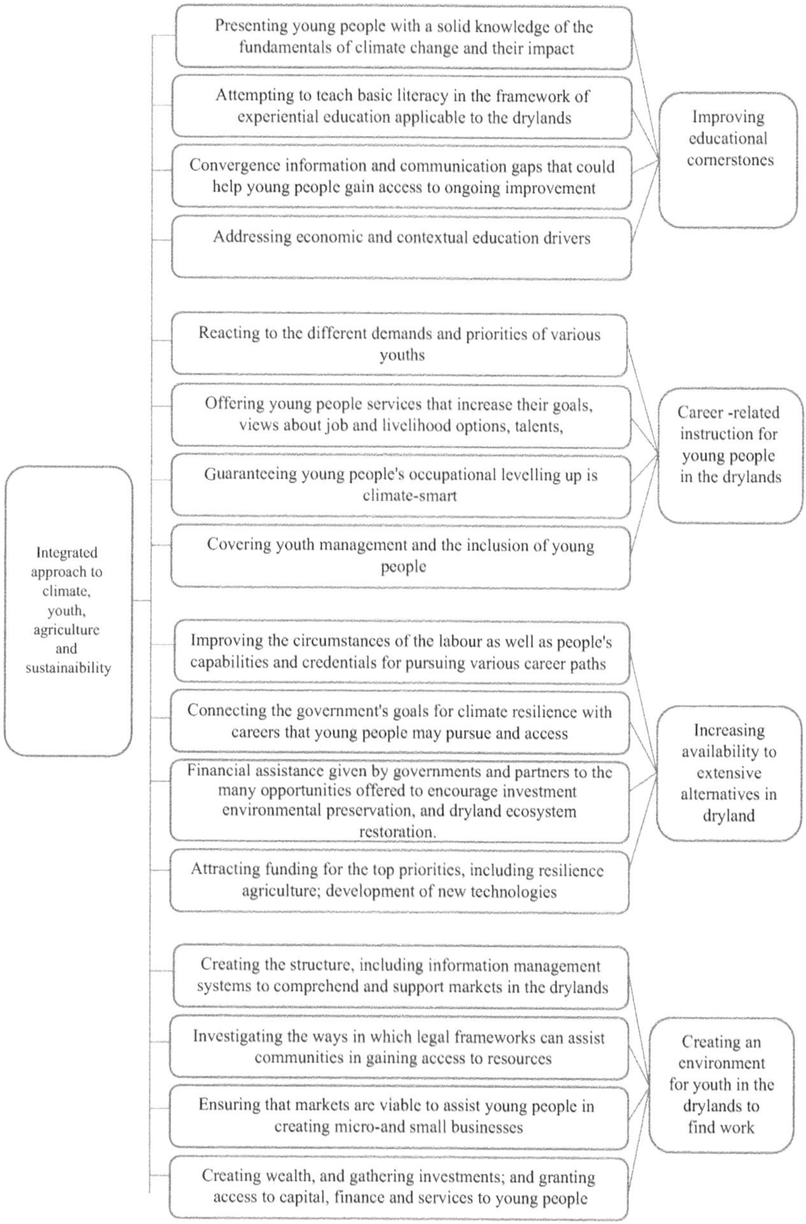

Diagram 3.2 Integrated approach towards sustainability, drylands and agricultural youth

pastoralist origins, to consult, collaborate with, and develop their leadership and decision-making abilities. Natural resources (such land and water) must be accessed or owned in order for rural youth to actively participate in a typical agricultural activity (Geza et al., 2021). Additionally, one has to have access to financial resources so they may buy the tools, services, and technology needed to successfully launch and oversee agricultural operations along the value chain. Additionally required are the abilities, education, and understanding required to manage and conduct such tasks. Due to their underrepresentation in policy-making processes, young people from rural, dryland backgrounds, particularly those with a pastoralist upbringing, do not have their needs, priorities, vulnerabilities, and talents taken into consideration.

The identification and maintenance of a balance between the social, economic, and environmental goals of agriculture as well as between agriculture and other economic sectors are seen as an ongoing process towards achieving sustainability in agriculture in drylands (Diagram 3.3).

6 Conclusion

Agriculture in drylands requires integrated strategies that link the social and environmental challenges that farmers there must overcome. In order to reduce rural youth unemployment and improve the inadequate succession plan in smallholder agriculture, it is crucial to identify the agricultural activities that rural youth would be interested in participating in as well as the variables that enable and restrict their involvement.

In the dryland regions, there are additional chances to help young people making the transition to an agroecological system. Cooperation and social support networks, natural resources, the potential of agroecology for livestock production, strategic livestock market locations, and the potential of natural resources can all be mobilised and tapped to promote successful agroecological transition and guarantee food security in the study locations. To accurately depict the difficulties of agricultural production in drylands and the impacts of climate change on agricultural productivity, all of this should be taken into consideration.

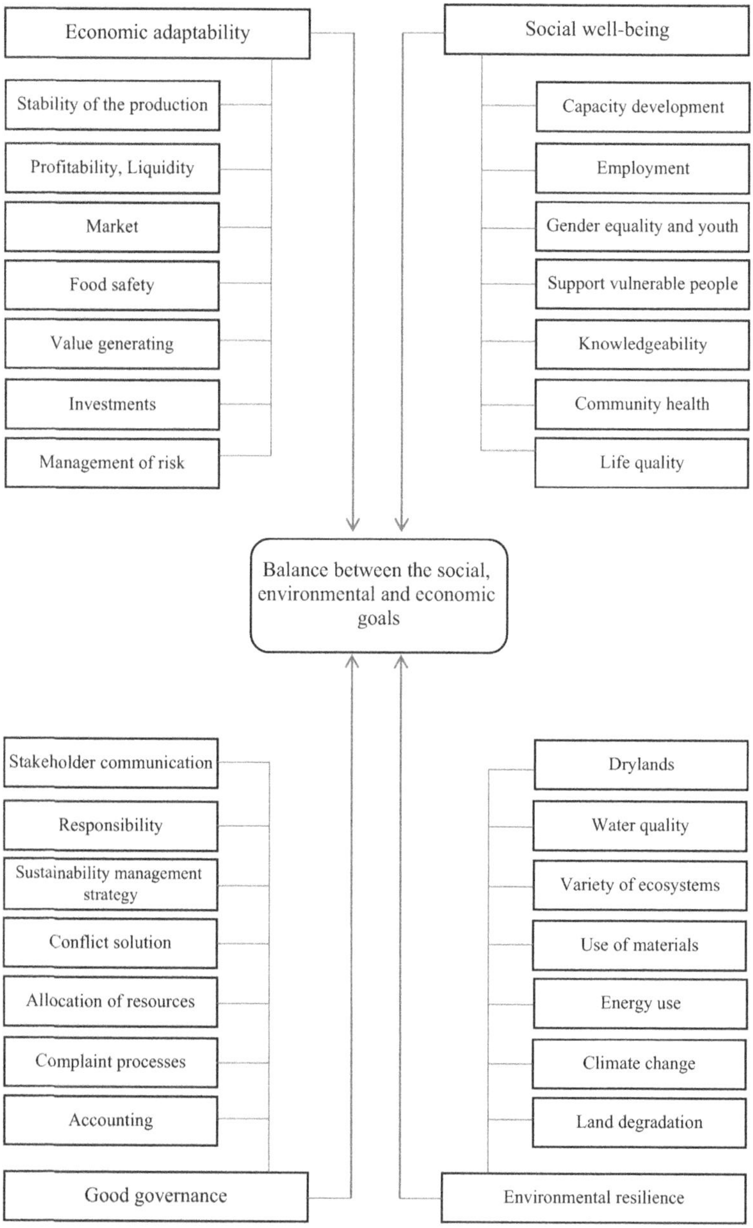

Diagram 3.3 Balance between the social, environmental, and economic goals

More comprehensive proposals for actions that contribute to the sustainability of young people in drylands include: enhancing the educational foundations for decent work by teaching fundamental literacy and numeracy in the context of applied learning that is relevant to the drylands; ensuring that young people have a solid understanding of the fundamentals of climate change and its implications; addressing the socioeconomic and culturally specific drivers of school absence; bridging information and communication barriers that might provide young people access to lifelong learning; modifying lesson plans to take pastoralist communities' unique needs into consideration.

Even in the long term, it is improbable that enough jobs will be created to accommodate all of the active job searchers due to the pandemic's effects and the economy's persistently weak growth rate. For this reason, self-employment has also been highlighted by policymakers, academics, and government officials as a viable way to help reduce unemployment, particularly among young people.

The corresponding importance of agriculture, the level of agricultural production intensification currently in place, the opportunities and constraints posed by the availability of agricultural resources in drylands, as well as the needs of individuals in communities, must all be considered when developing sustainable approaches. It is essential that the configuration of agriculture and the tools for promoting sustainable processes will change depending on the circumstances. In order to assist the youth who are involved in agriculture in drylands and to optimise productivity and production, sustainable agriculture will require ongoing adjustment, innovation, and development in strategies, policies, and technology.

For the growth of rural people as well as the rehabilitation of the drylands, it is essential to create the conditions for young people in rural areas to actively engage in the agricultural value chain. This is due to the fact that participating in these activities might have benefits that go beyond just them. Through the backward and forward links, there will be several advantages for the larger community, including multiple spillover impacts including job creation chances and skill development.

A continuing process towards attaining sustainability in the agricultural sector in drylands is the identification and maintenance of a balance between the social, environmental, and economic goals as well as between agriculture and other economic sectors in drylands. The integrated approach emphasises the need for a shift in public attitudes and knowledge base.

References

Alliance for a Green Revolution in Africa. (2020). *Annual Report 2020: Nurturing Change Across African Agriculture*. AGRA, Addis Ababa, Ethopia.

Arslan, A., Tschirley, D. L., Di Nucci, C., & Winters, P. (2021). *Youth inclusion in rural transformation*. Taylor & Francis.

Bello, L. O., Baiyegunhi, L. J. S., Mignouna, D., Adeoti, R., Dontsop-Nguezet, P. M., Abdoulaye, T., Manyong, V., Bamba, Z., & Awotide, B. A. (2021). Impact of youth-in-agribusiness program on employment creation in Nigeria. *Sustainability, 13*(14), 7801.

Bennell, P. (2017). Promoting livelihood opportunities for rural youth. IFAD, Rome, Italy, 2007. https://www.ifad.org/documents/10180/05f77557-2567-4c7c-8326-e26d2fbabeb5

Bentley, R. A., Maddison, E. J., Ranner, P. H., Bissell, J., Caiado, C. C. S., Bhatanacharoen, P., et al. (2014). Social tipping points and Earth systems dynamics. *Frontiers in Environmental Science, 2*, 35. https://doi.org/10.3389/fenvs.2014.00035

Berry, H. L., Waite, T. D., Dear, K. B. G., Capon, A. G., & Murray, V. (2018). The case for systems thinking about climate change and mental health. *Nature Climate Change, 48*(4), 282–290. https://doi.org/10.1038/s41558-018-0102-4

Bigliardi, B., & Galanakis, C. (2020). Innovation management and sustainability in the food industry: Concepts and models. In C. Galanakis (Ed.), *The interaction of food industry and environment* (pp. 315–340). Academic Press. https://doi.org/10.1016/B978-0-12-816449-5.00010-2

Bouzidi, Z., Faysse, N., Kuper, M., & Billaud, J.-P. (2015). Les Projets des Jeunes Ruraux: Des Stratégies Diversifiées pour Accéder au Foncier et Obtenir l'Appui de l'État. http://alternatives-rurales.org/les-projets-des-jeunes-ruraux-des-strategies-diversifiees-pouracceder-au-foncier-et-obtenir-lappui-de-letat/

Cavallo, R. E. (1982). *Systems methodology in social science research, recent developments*. Kluwer-Nijhoff Publishing.

Chauhan, N., Shukla, R., & Joshi, P. K. (2020). Assessing impact of varied social and ecological conditions on inherent vulnerability of Himalayan agriculture communities. *Human and Ecological Risk Assessment: An International Journal, 26*, 2628–2645.

Dupar, M., & Lovel, E. (2021). Issue brief resilient generation: Supporting young people's prospects for decent work in the drylands of east and west Africa. SPARC, Supporting Pastoralism and Agriculture in Recurrent and Protracted Crises.

Endris, G. S., Wordofa, M. G., Aweke, C. S., Hassen, J. Y., Hussien, J. W., Moges, D. K., Sileshi, M., Ibrahim, M. A., Kadiro, K., & Sebsibe, K. (2022). A review of the socio-ecological and institutional contexts for youth livelihood transformation in Miesso Woreda, Eastern Ethiopia. *Cogent Social Sciences, 8*, 2152210. https://doi.org/10.1080/23311886.2022.2152210

Food and Agriculture Organization of the United Nations—FAO. (2014). SAFA—Sustainability Assessment of Food and Agriculture Systems Guidelines (version 3.0), E-ISBN 978-92-5-108486-1. Retrieved January 30, 2023, from https://www.fao.org/3/i3957e/i3957e.pdf

FAO. (2018). Transforming food and agriculture to achieve the SDGs, 20 interconnected actions to guide decision-makers.

FAO. (2019). Dimensions of need—Sustainable agriculture and rural development. https://www.fao.org/3/u8480e/U8480E0l.htm

FAO. (2021). The state of food security and nutrition in the world. FAO. https://www.fao.org/publications/sofi/2021/en/

Farrugia, D. (2016). The mobility imperative for rural youth: The structural, symbolic and non-representational dimensions rural youth mobilities. *Journal of Youth Studies, 19*(6), 836–851.

Fishbein, M., & Ajzen, I. (2011). *Predicting and changing behavior: The reasoned action approach.* Taylor & Francis Group.

Gallai, N., Salles, J. M., Settele, J., & Vaissière, B. E. (2009). Economic valuation of the vulnerability of world agriculture confronted with pollinator decline. *Ecological Economics, 68*, 810–821.

Gaupp, F., Ruggeri Laderchi, C., Lotze-Campen, H., DeClerck, F., Bodirsky, B. L., Lowder, S., et al. (2021). Food system development pathways for healthy, nature-positive and inclusive food systems. *Nature Food, 2*(12), 928–934. https://doi.org/10.1038/s43016-021-00421-7

Geza, W., Ngidi, M., Ojo, T., Adetoro, A., Slotow, R., & Mabhaudhi, T. (2021). Youth participation in agriculture: A scoping review. *Sustainability, 13*, 9120.

Ghanem, H. (2015). *Agriculture and rural development for inclusive growth and food security in Morocco*. Brookings, Global Working Paper Series. Global Economy and Development, Washington, DC, pp. 1–19.

Gony, R. H., Gai, T. J., & Humphrey, A. (2021). The impacts of Covid-19 on farmers and herders in South Sudan: One cannot farm alone. London: SPARC.

Grant, M. J., & Furstenberg, F. F. (2007). Changes in the transition to adulthood in less developed countries. *European Journal of Population, 23*, 415–428.

Greiner, C., & Sakdapolrak, P. (2013). Rural-urban migration, Agrarian change, and the environment in Kenya: A critical review of the literature. *Population and Environment, 34*(4), 524–553. https://doi.org/10.1007/s11111-012-0178-0

Guo, Y., Chen, P., Zhang, H., & Jiang, Z. (2022). Evaluation of the perception and experience of rural natural landscape among youth groups: An empirical analysis from three villages around Hefei. *Sustainability, 14*, 16298. https://doi.org/10.3390/su142316298

Hoffmann, R. (2022). Contextualizing climate change impacts on human mobility in African drylands. *Earth's Future, 10*, e2021EF002591. https://doi.org/10.1029/2021EF002591

Hynes, W., Lees, M., & Marco Müller, J. (2020). *Systemic thinking for policy making: The potential of systems analysis for addressing global policy challenges in the 21st century*. OECD Publishing.

IOM. (2021). Migration, environment and climate change. The International Organization for Migration. https://www.iom.int/migration-environment-and-climate-change-climate

Irungu, K., Mbugua, D., & Muia, J. (2015). Information and communication technologies (ICTs) attract youth into profitable agriculture in Kenya. *East African Agricultural and Forestry Journal, 81*(1), 24–33.

Khan, N. A., Gao, Q., Abid, M., & Shah, A. A. (2021). Mapping farmers' vulnerability to climate change and its induced hazards: Evidence from the rice-growing zones of Punjab, Pakistan. *Environmental Science and Pollution Research, 28*, 4229–4244.

Lemos, M. C. (2015). Usable climate knowledge for adaptive and co-managed water governance. *Current Opinion in Environmental Sustainability, 12*, 48–52. https://doi.org/10.1016/J.COSUST.2014.09.005

Levine, S., Humphrey, A., Abdilatif, M., Rashid, S., Said, A., Adan, A., & Warsame, H. (2021). One more of life's difficulties: The impacts of Covid-19 on livelihoods in Somalia. London: SPARC.

Leyva, D., De la Torre, M., & Coronado, Y. (2021). Sustainability of the agricultural systems of Indigenous people in Hidalgo, Mexico. *Sustainability, 13*, 8075. https://doi.org/10.3390/su13148075

Li, J. W., Liu, Z. F., He, C. Y., Tu, W., & Sun, Z. X. (2016). Are the drylands in northern China sustainable? A perspective from ecological footprint dynamics from 1990 to 2010. *Science of the Total Environment, 553*, 223–231. https://doi.org/10.1016/j.scitotenv.2016.02.088

Montano, D. E., & Kasprzyk, D. (2015). Theory of reasoned action, theory of planned behavior, and the integrated behavioral model. In *Health behavior: Theory, research and practice* (pp. 95–124). Jossey-Bass/Wiley.

Parkinson, S., Woods, S. M., Sprinks, J., & Ceccaroni, L. A. (2022). Practical approach to assessing the impact of citizen science towards the Sustainable Development Goals. *Sustainability, 14*, 4676. https://doi.org/10.3390/su14084676

Pashaei Kamali, F., Borges, J. A. R., Meuwissen, M. P. M., de Boer, I. J. M., & Oude Lansink, A. G. J. M. (2017). Sustainability assessment of agricultural systems: The validity of expert opinion and robustness of a multi-criteria analysis. *Agricultural Systems, 157*, 118–128.

Piguet, E., Kaenzig, R., & Guélat, J. (2018). The uneven geography of research on 'environmental migration'. *Population and Environment, 39*(4), 357–383. https://doi.org/10.1007/s11111-018-0296-4

Raghavan, S. A., Funk, C., Aenis, T., Winker, P., & Breuer, L. (2018). Sensitivity analysis of a climate vulnerability index—A case study from Indian watershed development programmes. *Climate Change Responses*, 5.

Rao, C. S., Kareemulla, K., Krishnan, P., Murthy, G. R. K., Ramesh, P., Ananthan, P. S., & Joshi, P. K. (2019). Agro-ecosystem based sustainability indicators for climate resilient agriculture in India: A conceptual framework. *Ecological Indicators, 105*, 621–633.

Reddy, A. A., Bhattacharya, A., Reddy, S. V., & Ricart, S. (2021). Farmers' distress index: An approach for an action plan to reduce vulnerability in the drylands of India. *Land, 10*, 1236. https://doi.org/10.3390/land10111236

Rietveld, A. M., Van der Burg, M., & Groot, J. C. (2020). Bridging youth and gender studies to analyse rural young women and men's livelihood pathways in Central Uganda. *Journal of Rural Studies, 75*, 152–163.

Šedová, B., Čizmaziová, L., & Cook, A. (2021). A meta-analysis of climate migration literature. *CEPA Discussion Paper 29*. Center for Economic Policy Analysis.

Senders, A., Motz, M., Lentink, A., Vanderschaeghe, M., & Terrilon, J. (2014). Sustainable coffee as a family business. https://www.idhsustainabletrade.com/uploaded/2016/08/toolkit_total.pdf

Statistics South Africa. (2021). Quarterly labour force survey (2021). Statistics South Africa, Pretoria, South Africa.

Stavi, I., Roque de Pinho, J., Paschalidou, A. K., Adamo, S. B., Galvin, K., de Sherbinin, A., et al. (2021). Food security among dryland pastoralists and agropastoralists: The climate, land-use change, and population dynamics nexus. *The Anthropocene Review*. https://doi.org/10.1177/20530196211007512

Thalheimer, L., Otto, F., & Abele, S. (2021). Deciphering impacts and human responses to a changing climate in East Africa. *Frontiers in Climate, 3*, 84. https://doi.org/10.3389/FCLIM.2021.692114/BIBTEX

Thalheimer, L., Simperingham, E., & Jjemba, W. E. (2022). The role of anticipatory humanitarian action to reduce disaster displacement. *Environmental Research Letters, 17*(1), 014043. https://doi.org/10.1088/1748-9326/ac4292

Thrassou, A., Efthymiou, L., Vrontis, D., Weber, Y., Shams, S. M. R., & Tsoukatos, E. (2022). Editorial introduction: Crisis in context. In D. Vrontis, A. Thrassou, Y. Weber, S. M. R. Shams, E. Tsoukatos, & L. Efthymiou (Eds.), *Business under crisis, Volume I* (Palgrave Studies in Cross-disciplinary Business Research, In Association with EuroMed Academy of Business). Palgrave Macmillan. https://doi.org/10.1007/978-3-030-76567-5_1

Thrassou, A., Vrontis, D., Efthymiou, L., & Uzunboylu, N. (2022). An overview of business advancement through technology: Markets and marketing in transition. In A. Thrassou, D. Vrontis, L. Efthymiou, Y. Weber, S. M. R. Shams, & E. Tsoukatos (Eds.), *Business advancement through technology, Volume I* (Palgrave Studies in Cross-disciplinary Business Research, In Association with EuroMed Academy of Business). Palgrave Macmillan. https://doi.org/10.1007/978-3-031-07769-2_1

UN Environment Management Group. (2011). Education of the youth in drylands for agricultural production.

Vasileiou, K., & Morris, J. (2006). The sustainability of the supply chain for fresh potatoes in Britain. *Supply Chain Management, 11*, 317–327.

Vrontis, D., Thrassou, A., Weber, Y., Shams, R., Tsoukatos, E., & Efthymiou, L. (2022). *Business under crisis Volume I: Avenues for innovation, entrepreneurship and sustainability* (Palgrave Studies in Cross-Disciplinary Business Research, in Association with EuroMed Academy of Business). Palgrave Macmillan (Springer). https://doi.org/10.1007/978-3-030-76567-5

Wiggins, S., Levine, S., Allen, M., Elsamahi, M., Krishnan, V., Mosel, I., & Patel, N. (2021). Livelihoods and markets in protracted conflict: A review of evidence and practice. London: SPARC.

Wu, J. G., He, C. Y., Zhang, Q. Y., Yu, D. Y., Huang, G. L., & Huang, Q. X. (2014). Integrative modeling and strategic planning for regional sustainability under climate change. *Advances in Earth Science, 29*, 1315–1324.

4

Investigating the Supply Chain Performance of Agribusiness Firms from the IT Capability and Government Support Perspectives

Ranjan Chaudhuri, Sheshadri Chatterjee, and Demetris Vrontis

1 Introduction

The supply chain performance of agribusiness firms has been impacted over the past two decades by rapid market liberalization, globalization, stricter food safety and environmental regulations imposed by governments, and new trends in consumer lifestyles, which has led those firms to be increasingly concerned (Huggins & Valverde, 2018; Gaitan-Cremaschi et al., 2019). Along with environmental implications, they

R. Chaudhuri (✉)
Research Center, Léonard de Vinci Pôle Universitaire, Paris La Défense, France
e-mail: ranjanchaudhuri@hotmail.com

S. Chatterjee
Department of Computer Science and Engineering, Indian Institute of Technology Kharagpur, Kharagpur, India
e-mail: sheshadri.academic@gmail.com

D. Vrontis et al. (eds.), *Business for Sustainability, Volume I*, Palgrave Studies in Cross-disciplinary Business Research, In Association with EuroMed Academy of Business, https://doi.org/10.1007/978-3-031-37361-9_4

have also been experiencing unprecedented, entangled challenges with locational and traceability issues, treating farmers' interests fairly, and treating animals humanely (Irani & Sharif, 2016; Saitone & Sexton, 2017). The successful performance of an agribusiness firm mainly depends on how it can compete with others in terms of efficiently streamlining its supply chain activities (Panahifar et al., 2018; Wu et al., 2018). Presently, in different countries, agribusiness is undergoing modernization in business practices, resulting in the creation of some major problems for those who follow traditional business practices, especially in the context of supply chain activities (Zeng & Lu, 2021). Researchers have argued that information asymmetry is a major issue that weakens sustainability in the supply chain performance of agribusiness firms (Mesic et al., 2018; Gaitan-Cremaschi et al,. 2019; Shu et al., 2019).

However, the business community in the agriculture sector has realized that applying appropriate Information Technology (IT) with active government support is the most effective way for resolving these challenges in managing the supply chain (Oh et al., 2016; Ojha et al., 2019). Researchers have demonstrated that agribusiness firms that increase their IT capabilities in supply chain management activities can effectively mitigate the information asymmetry and enhance the relationships with their supply chain partners to ensure better supply chain performance (Ding et al. 2014; Fu et al., 2017). IT capabilities have introduced important changes in improving production quality (Migliore et al., 2020), production efficiency (Camanzi & Troiano, 2021), sustainability (Malorgio & Marangon, 2021), and supply chain performance of the agribusiness firms (Zeng & Lu, 2021). The increased use of IT-based capabilities, comprising employees and infrastructural abilities, has

D. Vrontis
Department of Management, School of Business, University of Nicosia, Nicosia, Cyprus

Department of Management Studies, Adnan Kassar School of Business, Lebanese American University, Beirut, Lebanon
e-mail: vrontis.d@unic.ac.cy

helped agribusiness to develop satellite-based global positioning systems that closely and flawlessly navigate the supply chain flow and monitor field conditions (Mariyono, 2020; Rambe & Khaola, 2022; Chatterjee et al., 2021a). Thus, the agriculture industry is optimistic that technological improvements, especially in IT capabilities, could improve supply chain performance and meet the growing consumer demands for agricultural products (Chege & Wang, 2020; Rambe & Khaola, 2022).

Therefore, it is important for agricultural firms to develop in-house IT capabilities to meet these changing demands in the agricultural market. This concept corroborates the Resource-Based View (RBV) (Barney, 1991) since IT capability is considered a valuable, rare, and non-replicable resource. IT capability can also be considered a dynamic capability, as it could address the dynamic needs of the agricultural market, which supplements the concept of dynamic capability view (DCV) (Teece et al., 1997). Previous research has indicated that the IT capabilities of agribusiness firms directly impact firm performance (Jin et al., 2014; Mendoza-Fong et al., 2018). But studies did not explicitly explore how the IT capabilities of agribusiness firms could directly improve supply chain performance and how active government support could affect a firm's IT capabilities (Zeng & Lu, 2021). In this vein, the present study is aimed at addressing the following research questions (RQs).

RQ1: How does IT capability impact the supply chain performance of agribusiness firms?
RQ2: Does government support have a moderating impact on the relationship between IT capability and supply chain performance of agribusiness firms?

2 Literature Review and Theoretical Underpinning

In emerging economies, agribusiness plays a significant role in enhancing household income, especially in rural communities (Sargani et al., 2018; Singh, 2019; Patel et al., 2020). In developing economies, the agriculture sector is a main contributor to economic growth (Ansari & Khan, 2018).

Studies refer to countries like India and Pakistan as agriculturally dependent regions (Iqbal et al., 2015; Ali, 2016). Zeren and Akkus (2020) observed that emerging economies are powerhouses for international trade and investment in agriculture. Several researchers have also shown growing scholarly interest in studying the supply chain performance of agribusiness firms (Odongo et al., 2016; Kirwan et al., 2017).

Ngwenyama and Morawczynski (2009) argued that the rapid economic growth of a country depends on the applications of high-quality information and communication technology. More recent studies have demonstrated that agribusiness firms that continuously invest in IT infrastructure are able to develop supply chain management systems (Cai et al., 2016; Gao, 2018). Studies have demonstrated that governments of different emerging economies are continuously funding agribusiness firms to properly train employees to strengthen their IT capabilities to improve their logistics systems, economic infrastructure, and supply chain systems (Peng et al., 2016; Zhou & Wan, 2017). Thus, to achieve better supply chain performance, agribusiness firms should improve their IT capability, comprising employee ability and infrastructural ability.

It has been observed that the IT capability of agribusiness firms is an intangible and immobile resource, which is difficult to replicate, but helps to ensure better firm performance and competitiveness (Wernerfelt, 1984). This concept is in consonance with the idea of RBV (Barney, 1991). Here it is necessary to understand the concept of competencies, which Amit & Schoemaker (1993) broadly categorized into "firm-resources" and "firm-capabilities". As RBV is related to firm performance, which principally depends on IT capability, it is important to note that resources can be easily acquired, whereas capability is a valuable, rare, inimitable, and non-substitutable resource for firms (Barney et al., 2001; Hart & Dowell, 2011).

IT capability is associated with the competency of firms to acquire external resources, combine and reconfigure them with their internal resources, and then deploy them to support the business flow, which affects the supply chain management activities of agribusiness firms. Thus, IT capability, in the context of above discussion, is considered a VRIN (Valuable, Rare, Imperfectly Imitable and Non-substitutable) ability, corroborating the concept of RBV (Barney, 1991).

Again, as the agricultural market is changing rapidly, to appropriately react and respond to such changes, agribusiness firms must possess dynamic capability to acquire the IT resources to strengthen the supply chain flow. This concept is in consonance with DCV (Teece et al., 1997). According to Zeng and Lu (2021), technological resources do not necessarily always produce better firm performance, but they are considered essential for IT capability and to improve human resource ability as well as the infrastructural ability of agribusiness firms. Dynamic capability is interpreted as a firm's "ability to integrate, build, and reconfigure internal and external resources/competencies to address and possibly shape rapidly changing business environments" (Teece, 2012, p. 1995). It is argued that if a firm possesses proper IT resources but lacks dynamic capability, it may still achieve better performance for a short period of time, but not in the long term (Teece, 2012). Agribusiness firms must possess dynamic capability by improving their human resources and infrastructural abilities to shape the market in ways that could facilitate value creation and realization (Katkalo et al., 2010). This concept supports DCV (Teece et al., 1997).

3 Hypotheses Development and Conceptual Model

With the inputs from the literature and the theories, it was possible to identify that IT capability, including personnel and infrastructural ability, could impact agribusiness firms' supply chain performance. We have also identified from these inputs that government support has a critical moderating influence on the relationships between agricultural firms' supply chain performance and their two predictors. These factors will be discussed in this section as we formulate the hypotheses for developing a theoretical model.

3.1 IT Capability

In many studies, IT capability has been considered important in the context of a firm's supply chain management system (Kim 2017; Mendoza-Fong et al., 2018). IT capability also helps agribusiness firms to efficiently gather, store, and analyze information about suppliers and consumers and to accurately ascertain market demand (Mehta et al., 2003; Zhou & Wan, 2017). This capability is considered an effective and significant enabler of supply chain management (Peng et al., 2016). Advantages include minimizing variability in the processes, improving the quality of the processes, and enhancing the output in the supply chain system (Wamba et al., 2019). With IT capability, agricultural products can be tracked and traced through the supply chain in order to safeguard their quality (Ding et al., 2014). For example, IT capability can facilitate supply chain visibility and traceability, as information is effectively and promptly shared to manage the risks of agricultural products becoming contaminated and thereby improve quality (Fu et al., 2017). This capability can be best utilized when employees are efficient and knowledgeable, provided they have the necessary skillsets and the firm has adequate infrastructural facilities (Basile et al., 2021). Because IT capability helps agribusiness firms to quickly access information, operational and transactional costs are reduced. It also helps to promote quality service, which is necessary to improve agribusiness firms' supply chain performance (Zeng & Lu, 2021).

The applications of IT in the supply chain management context include WeChat, WhatsApp, electronic data interchange, e-commerce, and the internet of things (IoT) to name a few applications that can improve the communication system and strengthen the efficiency of the supply chain flow (Yan et al., 2016). All these advantages of IT capability can be realized by agribusiness firms if they have adequately trained and skillful staff who can extract the best potential from the IT capability. Such IT infrastructure, along with adequate and efficient human resource capability, can also improve the supply chain management system of agribusiness firms (Chaudhuri, 2022). Accordingly, the following hypotheses are formulated.

H1: Manpower capability (MPC) positively impacts the supply chain performance of agribusiness firms (SCP).
H2: Infrastructure capability (INC) positively impacts the supply chain performance of agribusiness firms (SCP).

3.2 Moderating Role of Government Support (GS)

This study demonstrates that by improving IT capabilities, it is possible to improve the supply chain management process of agribusiness firms. This is because a huge investment is necessary to update their infrastructure so that they can effectively use modern technologies like artificial intelligence, blockchain technology, big data analytics, and internet of things for the betterment of the supply chain process (Chaudhuri, 2022; Chaudhuri et al., 2022; Thrassou et al., 2022a, 2022b). Agribusiness firms, especially in developing economies, often suffer from resource constraints (Nguyen, 2021). To help them to continue their businesses by improving supply chain activities, governments need to help the firms by subsidizing financial loans. They can also help agribusiness firms by providing tax incentives and acting as a guarantor against a business loan (Bhattacharjee et al., 2021).

To use modern technology, the employees of these firms must have updated training. Inadequate infrastructure needs to be modernized with technology to conduct online training sessions with the employees (Lyapina et al., 2019). Agribusiness firms experience challenges to impart technological training, as they frequently have a paucity of funds, and we can conjecture that government support should play a critical role (Agrawal, 2012). Thus, government support is perceived to help agribusiness firms improve their overall supply chain performance. Accordingly, it is hypothesized as follows.

H3: Government support (GS) moderates the relationship between the manpower capability (MPC) and supply chain performance of agribusiness firms (SCP).

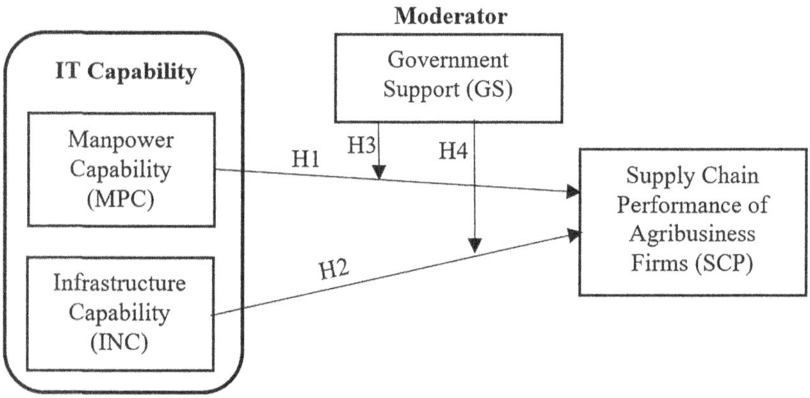

Fig. 4.1 The conceptual model (adopted from RBV and DCV)

H4: Government support (GS) moderates the relationship between the infrastructure capability (INC) and supply chain performance of agribusiness firms (SCP).

In terms of the above inputs, a theoretical model has been developed conceptually. It is shown in Fig. 4.1.

4 Research Methodology

To test the hypotheses and validate the proposed theoretical model, the Partial Least Squares (PLS) Structural Equation Modelling (SEM) approach was taken. As a multivariate technique, this approach is used for assessing the path relationships between the variables (Hair et al., 2016). PLS-SEM approach is deemed to be helpful to analyze an exploratory study like this and can analyze a complicated model that includes a moderator (Hair et al., 2016). The present study is an exploratory study possessing a complex model with a moderator. As such, PLS-SEM has been applied to analyze the data in the present study. The data obtained by conducting the survey was quantified with a 5-point Likert scale, anchored from 1 for Strongly Disagree (SD) to 5 for Strongly Agree (SA).

4.1 Research Instrument

The constructs in the set of questions were prepared based on knowledge from the existing literature. The questions in this questionnaire were prepared in the form of statements that were adjusted in terms of the context of this present study. All the questions were initially pretested with help from expert opinions. We consulted with seven experts who came from industries and were knowledgeable about the domain of this present study. Also, three academicians were consulted who have research experience in the field of this study. The opinion of these experts helped us to modify the language of the questionnaire, rendering them simpler.

After this pretest stage, the pilot test was conducted by analyzing the inputs from 25 respondents who were selected through the convenience sampling process. Those respondents were not included in the main survey. The outcomes of the pilot test help to improve the comprehensiveness, understandability, and readability of the set of questions. All these steps were taken with the intention to obtain unbiased replies from the respondents. In this way, 17 questions were finalized.

4.2 Collection of Data

To target respondents, some of the authors of this study attended conferences and seminars held between March 2022 and August 2022 in different places of India. The agendas of these events were aligned with the domain of this present study. At those conferences, resource persons were contacted who provided lists of employees who hold different positions at agribusiness firms spread across the northern and western parts of India. Those lists contained details of the prospective respondents who were willing to take part in the survey. The list contained 711 respondents in total.

Each prospective respondent was provided with a response sheet that contained the 17 questions. The respondents were also given a guideline that described that they needed to put one tick mark in one option out of five for each question. Also, all the prospective respondents were assured that their anonymity and confidentiality would be strictly

Table 4.1 Demographic information (N = 312)

Particulars	Category	Frequency (N)	Percentage (%)
Gender	Male	223	71.4
	Female	89	28.6
Age	Young adults (<35 years)	200	64.1
	Older adults (>35 years)	112	35.9
Educational qualification	Graduate	162	51.9
	Postgraduate	101	32.3
	PhD/Fellow	49	15.8
Hierarchy of employees	Individual contributors	119	38.2
	Junior managers	64	20.5
	Midlevel managers	54	17.3
	Senior managers	45	14.4
	Leaders	30	9.6

preserved, and they were requested to respond within two months. Within the stipulated time, 326 respondents returned the filled-in response sheets, which is a response rate of 45.8%. After reviewing the response sheets, it appeared that 14 responses were incomplete, and so those were not considered. Therefore, analysis was done on the inputs of 312 respondents against 17 items. The demographic information of 312 respondents is provided in Table 4.1.

5 Analysis of Data and Results

5.1 Measurement Properties

To verify the convergent validity, the loading factor (LF) of each of the items was estimated. Then, to examine the validity, reliability, as well as internal consistency of the constructs, AVE (average variance extracted), CR (composite reliability), and α (Cronbach's alpha) of all the constructs were assessed. The computed values of all the parameters were found to be within the specified range. The results are given in Table 4.2.

Table 4.2 Measurement properties

Constructs/Items	LF	AVE	CR	A	*t*-values
MPC		0.84	0.87	0.89	
MPC1	0.85				22.41
MPC2	0.96				23.56
MPC3	0.94				29.17
MPC4	0.90				32.67
MPC5	0.91				31.12
MPC6	0.95				27.17
INC		0.87	0.88	0.89	
INC1	0.87				26.01
INC2	0.84				34.19
INC3	0.95				31.67
INC4	0.95				30.66
INC5	0.90				25.02
INC6	0.97				26.11
SCP		0.75	0.81	0.86	
SCP1	0.87				24.17
SCP2	0.90				31.26
SCP3	0.91				19.38
SCP4	0.85				26.06
SCP5	0.78				27.11

Table 4.3 Discriminant validity test (Fornell and Larcker criteria)

Constructs	MPC	INC	SCP	AVE
MPC	0.92			0.84
INC	0.24	0.93		0.87
SCP	0.26	0.31	0.87	0.75

5.2 Discriminant Validity Test

We followed the Fornell and Larcker (1981) criteria to examine the discriminant validity of the constructs. With this process, the square roots of all the AVEs were estimated, and it was observed that they are greater than the corresponding bifactor correlation coefficients. The result satisfies the Fornell and Larcker criteria, confirming that the constructs have discriminant validity. The results are provided in Table 4.3.

Table 4.4 Moderator analysis (MGA)

Linkages	Hypotheses	*p*-value differences	Remarks
(MPC→SCP) × GS	H3	0.04	Significant
(INC→SCP) × GS	H4	0.01	Significant

5.3 Moderator Analysis (Multigroup Analysis)

This study considered that government support (GS) moderates the relationships covered by the linkages MPC→SCP (H1) and INC→SCP (H2). To verify the effects of the moderator GS on these two linkages, the impacts of GS have been categorized into two groups: Strong GS and Weak GS. Multigroup analysis was conducted to analyze the moderator, and the bootstrapping procedure was used to consider 5000 resamples. The criterion for significance of the moderating effects highlights that the *p*-value difference of the effects of the two categories of a moderator on the linkages should be either less than 0.05 or greater than 0.95 (Hair et al., 2016; Mishra et al., 2018). The results of the present study demonstrate that the effects of GS on H1 and on H2 are significant. The results are shown in Table 4.4.

5.4 Common Method Bias (CMB)

The study results were dependent on survey data. Hence, the possibility of having common method bias (CMB) cannot be overruled. As such, for mitigating the chance of CMB, we initially adopted some procedural measures. In the survey process and preparing the questionnaire, we conducted a pretest and pilot test to enhance the readability, understandability, and comprehensiveness of the questions so that the respondents would be able to understand them and respond without any bias. Additionally, potential respondents were assured that their identity would not be known, and their answers were completely confidential. Even then, to assess the severity of CMB, Harman's single factor test (SFT) was conducted. The results demonstrated that the first factor was 20.03%, being less than the recommended highest value of 50% (Podsakoff et al., 2003). Another study observed that Harman's SFT is not robust to be a conclusive test for the CMB (Ketokivi & Schroeder, 2004). Therefore, the marker correlation test was also conducted (Lindell & Whitney, 2001), and the results of this test did not highlight any distinct evidence of CMB either. So, it can be safely inferred that CMB could not pose a threat in this study.

5.5 Hypotheses Testing

To test the hypotheses, structural equation modelling technique (SEM) was followed by the bootstrapping procedure to consider 5000 resamples. By considering an omission distance 7, the cross-validated redundancy was assessed, and the Q^2 value emerged as 0.059, which is positive. Thus, the result indicates that the proposed theoretical model has accurate predictive relevance (Mishra et al., 2018). Again, to estimate the model fit, recommendations laid down by Henseler et al. (2014) were followed. Here the standardized root mean square residual (SRMR) is considered as a standard index. The SRMR values were duly estimated, and they are 0.061 for PLS and 0.033 for PLSc. Both values are found to be less than the highest recommended value of 0.08 (Hu & Bentler, 1999). The results highlight that the proposed theoretical model is in order.

The path coefficients of all the linkages, along with the corresponding *p*-values and other parameters, have duly been computed. The results are presented in Table 4.5 (Fig. 4.2).

Table 4.5 Structural equation modelling (SEM)

Linkages	Hypotheses	Path coefficients	*p*-values	Remarks
MPC→SCP	H1	0.23	$p < 0.001$(***)	Supported
INC→SCP	H2	0.31	$p < 0.01$(**)	Supported
(MPC→SCP) × GS	H3	0.17	$p < 0.05$(*)	Supported
(INC→SCP) × GS	H4	0.24	$p < 0.01$(**)	Supported

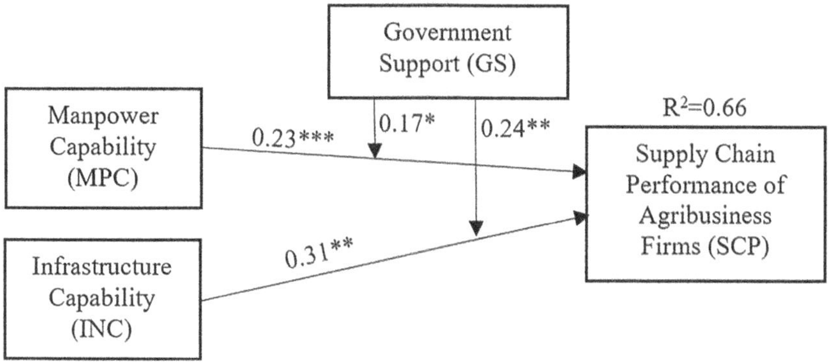

Fig. 4.2 Validated model (SEM)

6 Results and Discussion

The present study has formulated four hypotheses out of which two are concerned with the moderating effects of government support (GS) on the linkages H1 and H2. The study demonstrates that MPC and INC significantly and positively impact SCP, as the concerned path coefficients are 0.23 and 0.31 and the respective levels of significance are $p < 0.001$(***) and $p < 0.01$(**). The moderator GS significantly and positively impacts the linkages H1 and H2, since the path coefficients are 0.17 and 0.24, respectively, with levels of significance as $p < 0.05$(*) and $p < 0.01$(**). In terms of the coefficient of determination (R^2), it appears that MPC and INC could simultaneously predict SCP to the extent of 66% ($R^2 = 0.66$), which is the explanatory power of the proposed theoretical model.

The present study shows that MPC and INC are the two salient factors of IT capability and have a significant impact on SCP. This finding was also supported by Zeng and Lu (2021). The relationship between IT capability and supply chain performance of agribusiness firms was investigated through the lenses of RBV and DCV. This study highlights that IT capability stems from the personnel capability and infrastructural ability of agribusiness firms. Therefore, their employees must possess appropriate competencies to use modern technologies and the firms must have adequate infrastructure so that the employees have opportunities to use modern technologies to strengthen the firms' supply chain management system. This study has highlighted that government support acts as a moderator facilitating the relationships between MPC→SCP and INC→SCP. This has been verified by multigroup analysis.

Here the effects of this moderator GS on H1 and H2 are discussed through graphical presentation. Figures 4.3 and 4.4 present the effects of Strong GS (continuous lines) and Weak GS (dotted lines), respectively, on H1 and H2.

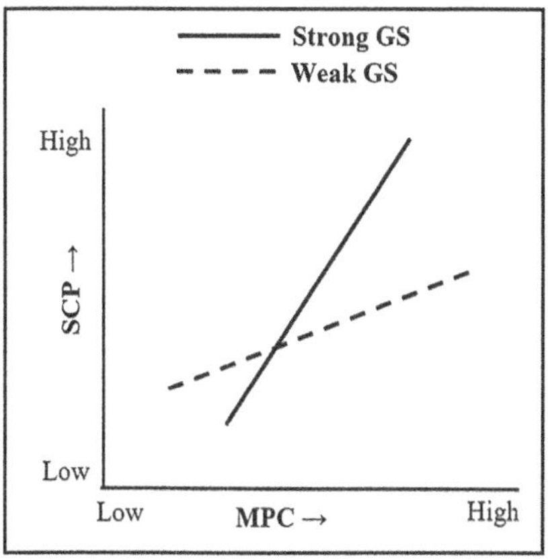

Fig. 4.3 Effects of GS on H1

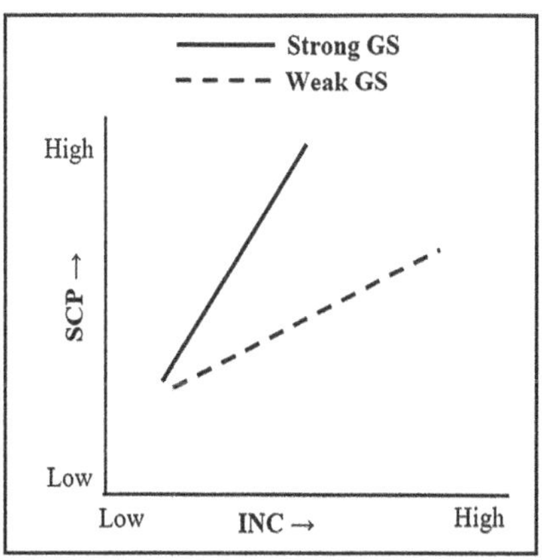

Fig. 4.4 Effects of GS on H2

In the two graphs, it appears that as MPC (Fig. 4.3) increases and INC (Fig. 4.4) increases, the rates of increase in SCP are effected more by Strong GS than by Weak GS, since the gradients of the continuous lines in both graphs are greater than the gradients of the dotted lines, which supplement the results of multigroup analysis (MGA).

7 Implications

Several theoretical contributions have been made by the present study. It is a fact that the role of IT capability in supply chain management is not a new topic of research. However, there are studies which have demonstrated that there are still many critical issues which need to be addressed (Zeng & Lu, 2021; Chatterjee et al., 2021b). From this perspective, we claim that, compared to the earlier studies, the present study is able to contribute precious theoretical implications to various key areas to advance the scope for future research.

Extant literature reveals that previous studies have considered the application of IT as the principal explanatory variable, though a limited number of studies have focused on the contributions of IT capability to the supply chain flow of agribusiness firms, especially as concerns developing countries (Sun & Bao, 2011; Zhou & Wan, 2017). Thus, the present study has supplemented the suggestions of Cai et al. (2016) by investigating the importance of IT capability in the supply chain management of agribusiness firms.

Various studies have demonstrated the direct correlation between IT capability and the performance of the firms in the context of industrial supply chain activities (Hwang et al., 2015; Peng et al., 2016). The present study has extended the concept of those previous studies and explored that IT capability, comprising workforce ability and infrastructure ability, could create value by improving the supply chain process of agribusiness firms. This has added knowledge to the extant literature.

The present study has used RBV (Barney, 1991) and DCV (Teece et al., 1997) and extended the ideas of these two views. With the concept of RBV, we have successfully demonstrated that IT capability, including personnel and infrastructure ability of agribusiness firms, is an in-house

VRIN capability. Similarly, we applied the concept of DCV to show that IT capability can also function as a dynamic ability to integrate the in-house capabilities with the externally sensed and seized opportunities to address the dynamic needs of agribusiness firms.

This study also provides some implications to practitioners, leaders, and policy makers of agribusiness firms. The primary implication is that agricultural firms must improve their IT capability to improve their overall supply chain performance. However, the leaders of these firms, especially in developing countries, should realize that merely investing in IT systems will not sufficiently improve their supply chain management process. They should also emphasize improving their employees' technological skillsets by arranging training sessions to develop their knowledge and efficiency in using modern technologies, which will ultimately improve the supply chain process of their firms. If the leaders and managers of the agribusiness firms also make efforts to modernize the IT infrastructure of their firms, which the skillful and trained employees can use efficiently, their businesses will succeed. Agribusiness firms need to design and execute appropriate strategies helpful for maximizing the returns from IT investment. In the context of improving a supply chain management system, the leader should focus on developing long-term partnerships with upstream and downstream firms of the entire supply chain management system.

Finally, the study has demonstrated that government support will improve the supply chain performance of agribusiness firms. This implies that the relevant government ministries and departments should come forward to help agribusiness firms by granting them adequate incentives, like loans from financial institutions that are easily processed with simple terms and conditions. In this respect, firms will benefit more if the government can act as a facilitator in the disbursement of such loans.

8 Limitations and Future Scope

The results of the present study depended on cross-sectional data, which invites defects of causality among the relationships between the constructs, such as endogeneity errors. To avoid this problem, future researchers should undertake longitudinal studies. The results are based on the analysis of the inputs from respondents in India. This invites external validity issues. Future researchers should consider including respondents in countries around the world so that the results could be more universal in nature. Also, the sample of 312 respondents does not represent the entire population. It is suggested that future researchers should consider including more respondents in the sample size to arrive at a result which has more generalizability.

The study has used DCV, which is criticized for being context insensitive (Ling-Yee, 2007). DCV is unable to identify the accurate conditions under which an agribusiness firm could derive the best supply chain performance from its IT capability (Dubey et al., 2019). It is suggested that future researchers should explore which conditions would be best for agribusiness firms to use their IT capability to improve their supply chain performance. The explanatory power of the proposed theoretical model is 66%. It is suggested that future researchers should consider other constructs and other boundary conditions, for example leadership support and technological turbulence, to verify if their inclusion could enhance the explanatory power of the proposed theoretical model.

References

Agrawal, T. (2012). Vocational education and training in India: Challenges, status, and labour market outcomes. *Journal of Vocational Education and Training, 64*(4), 453–474.

Ali, J. (2016). Performance of small and medium-sized food and agribusiness enterprises: Evidence from Indian firms. *International Food and Agribusiness Management Review, 19*(4), 53–64.

Amit, R., & Schoemaker, P. J. H. (1993). Strategic assets and organizational rent. *Strategic Management Journal, 14*(1), 33–46.

Ansari, S. A., & Khan, W. (2018). Relevance of declining agriculture in economic development of South Asian countries: An empirical analysis. *AGRIS on-Line Papers in Economics and Informatics, 10*(2), 3–14.

Barney, J. (1991). Firm resources and sustained competitive advantage. *Journal of management, 17*(1), 99–120.

Barney, J., Wright, M., & Ketchen, D. J. (2001). The resource-based view of the firm: Ten years after 1991. *Journal of Management, 27*(6), 625–641.

Basile, G., Chaudhuri, R., & Vrontis, D. (2021). Digital transformation and entrepreneurship process in SMEs of India: A moderating role of adoption of AI-CRM capability and strategic planning. *Journal of Strategy and Management, 15*(3), 416–433.

Bhattacharjee, K. K., Tsai, C. W., & Agrawal, A. K. (2021). Impact of peer influence and government support for successful adoption of technology for vocational education: A quantitative study using PLS-SEM technique. *Journal of Quality and Quantity, 55*(1), 2041–2064.

Cai, Z., Huang, Q., Liu, H. F., & Liang, L. (2016). The moderating role of information technology capability in the relationship between supply chain collaboration and organizational responsiveness evidence from China. *International Journal of Operations and Production Management, 36*(10), 1247–1271.

Camanzi, L., & Troiano, S. (2021). The evolutionary transformation of modern agri-food systems: Emerging trends in consumption, production, and in the provision of public goods. *Agricultural and Food Economics, 9*(24), 1–14.

Chatterjee, S., Chaudhuri, R., Galati, A., & Vrontis, D. (2021a). Adoption of ubiquitous CRM for operational sustainability of the firms: Moderating role of technology turbulence. *Sustainability, 13*(18), 1–18.

Chatterjee, S., Rana, N., & Dwivedi, Y. K. (2021b). How does business analytics contribute to organizational performance and business value? A resource-based view. *Information Technology & People*. In Press. https://doi.org/10.1108/ITP-08-2020-0603.

Chaudhuri, R. (2022). Supply chain sustainability during turbulent environment: Examining the role of firm capabilities and government regulation. *Operations Management Research, 15*(1), 1081–1095.

Chaudhuri, R., Chatterjee, S., & Vrontis, D. (2022). Digital transformation of the organisations using AI integrated partner relationship management. In A. Thrassou, D. Vrontis, L. Efthymiou, Y. Weber, S. M. R. Shams, & E. Tsoukatos (Eds.), *Business advancement through technology volume I* (Palgrave Studies in Cross-disciplinary Business Research, in Association with EuroMed Academy of Business). Palgrave Macmillan. https://doi.org/10.1007/978-3-031-07769-2_2

Chege, S. M., & Wang, D. (2020). The impact of technology transfer on agribusiness performance in Kenya. *Technology Analysis & Strategic Management, 32*(3), 332–348.

Ding, M. J., Jie, F., Parton, K. A., & Matanda, M. J. (2014). Relationships between quality of information sharing and supply chain food quality in the Australian beef processing industry. *International Journal of Logistics Management, 25*(1), 85–108.

Dubey, R., Gunasekaran, A., Childe, S. J., Blome, C., & Papadopoulos, T. (2019). Big data and predictive analytics and manufacturing performance: Integrating institutional theory and resource based view. *British Journal of Management, 30*(2), 341–361.

Fornell, C., & Larcker, D. F. (1981). Evaluating structural equation models with unobservable variables and measurement error. *Journal of Marketing Research, 18*(1), 39–50.

Fu, S. L., Han, Z. J., & Huo, B. F. (2017). Relational enablers of information sharing: Evidence from Chinese food supply chains. *Industrial Management and Data Systems, 117*(5), 838–852.

Gaitan-Cremaschi, D., Klerkx, L., Duncan, J., Trienekens, J. H., Huenchuleo, C., Dogliotti, S., Contesse, M. E., & Rossing, W. A. H. (2019). Characterizing diversity of food systems in view of sustainability transitions. A review. *Agronomy for Sustainable Development, 39*(1), 1–22.

Gao, Y. Y. (2018). How does Internet information technology promote rural social and economic development. *Modern Economic Research, 4*, 94–100.

Hair, J. F., Jr., Hult, G. T. M., Ringle, C., & Sarstedt, M. (2016). *A primer on partial least squares structural equation modeling (PLS-SEM)*. Sage Publications.

Hart, S. L., & Dowell, G. (2011). A natural-resource-based view of the firm: Fifteen years after. *Journal of Management, 37*(5), 1464–1479.

Henseler, J., Dijkstra, T. K., Sarstedt, M., Ringle, C. M., Diamantopoulos, A., Straub, D. W., & Calantone, R. J. (2014). Common beliefs and reality about PLS: Comments on Rönkkö and Evermann. *Organizational Research Methods, 17*(2), 182–209.

Hu, L., & Bentler, P. M. (1999). Fit indices in covariance structure modeling: Sensitivity to under parameterized model misspecification. *Psychological Methods, 3*(4), 424–453.

Huggins, C., & Valverde, A. (2018). Information technology approaches to agriculture and nutrition in the developing world: A systems theory analysis of the mNutrition program in Malawi. *Food Security, 10*(1), 151–168.

Hwang, D., Yang, M. G., & Hong, P. (2015). Mediating effect of IT-enabled capabilities on competitive performance outcomes: An empirical investigation of ERP implementation. *Journal of Engineering and Technology Management, 36*, 1–23.

Iqbal, M. A., Iqbal, A., Afzal, S., Akbar, N., Abbas, R. N., & Khan, H. Z. (2015). In Pakistan, agricultural mechanization status and future prospects. *American-Eurasian Journal of Agricultural and Environmental Sciences, 15*(1), 122–128.
Irani, Z., & Sharif, A. M. (2016). Sustainable food security futures perspectives on food waste and information across the food supply chain. *Journal of Enterprise Information Management, 29*(2), 171–178.
Jin, Y., Vonderembse, M., Ragu-Nathan, T. S., & Smith, J. T. (2014). Exploring relationships among IT-enabled sharing capability, supply chain flexibility, and competitive performance. *International Journal of Production Economics, 153*, 24–34.
Katkalo, V. S., Pitelis, C. N., & Teece, D. J. (2010). Introduction: On the nature and scope of dynamic capabilities. *Industrial and Corporate Change, 19*(4), 1175–1186.
Ketokivi, M. A., & Schroeder, R. G. (2004). Perceptual measures of performance: Fact or fiction? *Journal of Operations Management, 22*(3), 247–264.
Kim, H. J. (2017). Information technology and firm performance: The role of supply chain integration. *Operations Management Research, 10*(1/2), 1–9.
Kirwan, J., Maye, D., & Brunori, G. (2017). Acknowledging complexity in food supply chains when assessing their performance and sustainability. *Journal of Rural Studies, 52*, 21–32.
Lindell, M. K., & Whitney, D. J. (2001). Accounting for common method variance in cross-sectional research designs. *Journal of Applied Psychology, 86*(1), 114–121.
Ling-Yee, L. (2007). Marketing resources and performance of exhibitor firms in trade shows: A contingent resource perspective. *Industrial Marketing Management, 36*(3), 360–370.
Lyapina, I., Sotnikova, E., Lebedeva, O., Makarova, T., & Skvortsova, N. (2019). Smart technologies: Perspectives of usage in higher education. *Interna tional Journal of Educational Management, 33*(3), 454–461.
Malorgio, G., & Marangon, F. (2021). Agricultural business economics: The challenge of sustainability. *Agricultural and Food Economics, 9*(6), 1–4.
Mariyono, J. (2020). Improvement of economic and sustainability performance of agribusiness management using ecological technologies in Indonesia. *International Journal of Productivity and Performance Management, 69*(5), 989–1008.
Mehta, R., Dubinsky, A., & Anderson, R. (2003). Leadership style, motivation and performance in international marketing channels. *European Journal of Marketing, 37*(1/2), 50–85.

Mendoza-Fong, J. R., Garcia-Alcaraz, J. L., Macias, E. J., Ibarra Hernandez, N. L., Diaz-Reza, J. R., & Fernandez, J. B. (2018). Role of information and communication technology in green supply chain implementation and companies' performance. *Sustainability, 10*(6), e1793.

Mesic, Z., Molnar, A., & Cerjak, M. (2018). Assessment of traditional food supply chain performance using triadic approach: The role of relationships quality. *Supply Chain Management—an. International Journal, 23*(5), 396–411.

Migliore, G., Thrassou, A., Crescimanno, M., Schifani, G., & Galati, A. (2020). Factors affecting consumer preferences for "natural wine": An exploratory study in the Italian market. *British Food Journal, 122*(8), 2463–2479.

Mishra, A., Maheswarappa, S. S., Maity, M., & Samu, S. (2018). Adolescent's eWOM intentions: An investigation into the roles of peers, the Internet and gender. *Journal of Business Research, 86*, 394–405.

Nguyen, B. (2021). Value co-creation and social media at bottom of pyramid (BOP). *The Bottom Line, 34*(2), 101–123.

Ngwenyama, O., & Morawczynski, O. (2009). Factors affecting ICT expansion in emerging economies: An analysis of ICT infrastructure expansion in five Latin American countries. *Information Technology for Development, 15*(4), 237–258.

Odongo, W., Dora, M., Molnar, A., Ongeng, D., & Gellynck, X. (2016). Performance perceptions among food supply chain members: A triadic assessment of the influence of supply chain relationship quality on supply chain performance. *British Food Journal, 118*(7), 1783–1799.

Oh, S., Ryu, Y. U., & Yang, H. (2016). Supply chain capabilities and information technology characteristics: Interaction effects on firm performance. In *Proceedings of the 49th annual Hawaii international conference on system sciences* (pp. 1417–1425).

Ojha, D., Sahin, F., Shockley, J., & Sridharan, S. V. (2019). Is there a performance tradeoff in managing order fulfillment and the bullwhip effect in supply chains? The role of information sharing and information type. *International Journal of Production Economics, 208*, 529–543.

Panahifar, F., Byrne, P. J., Salam, M. A., & Heavey, C. (2018). Supply chain collaboration and firm's performance the critical role of information sharing and trust. *Journal of Enterprise Information Management, 31*(3), 358–379.

Patel, P. K., Patel, C. R., Chaitra, G. B., & Patil, C. (2020). Performance of agriclinics and agribusiness centers progra in India–a case of Gujarat. *International Journal of Current Microbiology and Applied Sciences, 9*(2), 1541–1549.

Peng, J., Quan, J., Zhang, G., & Dubinsky, A. J. (2016). Mediation effect of business process and supply chain management capabilities on the impact of IT on firm performance: Evidence from Chinese firms. *International Journal of Information Management, 36*(1), 89–96.

Podsakoff, P. M., MacKenzie, S. B., Lee, J. Y., & Podsakoff, N. P. (2003). Common method biases in behavioral research: A critical review of the literature and recommended remedies. *Journal of Applied Psychology, 88*(5), 879–883.

Rambe, P., & Khaola, P. (2022). The impact of innovation on agribusiness competitiveness: The mediating role of technology transfer and productivity. *European Journal of Innovation Management, 25*(3), 741–773.

Saitone, T. L., & Sexton, R. J. (2017). Agri-food supply chain: Evolution and performance with conflicting consumer and societal demands. *European Review of Agricultural Economics, 44*(4), 634–657.

Sargani, G. R., Deyi, Z., Magsi, H., Noonari, S., Joyo, A., Muhammad, S., & Kazmi, M. (2018). An empirical study of attitude towards entrepreneurial intention among Pakistan and China agricultural graduates in agribusiness. *The International Journal of Business Management and Technology, 2*(5), 21–34.

Shu, C., De Clercq, D., Zhou, Y., & Liu, C. (2019). Government institutional support, entrepreneurial orientation, strategic renewal, and firm performance in transitional China. *International Journal of Entrepreneurial Behavior & Research, 25*(3), 433–456.

Singh, S. (2019). Examining global competitiveness of Indian agribusiness in the twenty-first-century Asian context: Opportunities and challenges. *Millennial Asia, 10*(3), 299–321.

Sun, X. W., & Bao, J. L. (2011). Study on e-commerce development model of modern agriculture-take Suzhou as an example. In *Tenth Wuhan international conference on E-Business*, Wuhan, I(II), 276–280.

Teece, D. J. (2012). Dynamic capabilities: Routines versus entrepreneurial action. *Journal of Management Studies, 49*(8), 1395–1401.

Teece, D. J., Pisano, G., & Shuen, A. (1997). Dynamic capabilities and strategic management. *Strategic Management Journal, 18*(7), 509–533.

Thrassou, A., Vrontis, D., Efthymiou, L., & Uzunboylu, N. (2022a). An Overview of Business Advancement through technology: Markets and marketing in transition. In A. Thrassou, D. Vrontis, L. Efthymiou, Y. Weber, S. M. R. Shams, & E. Tsoukatos (Eds.), *Business Advancement through technology volume I* (Palgrave Studies in Cross-disciplinary Business Research, in Association with EuroMed Academy of Business). Palgrave Macmillan. https://doi.org/10.1007/978-3-031-07769-2_1

Thrassou, A., Vrontis, D., Efthymiou, L., & Uzunboylu, N. (2022b). An Overview of Business Advancement through technology: The changing landscape of work and employment. In A. Thrassou, D. Vrontis, L. Efthymiou, Y. Weber, S. M. R. Shams, & E. Tsoukatos (Eds.), *Business advancement through technology volume II* (Palgrave Studies in Cross-disciplinary Business Research, in Association with EuroMed Academy of Business). Palgrave Macmillan. https://doi.org/10.1007/978-3-031-07765-4_1

Wamba, S. F., Gunasekaran, A., Akter, S., & Dubey, R. (2019). The performance effects of big data analytics and supply chain ambidexterity: The moderating effect of environmental dynamism. *International Journal of Production Economics, 222*(4), 107498.

Wernerfelt, B. (1984). A resource-based view of the firm. *Strategic Management Journal, 5*(2), 171–180.

Wu, J. H., Zhang, X. F., & Lu, J. J. (2018). Empirical research on influencing factors of sustainable supply chain management—evidence from Beijing. *China. Sustainability, 10*(5), 1595–1605.

Yan, B., Yan, C., Ke, C. X., & Tan, X. C. (2016). Information sharing in supply chain of agricultural products based on the Internet of Things. *Industrial Management and Data Systems, 116*(7), 1397–1416.

Zeng, M., & Lu, J. (2021). The impact of information technology capabilities on agri-food supply chain performance: The mediating effects of interorganizational relationships. *Journal of Enterprise Information Management, 34*(6), 1699–1721.

Zeren, F., & Akkus, H. T. (2020). The relationship between renewable energy consumption and trade openness: New evidence from emerging economies. *Renewable Energy, 147*, 322–329.

Zhou, S. H., & Wan, G. H. (2017). The impact of E-Business on supply chain performance of manufacturing enterprises: An empirical study from information integration perspective. *Management Review, 29*(1), 199–210.

5

Sustainable Partnership Responses to Prevent Homelessness from Hospital Discharges and Prison Releases: The Case of Leeds City Council in the UK

Kate Daly and Niki Kyriakidou

1 Introduction

Social sustainability concerns the need to maintain structures in societies and communities (Rasouli & Kumarasuriyar, 2016) and covers both the physical needs and wellbeing of individuals (e.g. housing and health) and the quality of life and equity (e.g. communication and participation). This chapter focuses on creating community place-based leadership and governance structures that empower community-minded stakeholders to lead and deliver sustained social change to prevent the detrimental

K. Daly (✉)
Leeds City Council, Leeds, West Yorkshire, UK
e-mail: kate.daly@leeds.gov.uk

N. Kyriakidou
Leeds Business School, Leeds Beckett University, Leeds, UK
e-mail: n.kyriakidou@leedsbeckett.ac.uk

D. Vrontis et al. (eds.), *Business for Sustainability, Volume I*, Palgrave Studies in Cross-disciplinary Business Research, In Association with EuroMed Academy of Business, https://doi.org/10.1007/978-3-031-37361-9_5

impacts of homelessness and rough sleeping on the health and wellbeing of individuals and the prosperity of communities and neighbourhoods.

The Homelessness Reduction Act (HRA, 2017) places a duty on English local authorities to intervene early to prevent and relieve homelessness within their districts and requires them to form effective partnerships and working arrangements with other public bodies (including hospitals, prisons, the probation service) to facilitate referrals into their statutory homelessness services.

Leeds City Council is a metropolitan district council with the second-largest population of any council in the United Kingdom (approximately 800,000 inhabitants). It provides a wide range of public services, including education, housing, planning, libraries, leisure, waste collection, social services, and environmental health in accordance with its corporate strategy, which is subject to local government control. The council has a tall hierarchical management structure with a number of departments providing services relevant to this research, including statutory homelessness service (Leeds Housing Options), homelessness support services commissioned by the Adults & Health Integrated Commissioning Team and the Safer Leeds team that works in partnership to help people in Leeds feel safe, including leading on the rough sleeping agenda within the city centre.

The council's vision is for Leeds to be the best city in the UK with a strong economy and compassionate city, which tackles poverty and reduces inequalities. The drivers for this vision are the city's Inclusive Growth Strategy, Health & Wellbeing Strategy and Climate Emergency declaration, with locality working as a core principle. Housing is a key theme with a specific priority concerning "minimising homelessness through a greater focus on prevention". The underpinning housing strategy (2022–25) also has key themes around reducing homelessness and rough sleeping by improving the council's offer to marginalised groups and ensuring the right housing and support is offered.

Various partnership arrangements already exist within Leeds around preventing homelessness and rough sleeping, including the Housing Offenders Group (HOG), a strategic group aimed at addressing key issues and barriers and improving housing outcomes for offenders. In addition, the out-of-hospital care project team is a multi-agency response to prevent unnecessary hospital admissions and help achieve timely discharges while delivering better-integrated care and achieving person-centred wellbeing outcomes for people at risk of rough sleeping.

Despite extensive partnerships working within Leeds, there is still an identified risk of homelessness and rough sleeping for individuals leaving the hospital or being released from prison. This chapter reviews existing partnerships and working practices to identify ways to strengthen partnerships by enabling community-based leadership and governance to deliver sustainable change and innovation to prevent homelessness from hospital discharges and prison releases. This outcome will help to save the council and its partners' resources and improve the health and wellbeing outcomes for some of the city's most vulnerable residents.

2 Literature Review

Recognising the duties placed on the council and public bodies through the HRA (2017), the chapter intends to identify a potential leadership strategy to deliver sustainable change through effective partnership responses to prevent homelessness from hospital discharges and prison releases in Leeds. The key underpinning requirements considered are stakeholder management, place-based leadership and governance and strategic management.

2.1 The Impact of Homelessness on Social Sustainability

The three interrelated aspects of sustainable development are environmental, economic and societal. Human activity is often considered the most influential factor affecting all these aspects, and social sustainability refers to the need to sustain structures in societies and communities (Rasouli & Kumarasuriyar, 2016). It covers both the physical needs and wellbeing of individuals (e.g. housing and health) and the quality of life and equity (e.g. communication and participation).

The economic impact of homelessness and rough sleeping on the public sector and society is well known, and it is estimated that individuals who experience homelessness for more than three months cost on average £4298 per person to the NHS, £2099 per person for mental health services and £11,991 per person to the criminal justice system on a yearly basis (Pleace & Culhane, 2016). However, the real costs of homelessness are the damage it does to an individual's health, wellbeing and life chances (Pleace & Culhane, 2016). Concerns also exist that this damage is exacerbated by poor recovery outcomes for people experiencing homelessness who are left unsupported after a hospital stay (Tinelli et al., 2022).

The environmental impacts of homelessness are complex and broad in range but include physical impacts around littering and uncleanliness within the city. In addition, rough sleeping people are exposed to various environmental hazards, including poor air quality and pollution, which will further impact their health and wellbeing.

2.2 The Importance of Stakeholders and Partners in Terms of Preventing Homelessness

A stakeholder is a group and individuals who can affect, or are affected by, the achievement of an organisation's objectives (Freeman, 1984). Stakeholders can depend on an organisation to fulfil their own goals, and in turn, an organisation can depend on the theme (Johnson et al., 2017). With respect to preventing homelessness arising from hospital discharges and prison releases, LCC has many different stakeholders, both internal and external to the organisation, and has diverse relationships with them.

The influence of stakeholders and partners depends on the power they process and their level of interest in supporting or opposing the change/response (Lafley & Martin, 2013). Power is defined as the ability of individuals or groups to persuade, induce, or coerce others into following certain courses of action (Johnson et al., 2017). Other stakeholder attributes include legitimacy in terms of being willing to work for the good of others rather than their own self-interest, and urgency, which concerns the degree to which the stakeholder can call for immediate attention (Mitchell, 1997). Finally, a partner stakeholder is an individual, group, organisation and/or network that have the power to influence a partnership and/or an interest in it and may assume or bear risks for a partnership and/or stand to gain benefits from it (Stott, 2009).

2.3 Place-based Leadership and Governance

A partner stakeholder can provide leadership where they are able to influence and interact with other individuals or organisations to achieve shared objectives (Stott, 2009). Place-based leadership concerns leadership activity that serves a public purpose in a prescribed area, meaning that those exercising decision-making power are concerned for and know about the communities living in a particular "place" (Hambleton, 2009). It is an effective partnership strategy (Bratton, 2020) as the leaders are well-connected to the local agenda and current regarding the key ongoing challenges and drivers (Trickett & Lee, 2010). In addition, leaders can use their knowledge to lead and manage stakeholders to ensure all their views underpin the partnership's strategy development and governance structures (Mitchell, 1997).

Hambleton (2018) developed the notion of place-based governance, which encompasses the five overlapping realms of place-based leadership: political leadership meaning the work of elected members; public managerial/professional leadership referring to the work of the council officers to plan and manage public services and promote community wellbeing; community leadership recognising social movements or work undertaken by community-minded people; business leadership meaning the local business community and social entrepreneurs; and trade-union leadership, concerning the work of the trade unions to improve employee pay and conditions (Hambleton, 2018).

George and Reed (2017) developed a framework for place-based governance, proposing that organisations seeking sustainable solutions in a geographical area must process three underpinning requirements: comprehensive understanding, community empowerment, and community-based outcomes. Building on these requirements, this framework proposes five procedural drivers for successful implementation: local leadership, strong networks, diverse community engagement, learning together and information sharing.

2.4 Strategic Management

Strategic management does not relate to market competitiveness or profitability within public services; it is about considering options to decide on the strategic direction and can incorporate innovation to create value from ideas (Tidd & Bessant, 2014; Vlados, 2022; Thrassou et al., 2022). Community leadership is unlikely to involve radical innovation with wholescale changes or move away from what the partnerships/organisations have always done. Instead, the strategic process aims to deliver incremental changes and innovative solutions to benefit local citizens and communities.

Despite the different emphasis, the strategic development within the public service aligns with the Strategy Choice Cascade (Lafley & Martin, 2013), which comprises five interlinked questions to identify the choices made:

- What is our winning aspiration?
- Where will we play?
- How will we win where we have chosen to play?
- What capabilities must be in place to win?
- What management systems are required to ensure the capabilities are in place?

These questions help community leaders identify the procedural drivers required for a strategic change in terms of setting a clear scope, identifying the outcomes, ensuring the required resources and competencies are in place, and there are processes to implement, manage and monitor the strategy. These drivers could further strengthen the local governance structures to deliver social sustainability.

2.5 Theoretical Framework

This research evaluates the effectiveness of the existing community leadership structures in providing opportunities for collaborative working, creative thinking and peer support (Clore Social Leadership, 2020). It identifies the potential to deliver sustainable social change in terms of

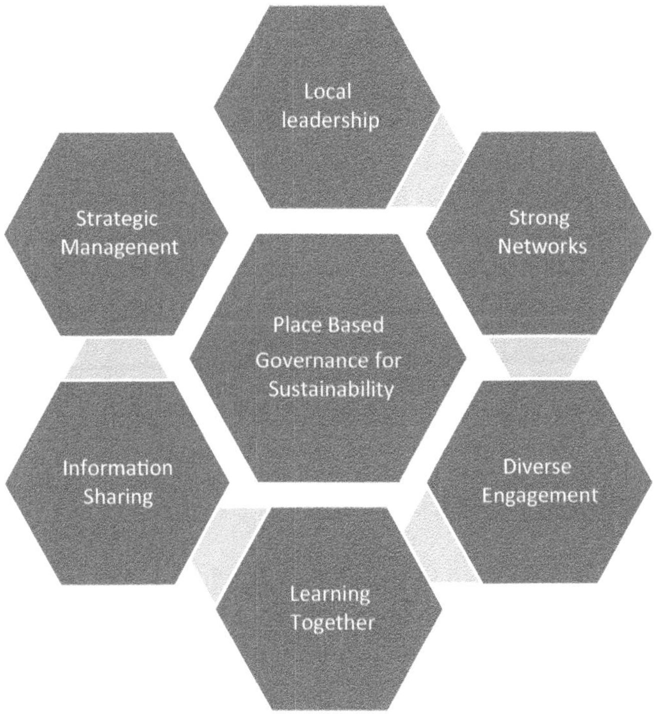

Fig. 5.1 Theoretical framework

preventing homelessness from hospital discharges and prison releases. This evaluation is based on the procedural drivers for place-based governance (George & Reed, 2017) and expanded to include strategic management (Lafley & Martin, 2013), as shown in Fig. 5.1.

3 Methodology

3.1 Secondary Data Collection

The project used a mix of quantitative and qualitative information from a range of sources (Biggs, 2010). The secondary data collection and analysis focused on identifying the key partner stakeholders involved in preventing homelessness arising from hospital discharges and prison releases in Leeds.

This analysis identified the key public bodies and organisations involved in making referrals to Leeds Housing Options to prevent homelessness using the duty-to-refer processes and showed that the number of referrals generally increased each year to around 1500 individuals in 2022, with all public bodies now making more referrals. The organisations referring to the out-of-hospital care project were also identified, and include Leeds Housing Options, health partners and third-sector organisations. In addition, the number of prisoners with a housing need being discussed during the weekly operational meetings was analysed to identify the scale of the problem and the key prisons making releases into Leeds.

3.2 Primary Data Collection

The study was conducted in two phases. In Phase I, one of the chapter's authors interviewed key colleagues from the Leeds City Council and partner stakeholders. Key stakeholders were identified via the secondary data analysis. They were representatives of public bodies and organisations actively involved in making referrals to the Leeds Housing Options or the out-of-hospital care project or through their involvement in key strategic partnerships such as the HOG. Interviews were semi-structured using a series of set questions in English and lasted 30–60 minutes. The interviews were conducted remotely over MS TEAMS and recorded to enable a transcript to be made. An interview schedule using open-ended questions guided the semi-structured interviews with the partner stakeholders and was used to reflect on their experiences in partnership collaborations and the effectiveness of the channels (networks) they used. The interviews also helped identify enablers and barriers to preventing effective partnerships and how these could be overcome.

The thematic analysis of the interview data is presented in Table 5.1.

Ethical approval for this research was obtained prior to any data collection. The primary research was guided by key ethical principles such as integrity, respect of participants and avoidance of harm, ensuring informed consent and the privacy of those involved, the voluntary nature

Table 5.1 Interview content

Outcome	Procedural driver	Themes to be explored within the interviews	Thematic analysis—Key findings
Place-Based Governance for Sustainability	Local leadership	• Understanding of local leadership • Effectiveness of current local leadership to facilitate collaboration between partners	The key attributes identified: • Taking responsibility • Coordination • Collaboration • Having a strategic vision • Overcoming different organisational cultures
	Strong Networks (and Stakeholder Management)	• Identification of the key stakeholders • Effectiveness of the key stakeholder's involvement in local partnerships • Effectiveness of their own organisation within partnerships • Identification of key barriers and challenges	The key features highlighted: • Joint case management meetings • Sound governance arrangements • a team Leeds approach • Good working relationships • Treating partners equally • Issue with short term funding
	Diverse Engagement	• Effectiveness of their organisation seeking feedback from service users and partners.	The key points raised: • Listening to honest feedback • Exit surveys • Enable self-reflection • Priority for organisational development
	Learning Together	• Identification of work where their organisation collaborates creatively • Identification of examples of workforce peer support, including training and development opportunities	The key features identified: • Building good relationships • Culture change • Learning from others • Acknowledging failure • Peer to peer learning opportunities • Co-location to develop understanding
	Information sharing	• Identification of examples where information is shared to develop a comprehensive understanding • Ideas to improve the delivery community-based outcomes	The key requirements: • Good governance • Shared case management systems • Information governance barriers • Outcomes focused • System leadership
Strategy choice cascade	Strategy Choice Cascade	• Understanding of the strategies in place in the Leeds to prevent homelessness, • Views on the resources and competences in place to implement, manage and monitor these strategies	The key points raised: • Some awareness of key strategies • Tend to sit on the shelf • Need to embed them in day to day working • Issue when working at speed around transformation

of participation and the right to withdraw at any point of the research study and managing the data responsibly (Saunders 2019). Minimum personal data was collected as part of the study and stored following GDPR. The interviews produced a large quantity of qualitative data, which was analysed and collated to identify the key themes and observations. This data informed the development of Phase II of this study.

The second phase of the research study was focused on developing case studies as derived from three interviews with key partner participants from different organisations involved in the project. The interview transcripts were further analysed, paraphrased and summarised to create the case studies presented in the next section. This approach allowed the authors to draw additional information through a more focused investigation of participant organisations. In addition, it critically explored the effectiveness of the partnership and strategies in place whilst ensuring the key research questions are covered (Biggs, 2010).

3.3 Case Studies

Case studies have been derived from interviews with representatives from the HM Prison Service, a Health partner and a third-sector organisation who are a sample of different partner stakeholders. The purpose of the case studies is to share insight into their involvement within partnership responses and their effectiveness, identify key barriers and issues, and identify ideas and views to engage all partners to collaborate to deliver sustainable change fully. The semi-structured interviews were recorded and transcribed and the participant responses were analysed, paraphrased and summarised to create the following case studies.

4 Partner Stakeholder 1: Criminal Justice Partner

HM Prison Service has a large adult male prison in Leeds, West Yorkshire, that makes releases into the city. In addition, non-operational strategic housing roles that work with regional and local partners to trial new ideas and initiatives to prevent prison leavers from being released homeless.

The strategic housing role takes ownership to coordinate partners and facilitate access to the prison to prevent homelessness arising from prison releases. The weekly Leeds Housing Options prison release meetings where the statutory homelessness service brings forward a list of individuals potentially threatened with homelessness for discussion with key partners. This enables partners to develop a comprehensive understanding. However, the prison can only share limited risk information. The prison service would like to see an approach to these meetings replicated by other local authorities.

The COVID-19 pandemic has impacted the prison, contacting all partners and facilitating accommodation awareness events. With data still showing that people from Leeds are still being released homeless, they are now putting plans in place to have regular engagement events (e.g. resettlement days) to ensure increased involvement and accountability of partners who work directly with prison leavers.

The prison service still encounters logistical barriers (e.g. when someone is on leave) and staffing issues with partners, which prevents some from participating and actively inputting into partnership meetings despite arrangements being made well in advance. The prison does not seek or encourage feedback from partners and acknowledges that they should work on this.

They acknowledge that the prison could probably do more to engage with prisoners, especially those revolving door prisoners, to find out what did not work last time and what could this time, and understand why they are not engaging or not ready to settle into accommodation. They recognise that it would be beneficial to enable local authorities to converse with prisoners about the importance of engaging with services to prevent homelessness.

The prison service is aware of the Leeds homelessness and rough sleeping strategy but finds them quite time-consuming and unwieldy. They would prefer to access them in different formats, as people working in homelessness are often too overwhelmed to read a long strategy. It would be good to access the information in different ways.

Reflecting on the first case study, the existence of specialist strategic roles in the local prison indicates the level of priority that they place on preventing homelessness arising from prison releases. The prison makes releases across West Yorkshire and works with several local authorities. Throughout the interview, they often highlighted the proactive approach of Leeds Housing Options in identifying individuals at risk of homelessness and facilitating partner meetings as best practice.

The participant highlighted several risks and barriers to effective partnership working, including partner commitment, capacity to attend pre-arranged meetings and the high demand for support. Moving on from the COVID-19 pandemic, the prison plans to enable partners access to prisons and encourage prisoners to engage early with housing support services to prevent homelessness.

5 Partner Stakeholder 2: Health Partner Stakeholder

An NHS trust who provides community health services for the people of Leeds, including working with those that are either at risk of or are experiencing homelessness. A homeless integration lead role provides system leadership and actively participates within a range of city-wide partnerships around homelessness and rough sleeping.

From a health perspective, local leadership is about working with and coordinating local discharge pathways, including undertaking in-reach into the acute hospitals, working with Leeds City Council who is managing homelessness governance structures and homelessness services, and influencing third-sector organisations to provide support and accommodation services for those at risk of homelessness. This complex pathway has many interfacing elements and system dependencies, with many partners involved and none have overall management control.

Recently, there have been changes to the historical transactional relationships between the commissioner and the provider, which generally caused organisations to work within their internal silos with in-house service pathways. People are now more joined up and developing a "team Leeds" ethos where everyone works together more cohesively and does not consider which organisation they are from (either third sector or public body). This has created better relationships leading to improvements in systems around information sharing. However, there is still no organised way to seek the lived experience's views and feedback, and the reason for this is the perceived difficulties in engaging with them.

Understanding the homelessness agenda across the NHS trust needs to be improved, and senior leaders could be more involved within the city-wide partnership structures. The dedicated health inclusion team is a specialist team and is not integral to or part of the overall health system operating across the neighbourhood teams across Leeds. This approach can cause barriers for the team to deliver inclusive health and ensure mainstream services are accessible for all.

The multi-disciplinary team working on the out-of-hospital project are all from different organisations, which is unique in terms of enabling creativity and empowering team members to speak up and share their ideas. This enables challenge between the team as people feel safe to do so whilst also learning from each other. Team members are treated as equal partners bringing their expertise; therefore, no strict management hierarchy blocks creative thinking. It also enables learning to be disseminated to people's own organisations, which has been helpful. Unfortunately, this project is funded using short-term funding, and there is a risk that the project will lose momentum now that the funding is ending. Considering all the time and energy invested in setting up the project and systems, this is not very reassuring.

Despite health and homelessness services having different case management systems, there are processes in place to share information with each other, and partners need to be more confident in sharing information where it keeps patients and the public safe. Whilst partners need to be mindful and careful about people's information, it should not be a barrier to sharing information.

This community NHS trust has created a dedicated health inclusion team to work with those who are rough sleeping or at risk of rough sleeping; the leader of this team is able to fully particulate in city-wide governance structures and work with partners to develop streamlined discharge pathways for this cohort. However, the existence of this dedicated team can mean that inclusion health is not integrated within the mainstream neighbourhood services, and therefore universal services are not accessible to all.

The participant recognises the importance of creating safe spaces for multi-disciplinary partnership working where partners are empowered and treated equally so that they can challenge each other to enable creative and innovative solutions. This way of working increases understanding across organisations and breaks down organisational and hierarchical barriers, especially around information sharing. However, there is an ongoing risk where these partnership arrangements rely on short-term temporary funding.

6 Partner Stakeholder 3: Third-Sector Partner

A consortium of third-sector organisations provides supported accommodation for those at risk of homelessness, a service commissioned by Leeds City Council. The service coordinator oversees several intensive support accommodation units and around 200 community properties and provides leadership for the partnership in terms of contract performance and strategy delivery.

From their perspective, local leadership is about having the right people have the right conversations to ensure they are doing their best for their organisations and the clients being discharged from hospitals and prisons to prevent homelessness. Good leadership is about making difficult decisions, being accountable and being committed to delivering change. Leadership should be about looking at what works and what does not, including how the partnership can constantly improve ways of working and professionally challenge each other.

There are some strong strategic partnerships within Leeds focused around themes or groups of individuals (the street support partnership is a good example that has a shared vision and values to stop rough sleeping in the city centre). However, if organisations are part of a partnership, they should also be accountable for its outcomes. Time and resources (especially a disparity of funding) are barriers to effective partnership working and can cause disharmony.

The COVID-19 pandemic caused closer integration between the service and health inclusion services, which has continued, for example, through the provision of surgeries within the accommodation settings. Operational conversations are now embedded and have led to positive outcomes for clients. It can be helpful for these working practices to be formalised through joint protocols, which are regularly updated and reviewed to ensure effective information sharing.

They proactively initiate city-wide conversations and partnerships to ensure they are connected and integrated and can influence what is happening in Leeds. For example, they can struggle to communicate and integrate with larger public bodies (e.g. probation, health) who may have different cultures and visions of their own organisation. They also co-locate with Leeds Housing Options and street support services to improve understanding and information sharing. They aim to be inclusive and ensure the clients' voice is represented in these partnership discussions to be creative and improve their outcomes.

Multi-disciplinary teams need to pool resources and develop creative solutions to address the wider issues faced by people at risk of homelessness (e.g. mental health, trauma and self-neglect). Some partners reflect and review recent cases and include partners to ensure learning is disseminated, often about developing closer relationships and better communications with partners (e.g. drug and alcohol services). It would be beneficial if this were expanded so that all organisations can reflect on what is not working well and share learning experiences. Time and resource pressures mean this does not always happen but could deliver positive outcomes. It would also help to compare and benchmark the partnership work within Leeds with local authorities.

They support peer networks with other partners (e.g. third sector and the council) where staff can come together and discuss the roles, support each other and offer support and feedback. They share inductions and are co-located with partners, including Leeds Housing Options. This work helps form good relationships and build understanding with our partners. The service has undertaken some training for our workforce on conduct at multi-agency meetings and the importance of sharing information effectively at a practitioner-to-practitioner level.

The management of strategies within Leeds could be improved with partnerships becoming more accountable for the strategy implementation by more active and regular strategic management. At present, strategies are only reviewed when they are due for a refresh and review.

The final case study recognises the importance of local leadership and partnerships to pool resources and expertise together to deliver positive change, which can only be achieved if partners are accountable for their contribution. This organisation takes a proactive approach within partnerships to ensure they can influence larger stakeholders, including co-locating with Leeds Housing Options to develop understanding and improve information sharing. They also try to ensure their service users' voices are heard within the partnerships.

The participant notes the importance of partners reflecting and learning together, especially where positive outcomes may not have been achieved. However, they note that not all partners engage in this process, and time and resource pressures cause barriers to its success. They recognise the fast pace and challenging nature of their work means that peer-to-peer support is vital and look for opportunities to enable joint work and co-location with partners. They also provide training to empower their workforce to contribute to multi-agency meetings and share information effectively.

7 Discussion and Recommendations

Place-based governance concerns mobilising change by empowering communities (Dale, 2001), and analysis of the three case studies using the theoretical framework revealed some common themes.

7.1 Local Leadership

Place-based leadership within this research involves exercising decision-making and leadership based on a concern for and knowledge of individuals who are homeless or at risk in Leeds (Hambleton, 2009). All case studies recognised that there was no single leader within the city, but there was a need for joint ownership and collaboration to achieve the overarching vision for positive health and wellbeing outcomes for individuals and the strategic aims of the city.

The case studies highlighted the need for leaders to be well-connected with the local homelessness agenda and updated with the ongoing challenges and drivers (Trickett & Lee, 2010) whilst not working in isolation within their own organisation. In addition, they identified the need to be open and willing to develop an understanding of all the services and facilitate conversations to identify what is working well and what is not, as illustrated in the case study with the third-sector partner.

Evidence suggests that the effectiveness of the leadership to facilitate collaborative and creative partnership working has been strengthened in Leeds in recent years. For example, the case studies highlighted in the multi-partnership response to the COVID-19 pandemic helped establish more positive and equal relationships across services and organisations. In addition, all the cases provided positive examples of city governance structures and working practices. However, issues were raised concerning different organisational cultures and hierarchical structures, which means getting the right people involved in the partnerships and conversations can be more difficult.

Recommendation 1 Organisations should proactively look across partnerships to identify what works well and what does not to identify how the partnership can constantly improve working methods and professionally challenge each other.

7.2 Strong Networks

Strong networks and place-based leadership allow collaborative working, creative thinking and peer support, which can deliver sustainable social change (Clore Social Leadership, 2020) and build trusting relationships (George & Reed, 2017). The case studies indicated that their organisations are active within partnerships, either at a strategic or operational level or both. Examples of activity included attending and contributing to meetings and co-locating their workforce within the partner's premises. Networks and partnerships also provide the catalyst for securing additional investment into the city, evidenced by the out-of-hospital care project described in the health partner case study.

Forming effective networks was recognised as resource-intensive within the case studies, which is challenging for many organisations within the current financial climate where there is a need to address different and potentially conflicting priorities whilst facing increasing service demand. For example, HM Prison partner identified barriers to developing strong networks, including knowing whom to contact, staffing turnover and partner commitment.

Recommendation 2 Partnerships need to reflect and review working practices to ensure each meeting or network has a clear purpose with independence clearly defined to ensure resource use is maximised.

7.3 Diverse Engagement

Seeking feedback from a mix of service users and partners is considered integral to ensuring effective place-based organisations, leadership and governance (Tessler Lindau et al., 2011), with the third-sector case study illustrating how they try to include service user voice within their partnership working. The prison case study notes that service user engagement is a priority area for development, including working with the revolving door prisoners to find out what did not work last time and how things could be done differently this time.

Recommendation 3 Partners should work together more closely to learn from each other so all can adopt the most appropriate engagement approaches that recognise the vulnerability of the individuals involved with homelessness services.

7.4 Learning Together

Learning together through interacting with colleagues and partners effectively develops shared understanding, collective views and new creative ideas (Lebel et al., 2010). All the case studies recognised that good relationships were key to establishing forums and working practices to enable creative thinking and learning to overcome issues and challenges around homelessness. For example, the health partner referred to the need for a safe space, removing organisational walls and treating all partners equally, where failure can be acknowledged openly.

Despite this willingness to work together creatively, there is limited training and development opportunities for staff apart from ad hoc shadowing and lunchtime seminars. Capacity and budget pressures are the main barriers, along with managing the expectations of partners and staff. However, the third-sector organisation case study illustrates that they are overcoming these issues through co-location across organisations, including Leeds Housing Options.

Recommendation 4 Partners should build relationships and understanding across the workforce through co-location opportunities and open and honest conversations, instilling a common purpose and commitment.

7.5 Information Sharing

Sharing the right and appropriate information helps partners support individuals, and good communication effectively builds trust and legitimacy across partnerships (Lockwood et al., 2010). However, there are still barriers in terms of sharing information, especially around consent and GDPR regulations, the prison and probation service sharing risk information, and health partners using different case management systems for homelessness services. Partners have amended working practices to overcome these barriers; for example, Leeds Housing Options coordinating and facilitating prison release meetings to ensure key partners have a common understanding.

In terms of sharing information on best practices or lessons learnt, the third-sector organisation recognised that there is only limited reflection (Kolb, 1984) or measurement of a strategy success happening between partners in Leeds. Short-term funding was also identified as an issue as activities and services lose momentum and knowledge when the funding period ends, for example, when staff start looking for alternative employment.

Recommendation 5 Partners should facilitate workforce training to build confidence to share the right information at a practitioner-to-practitioner level.

7.6 Strategy Choice Cascade

The case studies indicate only some awareness of the key city-wide strategies, and therefore a lack of knowledge of the key elements of the strategy choice cascade in terms of the vision, scope, processes, required capabilities or management/monitoring systems to successfully implement a strategy (Lafley & Martin, 2013). The case studies illustrate that partnerships generally work at speed, addressing new emerging situations or around service transformation and that activities and progress tend not to be effectively monitored or measured with strategies that are only looked at when they are due for review.

Recommendation 6 The partnership should ensure closer integration of the key strategies into the day-to-day performance management of the partnership to effectively measure progress and enable partnerships to become more accountable and celebrate success together.

8 Conclusions and Contributions

Place-based governance for sustainability underpinned by comprehensive understanding, community empowerment and community-based outcomes can catalyse innovation to create sustainable partnership responses to deliver social change (George & Reed, 2017). This evaluation suggests that the five procedural drivers (local leadership, strong networks, diverse community engagement, learning together and information) (George & Reed, 2017), along with strategic management, are present in some capacity within the partnership arrangements operating in Leeds. However, the extreme demands on organisations and partnerships and the constant need to transform to meet changing needs and priorities mean that the potential for the partnerships to achieve effective place-based governance to enable innovation and lead social change is not fully maximised. Organisational culture and communication across large organisation hierarchies should also be addressed to strengthen the potential outcomes. The partnerships need to self-review working practices to ensure each meeting or workstream aims to achieve positive outcomes while empowering their workforce to act as local leaders.

Closer integration of the strategies into the day-to-day performance management of the partnerships would effectively measure progress and enable partnerships to become more accountable and celebrate success together.

References

Biggs, D. (2010). *Management consulting: A guide for students.* South-Western Centage Learning. ISBN: 9781408007914.

Bratton, J. (2020). *Organisational leadership.* SAGE Publications. ISBN: 9781529793604.

Clore Social Leadership. (2020, October 23). *The power of a place-based approach to leadership*. Retrieved from Clore Social Leadership. https://cloresocialleadership.org.uk/blogpost/1885781/359296/The-power-of-a-place-based-approach-to-leadership

Dale, A. (2001). *At the edge: Sustainable development in the 21st century.* UBC Press.

Freeman, R. (1984). *Strategic management: A stakeholder approach.* Pitman. ISBN: 9780774808361.

George, G., & Reed, M. G. (2017). Operationalising just sustainability: Towards a model for place based governance. *Local Environment, 22*(9), 1105–1123. https://doi.org/10.1080/13549839.2015.1101059

Hambleton, R. (2009, November 1). Place-based leadership & public service innovation. Retrieved from Researchgate: https://www.researchgate.net/profile/Robin-Hambleton/publication/254251177_Place-Based_Leadership_and_Public_Service_Innovation/links/00b7d53b5359005216000000/Place-Based-Leadershipand-Public-Service-Innovation.pdf

Hambleton, R. (2018, October 9). *Inclusive place-based leadership: Lesson-drawing from urban governance innovation in Bristol, UK.* Retrieved from Metropolitics. https://metropolitics.org/Inclusive-Place-Based-Leadership-Lesson-Drawing-from-Urban-Governance.html

Johnson, G. W., Whittingham, R., Scholes, K., Angwin, D., & Regner, P. (2017). *Exploring strategy: Text and cases.* Pearson. ISBN-13: 978-1292002545.

Kolb, D. A. (1984). *Experiential learning: Experience as the source of learning and development*. Prentice Hall. http://academic.regis.edu/ed205/Kolb.pdf

Lafley, A., & Martin, R. G. (2013). Playing to win—How strategy really works. Harvard Business Review Press. ISBN-10: 9781422187395.

Lebel, L., Grothmann, T., & Siebenhüner, B. (2010). The role of social learning in adaptiveness: Insights from water management. *International Environmental Agreements: Politics, Law and Economics, 10*, 333–353. https://doi.org/10.1007/s10784-010-9142-6

Leeds City Council. (2022a, August 19). *Best Council Plan 2020–25*. Retrieved from Leeds City Council. https://www.leeds.gov.uk/docs/BCP%20 2020-2025.PDF

Leeds City Council. (2022b, August 24). *Current housing strategy 2022 to 2027*. Retrieved from Leeds.GOV.UK: https://www.leeds.gov.uk/housing/housing-strategy/leeds-housing-strategy/current-strategy

Lockwood, M., et al. (2010). Governance principles for natural resource management. *Society and Natural Resources, 23*(10), 986–1001. https://doi.org/10.1080/08941920802178214

Mitchell, R. (1997). Towards a theory of stakeholder identification and salience: Defining the principle of who and what really counts. *Academy of Management Review, 22*(4), 853–866. https://doi.org/10.2307/259247

Pleace, N., & Culhane, D. P. (2016). *Better than Cure? Testing the case for enhancing prevention of single homelessness in England*. Research Report. Crisis. https://orcid.org/0000-0002-2133-2667

Rasouli, A. H., & Kumarasuriyar, A. (2016, December). The social dimention of sustainability: Towards some definitions and analysis. *Journal of Social Science for Policy Implications, 4*(2). https://doi.org/10.15640/jsspi.v4n2a3

Saunders, M. L. (2019). *Research Methods for Business Students* (8th Edn.). Harlow: Pearson.

Stott, L. (2009). *Stakeholder Engagement in Partnerships. Who are the stakeholders, and how do we 'engage' with them*? Retrieved from BPD Research Series. https://doi.org/10.1016/j.hjdsi.2019.05.001

Tesslet Lindau, S., et al. (2011). Building community-engaged health research and discovery infrastructure on the south side of Chicago: Science in service to community priorities. *Preventive Medicine, 52*(3), 200–207. https://doi.org/10.1016/j.ypmed.2011.01.001

Thrassou, A., Vrontis, D., Efthymiou, L., & Uzunboylu, N. (2022). An overview of business advancement through technology: The changing landscape of work and employment. In A. Thrassou, D. Vrontis, L. Efthymiou,

Y. Weber, S. M. R. Shams, & E. Tsoukatos (Eds.), *Business advancement through technology volume II. Palgrave studies in cross-disciplinary business research, in association with EuroMed Academy of Business*. Palgrave Macmillan. https://doi.org/10.1007/978-3-031-07765-4_1

Tidd, J., & Bessant, J. (2014). *Strategic innovation management.* Wiley. ISBN: 9781118863381.

Tinelli, M., Wittenberg, R., Cornes, M., Aldridge, R. W., Clark, M., Byng, R., Foster, G., Fuller, J., Hayward, A., Hewett, N., Kilmister, A., Manthorpe, J., Neale, J., Biswell, E., & Whiteford, M. (2022). The economic case for hospital discharge services for people experiencing homelessness in England: An in-depth analysis with different service configurations providing specialist care. *Health & Social Care in the Community, 00*, 1–12. https://doi.org/10.1111/hsc.14057

Trickett, L., & Lee, R. (2010). Leadership of 'subregional' places in the context of growth. *Policy Studies, 31*(4), 429–440. https://doi.org/10.1515/admin-2016-0024

Vlados, C. (2022). Conceptual mutations of change management and the strategy–Technology–Management Innovation. In A. Thrassou, D. Vrontis, L. Efthymiou, Y. Weber, S. M. R. Shams, & E. Tsoukatos (Eds.), *Business advancement through technology volume II. Palgrave studies in cross-disciplinary business research, in association with EuroMed academy of business.* Palgrave Macmillan. https://doi.org/10.1007/978-3-031-07765-4_6

6

Green Economy and Credit Quality in the European Banking Industry: What are the Opportunities for Sustainability?

Elena Bruno, Giuseppina Iacoviello, and Mavillonio Maria Saveria

1 Introduction

In recent years, the increase in demand for "green" products by investors and borrowers as well as pressure from the community regulator have pushed banks towards a necessary consideration of Environmental, social and governance (ESG) risks in their credit risk management policies (Schultz et al., 2013; Bryant et al., 2020; Stiroh, 2020). The inclusion of ESGr in business models influences prudential requirements; ESG practices are therefore to be considered a strategic variable for both banks and authorities (EBA, 2020; ECB, 2020). ESGr should be meaningful for all stakeholders, although the imperative of achieving profitability and solvency objectives does not always guarantee the adoption of better ESG

E. Bruno (✉) • G. Iacoviello • M. Maria Saveria
Department of Economics and Management, University of Pisa, Pisa, Italy
e-mail: elena.bruno@unipi.it; giuseppina.iacoviello@unipi.it; mariasaveria.mavillonio@phd.unipi.it

D. Vrontis et al. (eds.), *Business for Sustainability, Volume I*, Palgrave Studies in Cross-disciplinary Business Research, In Association with EuroMed Academy of Business, https://doi.org/10.1007/978-3-031-37361-9_6

policies. The latter requires banks to achieve, among other things, higher qualitative standards of Corporate Social Responsibility (CSR) in order to be able to act with a view to containing environmental impacts and with greater commitment to implementing programmes of social responsibility (see for all, Bătae et al., 2020; Miralles-Quirós et al., 2019).

The relationship between ESGr and Credit Risk (CR) in banks has been investigated in previous literature (Bouslah et al., 2018; Gangi et al., 2019 and others for all); however, there is a lack of empirical data on whether such a relationship can mitigate the effect of the Non Performing Loans (NPL) index on solvency levels (Albertini, 2013; Birindelli et al., 2022).

Some authors have analyzed the impact of ESG activity on the value of the bank (Finger et al., 2018; Azmi et al., 2021; Ren et al., 2022), others have focused on the analyses of the correlation between ESG and bank stability (Di Tommaso & Thornton, 2020; Chiaramonte et al., 2022); still, other studies investigate the impact of ESG policies on the reduction of systemic risk (Berger et al., 2016; Anginer et al., 2018). There is still sparse literature regarding the possible effects of the ESGr on the NPL ratio and the solvency ratio (SLV ratio). If the focus shifts to the empirical results, it can be noted that these are even more limited and often conflicting, especially if the observation perimeter is extended to the European zone.

Based on current knowledge, although research has addressed the relationship between ESG and CR, our study is one of the first to consider the European banking sector and use a market-based measure of the Credit Default Swaps (CDS) spread (Drago et al., 2019) on a sample of European banks.

The innovative contribution is to have linked the solvency of the banks and the financial performance (FP) to the metrics of the CR, measured by the spread of the CDS and by the ESGr.

In the non-financial sector, ESGr appears to reduce losses and CDS spread levels, thereby improving credit ratings (Attig et al., 2013; Bouslah et al., 2018); the quality of the GCA and FP could be significantly improved. This result is achieved using the regression technique, by testing whether the green credit asset increase can reduce the NPL ratio and improve the SLV ratio.

The analysis was conducted on a panel of European banks, in both the Member States of the European Union and non-member countries, listed on the stock exchange in the period 2012–2021, on data extracted from various sources, although most refer to the Refinitiv Datastream.

Initially, the sample included 810 bank-year observations. After eliminating all the bank-year observations with at least one missing value among regression model variables, the number was reduced to 310 to create a balanced panel. Based on the total sample statistics, for the ESG combined score (ESG_{comb}), the average of the selected banks is less than 80%.

We postulate that the ESGr, NPLs and bank solvency linkage may give higher scores. The expectation is tested using a framework built around the analysis of three different regression models: the first to analyze the relationship between the CDS and ESG_{comb} score; the second to study the relationship between NPL and ESG scores; and the third to study the relationship between SLV ratio (Total Equity/Total Assets) and NPL.

The results of Zhang et al. (2016) support the hypothesis of moral hazard, that an increase in the NPL ratio will increase lending risk, which may lead to instability of the financial system. Moreover, the moral hazard issue will be accentuated due to the low solvency ratio and will then lead to a higher NPL ratio.

Ultimately, the models developed are a useful contribution to the existing literature as few previous studies have used more than one statistical model that correlates the indicators of ESG policies with those of the FP and banks' solvency. According to Buallay (2019), the study of the relationship between ESG dimensions, the performance, and banks'solvency are much more complex than a "simple cause-effect link". Therefore, each dimension of financial metrics relative to ESGr needs to be analyzed, as one might expect significant relationships between ESGr, financial performance, and SLV ratio. We analyze these relationships, in a disaggregated way, to support our findings more effectively than previous studies.

The chapter is organized as follows. Section 2 presents the literature review and development of hypotheses. In Sect. 3, we provide the research design and the methodological approach for empirical remarks. In Sect. 4, we discuss the empirical findings and, finally, in Sect. 5, we provide the conclusions, the main implication, and the future developments of our research.

2 Literature Review and Development of Hypotheses

In the last two decades, the attention of the regulator, economic operators, and academic scholars has mainly been directed to the understanding of the virtuous relationship between ESGr and FP. However, most of the published empirical studies have focused on the relationship between the level of NPLs and CR in banks with contrasting findings. Much research demonstrates a positive correlation between ESG and FP (Wu & Shen, 2013; Widyawati, 2020; Cornett et al., 2016; Buallay et al., 2021); indeed, other studies provide non-significant results on this relationship (Matuszak & Różańska, 2017; Mate et al., 2021).

In most empirical studies there is a greater interest in the use of proxies concentrated on a single pillar of ESG (for example Dowell et al., 2000; Konar & Cohen, 2001); corporate investments and activities voluntarily undertake to manage responsibly and account for its impact on society (Masulis & Reza, 2015; Liang & Renneboog, 2017); satisfaction of bank's employees and customers (Luo & Bhattacharya, 2006; Servaes & Tamayo, 2013). It is only recently that research has begun to take advantage of the increased availability and breadth of cross-company and industry data afforded by ESG disclosure scores (Liang & Renneboog, 2017; Trigo et al., 2022). From a regulatory point of view, the attention of authorities towards ESG issues has been interesting. In the first step, the European Union (EU) was keen to improve disclosure by banks on non-financial information by preparing specific reports on sustainability. In 2014, in fact, the first EU directive (2014/95/EU) also required banks to carry out the necessary non-financial reporting in order to disclose information on ESG activity strategies. By virtue of the completion of the Banking Union (BU) process, the European Banking Authority (EBA, 2020), in October 2020, published an ESG risk oversight document for banks and investment firms, succeeded by a consultation document, published at the end of November by the European Central Banking (ECB, 2020), which also made it mandatory for banks to include the ESG risk component in stress testing activity and to be completed by the end of 2022.

There have also been regulatory interventions in countries outside the EU zone. This is the document on the "Principles for Responsible Banking", the aim of which is to align the ESG strategy of the banks both with the Paris Climate Agreement and with the United Nations Sustainable Development Goals, of the "Climate Biennial Exploratory Scenario" (CBES) issued in the United Kingdom, for the assessment of the resilience of the financial system to environmental risks (Bank of England, 2021).

If we then consider the scientific production on the issues that have been highlighted, it is important to point out that, if there is substantial literature on the positive impacts of sustainability practices on the levels of corporate profitability (Gangi et al., 2019), there are, however, few studies on the analysis of the impact of ESG activities on credit risk, measured both by the ESGr and by the spread on CDS, and on the existing correlation between CR, FP, and bank solvency.

Our work fits precisely into this line of study and aims to contribute to bridging the gap in the literature through an empirical analysis of the correlation between financial performance and solvency indicator, referred to as $ESG_{\text{-comb}}$ scores. The intent is to seek solid evidence to identify a possible channel for CR reduction. In fact, if market operators tend to associate a satisfactory ESGr with lower CR, this would have a positive impact both on provisioning policies and on the agency costs component and the presence of asymmetric information (El Ghoul et al., 2011). This would lead to a virtuous process: the containment of capital constraints would guarantee better access to the financing channel (Cheng et al., 2014) with undisputed positive effects on the bank performance (García-Sánchez & García-Meca, 2017). Furthermore, in the non-financial sector, ESGr appears to reduce market share losses and CDS spread levels, which would then improve the CR (Attig et al., 2013).

Based on the above, we can formulate our first research hypothesis:

Hp 1: As ESG ratings improve, there is a positive effect on banks' credit risk (inverse relationship between ESGr and CR).

Using ESGr issued by Refinitiv and using CDS spread (the values as a proxy for creditworthiness), the relationship between ESGr and CR in the sample banks is analyzed. The analysis is referenced to the time range 2012–2021 (Sustainable Development Goals—SDGs—and Paris Agreement—COP 21) to identify the effects of exposure to ESG risk, discounting any distortions in CDS prices in earlier periods resulting from the succession of financial crises in 2008 and 2012.

The literature is more extensive; some scholars link credit quality to financial and economic variables (Naili & Lahrichi, 2020); other authors (Wu & Shen, 2013; Shen et al., 2016) indeed highlight a direct correlation between credit quality and CSR strategic choices, in terms of ESG activities, on reduction NPL levels. Compliant with the constraints of "green finance", they can reduce the riskiness of their loan portfolio through a reduction in the NPL level (Cui et al., 2018; Nizam et al., 2019) with positive effects on the SLV ratio.

Based on these remarks, we formulate our second and third hypotheses. Starting from the verification of geographic and size biases, statistical models could be developed with the aim of assessing whether the following assumptions are verified:

Hp 2: If there is an inverse relationship between ESGr and CR, there is also an inverse relationship between ESGr and NPL value (increasing the rating reduces the value of Npl);

Hp 3: The inverse relationship between ESGr and the value of NPls does not always generate a positive impact on the SLV.

We expect that an increase in ESG score has a positive effect on banks' CR, but a correlation between the ESG score and NPL is negative for all dimensions with a positive impact on SLV.

3 Methodology and Research Design

For the analysis, three different regression models were built: the first to analyze the relationship between CDS and ESG score, the second to study the relationship between NPL and ESG score, and the third to study the connection between SLV ratio and NPL. In Table 6.1, we present the description of the variables that we use for our analysis.

The dependent variable of the first model will therefore be the natural logarithm of annual 5-year senior unsecured CDS spread levels.

The dependent variable of the second model will be the natural logarithm of NPL.

The dependent variable of the third regression model is the solvency ratio, autonomously calculated based on Refinitiv Datastream data as ratio between total equity and total assets:

$$\text{SOLVRatio}_{it} = \frac{\text{Total Equity}_{it}}{\text{Total Asset}_{it}} \tag{6.1}$$

The model that analyzes the relationship between CDS and ESG score is:

$$\begin{aligned} \ln(\text{CDS})_{i,t} = {} & \beta_0 + \beta_1 \text{ESG}_{i,t} + \beta_2 \text{ENV}_{i,t} + \beta_3 \text{CG}_{i,t} + \beta_4 \text{SOC}_{i,t} \\ & + \beta_5 \text{ROENorm}_{i,t} + \beta_6 \text{CapAde}_{i,t} + \beta_7 \text{CostRatio}_{i,t} \\ & + \beta_8 \text{Size}_{i,t} + \beta_9 \text{NPLRatio}_{i,t} + \epsilon_{i,t} \end{aligned} \tag{6.2}$$

The main variables of the above model are all ESG scores. The control variables of the model are: ROENorm, normalized Return on Equity (ROE); CapAde, the capital adequacy ratio; CostRatio, the cost-to-income ratio; Size, the size of the company measured by logarithm of total assets; NPLRatio.

The model that analyzes the relationship between NPL and ESG is given below:

Table 6.1 Variables description

Variables	Role	Description	Calculation method	Source
Ln(CDS)	Dependent variable	Natural logarithm of CDS spreads	Ln(CDS Spread)	Autonomous calculations based on the data provided by Refinitiv Datastream
Ln(NPL)	Dependent variable	Natural logarithm of non performing loans	Ln(NPL)	Calculations based on the data provided by Refinitiv Datastream
Solvency Ratio	Dependent variable	Ratio of total equity to total assets	$\frac{Total\ Equity}{Total\ Asset}$	Calculations based on the data provided by Refinitiv Datastream
ESG	Independent variable	Combined ESG score	Refinitiv's ESG score is an overall company score based on the self-reported information in the environmental, social and corporate governance pillars.	Refinitiv Datastream
ENV_Score	Independent variable	Environmental ESG score	Refinitiv's Environment Pillar Score is the weighted average relative rating of a company based on the reported environmental information and the resulting three environmental category scores.	Refinitiv Datastream
GOV_Score	Independent variable	Corporate Governance ESG score	Refinitiv's Governance Pillar Score is the weighted average relative rating of a company based on the reported governance information and the resulting three governance category scores.	Refinitiv Datastream

SO_Score	Independent variable	Social ESG score	Refinitiv's Social Pillar Score is the weighted average relative rating of a company based on the reported social information and the resulting four social category scores.	Refinitiv Datastream
Cost to Income Ratio	Control variable	Cost-effectiveness Ratio: Ratio of operating expenses to net interest and other banking income	$\frac{Operating\ Expenses\ Total}{Net\ Interest\ Income}$	Autonomous calculations based on the data provided by Refinitiv Datastream
Capital Adequacy	Control variable	Adequacy Ratio: Ratio of TIER 1 capital to total Risk Weighted Assets (RWA).	$\frac{TIER\ 1\ Capital}{RWA}$	Autonomous calculations based on the data provided by Refinitiv Datastream
NPL Ratio	Control variable	Ratio of non performing loans to total amount of loans disbursed	$\frac{Non\ performng\ Loans}{Total\ loans}$	Autonomous calculations based on the data provided by Refinitiv Datastream
ROE_ Normalized	Control variable	Performance Index. Profitability of total operations net of the impact of extraordinary operations		Autonomous calculations based on the data provided by Refinitiv Datastream
Size	Control variable	Natural logarithm of the total asset	Ln(Total asset)	Autonomous calculations based on the data provided by Refinitiv Datastream
CDS SPread	–	*Credit Default Swap* spread with *maturity* 5 years express in basis point.		Refinitiv Datastream

$$\ln(\text{NPL})_{i,t} = \beta_0 + \beta_1\text{ESG}_{i,t} + \beta_2\text{ENV}_{i,t} + \beta_3\text{CG}_{i,t} + \beta_4\text{SOC}_{i,t} + \beta_5\text{ROENorm}_{i,t} + \beta_6\text{CapAde}_{i,t} + \beta_7\text{CostRatio}_{i,t} + \beta_8\text{Size}_{i,t} + \epsilon_{i,t} \quad (6.3)$$

Again, the main variables are represented by all ESG score. The control variables of the model are: ROENorm, normalized ROE; CapAde, the capital adeguacy ratio; CostRatio, the cost-to-income ratio; Size, the size of the company measured by logarithm of total assets.

Finally, the models that analyze the relationship between SLV ratio have two different points of view. On the one hand, with respect to ESG score, while on the other, with respect to the value of NPL.

The equations are the following:

$$\text{SolvRatio}_{i,t} = \beta_0 + \beta_1\text{ESG}_{i,t} + \beta_2\text{ENV}_{i,t} + \beta_3\text{CG}_{i,t} + \beta_4\text{SOC}_{i,t} + \beta_5\text{ROENorm}_{i,t} + \beta_6\text{CapAde}_{i,t} + \beta_7\text{CostRatio}_{i,t} + \beta_8\text{Size}_{i,t} + \beta_9\text{NPLRatio}_{i,t} + \epsilon_{i,t} \quad (6.4)$$

$$\text{SolvRatio}_{i,t} = \beta_0 + \beta_1\ln(\text{NPL})_{i,t} + \beta_2\text{ESG}_{i,t} + \beta_3\text{ENV}_{i,t} + \beta_4\text{CG}_{i,t} + \beta_5\text{SOC}_{i,t} + \beta_6\text{CapAde}_{i,t} + \beta_7\text{CostRatio}_{i,t} + \beta_8\text{Size}_{i,t} + \beta_9\text{NPLRatio}_{i,t} + \beta_{10}\text{ROENorm}_{i,t} + \epsilon_{i,t} \quad (6.5)$$

The main variables of this model are all ESG scores and NPLs.

The control variables of the systematic risk model are: ROENorm, normalized (ROE); CapAde, the capital adeguacy ratio; CostRatio, the cost-to-income ratio, Size, the size of the company measured by logarithm of total assets; NPLRatio.

The estimators used to perform the panel regression analysis on the models mentioned above are the Fixed model and the Random estimator. The Pooled estimator was discarded a priori, since this regression is most often unlikely to be adequate to implement a regression on panel data, since it has some serious limitations. As for the choice between the Fixed and Random models, Hausman" test (1978) was performed to check which of the two was the most appropriate, and the test indicated that the most suitable model was the Fixed model for all models exept the

Table 6.2 The Hausman Test

Dependent variable	*Independent variable*	*Models*	*Result of Hausman Test*	*Chosen model*
Ln(CDS)	***ESG***	Random vs Fixed Effects	chisq = 30.009, df = 10, p-value = 0.0008536 alternative hypothesis: one model is inconsistent	**Fixed Effects**
Ln(NPL)	***ESG***	Random vs Fixed Effects	chisq = 46.088, df = 8, p-value = 2.287e-07 alternative hypothesis: one model is inconsistent	**Fixed Effects**
Solvency Ratio	***ESG***	Random vs Fixed Effects	chisq = 43.803, df = 10, p-value = 3.572e-06 alternative hypothesis: one model is inconsistent	**Fixed Effects**
Solvency Ratio	***ESG & NPL***	Random vs Fixed Effects	chisq = 21.345, df = 10, p-value = 0.01881 alternative hypothesis: one model is inconsistent	**Random Effects**

model that shows the relationship between solvency ratio and NPL (see Table 6.2).

The total sample analyzed included 31 European banks listed with 310 bank-year obsevations from 31 December 2012 to 31 December 2021 (included). The Refinitiv Datastream database was used for data extraction.

Initially, the sample included 810 bank-year observations. After eliminating all the bank-year observations with at least one missing value among regression model variables, the number was reduced to 310 to create a balanced panel. The time horizon of analysis was the ten-year period from 2012 to 2021, with the intentional inclusion of the years 2020–2021, despite the COVID-19 pandemic.

As regards the geographical area considered in the selection of banks, it covered the whole European continent, both the Member States of the European Union and non-member countries.

Regarding total sample statistics, for ESG combined, the average of the selected banks is less than 80%.

Looking at the two tails of the distribution, on the left side we have the minimal value (19.23%) and the first percentile (23.71%). On the right side of the distribution range, we have the maximum value and the ninety-ninth percentile equal to 97.56% and 97.34%, respectively.

Environment, Corporate Governance and Social Score have a similar distribution, with averages of 62%, 73% and 58%, respectively.

The ROE is, on average 4.55%. Thus, we can conclude that the sample's banks are generally functioning at a profit.

On the left side of the distribution range, we find the banks that had the worst performance, with first percentile at -40%; on the other side, we find the intermendiate that had the best performance, with the ninety-ninth percentile being 26.3%.

As regards size descriptive statistics, the total asset is slightly lower than the 3 billion euros, on an average (see Table 6.3).

On a preliminary basis, we analyzed Pearson' correlation coefficients over the total sample with the purpose of observing the degree of correlation between the ESG score and the three dependent variables (CDS spread, NPL, and solvency ratio). The results are reported in Table 6.4.

We can see a negative correlation, both between the ESG score and CDS spread, and between ESG score and the solvency ratio, with the coefficients in question being -0.349 and -0.374, respectively.

In summary, this result is also in line with our assumptions, as it indicates that the increase in ESG score has a positive effect on banks' credit risk (RQ 1).

However, the correlation between the ESG score and NPL is negative for all scores, apart from the Social ESG score that has a positive coefficient, precisely 0.005. This confirms the initial assumption about the negative relationship between ESG score and NPL (RQ 2).

Pearson's correlation matrix is also useful for the determination of multi-collinearity among selected variables. According to Lind et al. (2017), the regression model analyzed should not show the problem of multi-collinearity because the coefficients of correlation between regressors are below 0.7.

Table 6.3 Descriptive statistics

Variables	Obs	Mean	Std. Dev.	Min	Max	p1	p99	Skew.	Kurt.
Total assets	310	2.720e+09	5.980e+09	54,753,000	4.113e+10	65,239,000	2.994e+10	3.705	17.475
Common Equity	310	2.420e+08	7.020e+08	-2,823,969	5.484e+09	4,041,361	3.848e+09	4.657	27.156
NPL	310	1.070e+08	3.150e+08	904,374	2.112e+09	1,157,604	1.711e+09	4.323	22.865
EBIT	310	50,600,000	1.780e+08	-1.259e+08	1.566e+09	-6,134,899	1.051e+09	5.433	35.975
EBITDA	310	55,300,000	1.910e+08	-1.048e+08	1.667e+09	-6,027,604	1.125e+09	5.351	35.022
Tier1 capital	310	2.380e+08	6.910e+08	3,685,426	5.412e+09	4,874,035	3.767e+09	4.614	27.021
Total liabilities	310	2.470e+09	5.280e+09	49,020,000	3.564e+10	60,126,000	2.546e+10	3.633	16.782
Deposits	310	1.630e+09	4.230e+09	15,362,572	2.727e+10	15,647,506	2.106e+10	3.79	17.483
RWA	310	1.850e+09	5.480e+09	32,207,000	3.772e+10	39,137,113	3.179e+10	4.229	21.899
ROE	310	4.555	14.117	-88.27	98.14	-40.46	26.34	0.077	21.793
ENVSCORE	310	79.001	16.713	19.23	97.56	23.71	97.34	-1.312	4.229
CGSCORE	310	62.33	21.425	12.86	97	14.48	94.33	-0.477	2.194
SOSCORE	310	73.448	14.85	14.83	98.61	25.92	97.03	-0.953	4.317
ESG	310	58.418	14.163	22.67	91.68	27	87.41	0.083	2.396
Size	310	20.489	1.525	17.818	24.44	17.994	24.123	0.305	2.765
Capital Adequacy	310	0.144	0.029	0.082	0.279	0.089	0.221	0.976	4.502
Cost to Income Ratio	310	2.667	1.334	0.807	9.246	0.906	7.197	1.849	7.538
Solvency Ratio	310	0.069	0.029	-0.041	0.156	0.028	0.149	0.853	3.916
NPL Ratio	310	0.052	0.081	0.002	0.533	0.003	0.46	3.459	16.428
ROE Normalized	310	0.595	0.327	0	1	0	1	-0.487	2.029
Ln(NPL)	310	16.842	1.484	13.715	21.471	13.962	21.26	1.16	4.654
CDS Spread	310	178.911	203.77	19.45	1312	23.46	975	2.42	9.69
Ln(CDS)	310	4.732	0.915	2.968	7.179	3.155	6.882	0.484	2.545

Table 6.4 Pearson correlation matrix

	ln(CDS)	ln(NPL)	SolvRatio	ESGScore	ESGENV	ESGCG	ESGSO	CapAde	CostRatio	Size	ROENor	NPLRatio
ln(CDS)	1	...	...	...	...	...	...	...	...	...	...	...
ln(NPL)	0.041	1	...	...	...	...	...	...	...	...	...	...
Solv Ratio	0.400	0.139	1	...	...	...	...	...	...	...	...	...
ESG Score	-0.349	-0.104	-0.374	1	...	...	...	...	...	...	...	...
ESGENV	-0.327	-0.081	-0.570	0.674	1	...	...	...	...	...	...	...
ESGCG	-0.276	-0.162	-0.262	0.847	0.445	1	...	...	...	...	...	...
ESGSO	-0.276	0.005	-0.282	0.859	0.533	0.489	1	...	...	...	...	...
Cap Ade	-0.392	-0.235	-0.013	0.178	0.148	0.157	0.118	1	...	...	...	...
Cos t Ratio	-0.006	0.028	-0.494	0.039	0.315	0.021	-0.048	-0.216	1	...	...	...
Size	-0.413	0.731	-0.099	0.128	0.124	0.056	0.163	0.143	-0.041	1	...	...
ROENor	-0.124	-0.046	0.051	0.054	-0.090	0.007	0.110	0.032	-0.176	-0.018	1	...
NPL Ratio	0.522	0.166	0.181	-0.268	-0.156	-0.225	-0.233	-0.234	0.137	-0.419	-0.110	1

4 Main Results and Discussion

As regards the first model, from the results using Fixed-effect model, we can observe that the coefficient associated with ESG score immediately appears to be statistically very significant based on the p-value (0.009561). The coefficient in question is very high and has a negative sign, precisely -9.086. This result further supports RQ 1 that the ESG score positively affects the decrease in credit risk of European banks (see Table 6.5).

For all other scores, the results show a significant and positive relation with CDS spread. We have a positive coefficient as 2.28(***), 3.50(**), and 4.29(*) for Environment, Corporate Governance, and Social.

The R2 coefficient of determination (0.2505) in regression indicates that the model can explain 25.05% of CDS spread.

The only control variable with statistically significant coefficients is the capital adeguacy ratio (-8.416***).

The other control variables, which are not characterized by statistically significant coefficients, are instead the cost ratio, the size, the ROE normalized, and the NPL ratio.

Using the Fixed-effect model for the second model—relationship between ESG score and NPL—we can see that the coefficient associated

Table 6.5 Effects of ESG on CDS spread

Variables	Estimate	Std. error	t-value	Pr(>|t|)	Signif. code
ESG Score	-9.086112	3.4812413	-2.61	0.009561	**
ESGENV	2.2826742	0.5743096	3.9746	9.06E-05	***
ESGCG	3.5070435	1.2874548	2.724	0.006872	**
ESGSO	4.2972306	1.9080818	2.2521	0.025121	*
Cap Ade	-8.4166194	1.5951899	-5.2762	2.72E-07	***
Cost Ratio	-0.0037161	0.0329289	-0.1129	0.910232	
Size	-0.0711322	0.1557196	-0.4568	0.648186	
ROENor	-0.106756	0.1132707	-0.9425	0.34679	
NPL Ratio	0.9425164	0.6628946	1.4218	0.156237	

Total Sum of Squares: 68.071
Residual Sum of Squares: 51.018
R-Squared: 0.25051
Adj. R-Squared: 0.13906
F-statistic: 8.9912 on 10 and 269 DF, p-value: 9.0553e-13
Signif. codes: 0 '***' 0.001 '**' 0.01 '*' 0.05 '.' 0.1 ' ' 1

Table 6.6 Effects of ESG on non performing loans

Variables	Estimate	Std. error	t-value	Pr(>|t|)	Signif. code
ESG Score	-4.714156	3.759643	-1.2539	0.21096	
ESGENV	1.37547	0.619031	2.222	0.02711	*
ESGCG	0.595103	1.396343	0.4262	0.67031	
ESGSO	2.305839	2.067776	1.1151	0.26578	
Cap Ade	-4.245735	1.729789	-2.4545	0.01474	*
Cost Ratio	0.076123	0.035419	2.1492	0.0325	*
Size	1.183918	0.167815	7.0549	1.44E-11	***
ROENor	-0.051076	0.098419	-0.519	0.60421	

Total Sum of Squares: 88.42
Residual Sum of Squares: 60.719
R-Squared: 0.31328
Adj. R-Squared: 0.21699
F-statistic: 15.4539 on 8 and 271 DF, p-value: < 2.22e-16
Signif. codes: 0 '***' 0.001 '**' 0.01 '*' 0.05 '.' 0.1 ' ' 1

with ESG score (Environment score) appears to be statistically significant and its value is negative, with an accuracy of 1.375(*) (see Table 6.6).

The other score is not statistically significant. The R^2 coefficient of determination (0.3132) in regression indicates that the model can explain 31.32% of NPL. The control variables with statistically significant coefficients are capital adeguacy ratio (-4.24 *), cost ratio (0.076*), and size (1.18***).

Whereas for the third model, from the results obtained by the Fixed-effect model, we can observe that the coefficient associated with ESG score appears to be statistically very significant in explaining the variance of the solvency ratio based on t-statistics (2.9628) and p-value (0.0033209) (see Table 6.7).

The coefficient in question has a positive sign, precisely 0.22 (**).

We have the opposite result for the three distinct scores; the coefficients are negative and statistically significant: -0.041 (**) for environment, -0.082 (**) for corporate governance and -0.08(.) for social score.

The R^2 coefficient of determination (0.4781) in regression indicates that the model can explain 47.81% of the solvency ratio variance.

The other control variables to which statistically significant coefficients have been associated are capital adeguacy ratio (0.13 ***), cost ratio (-0.004***), size (1.18***), ROE normalized (0.005*) and NPL ratio (0.09***).

Table 6.7 Effects of ESG on solvency ratio

Variables	Estimate	Std. error	t-value	Pr(>|t|)	Signif. code
ESG Score	0.228050	7.70E-02	2.9628	0.0033209	**
ESGENV	-0.041021	1.27E-02	-3.2306	0.0013891	**
ESGCG	-0.082825	2.85E-02	-2.9097	0.0039205	**
ESGSO	-0.080443	4.22E-02	-1.9068	0.0576112	.
ROE	-0.000307	6.11E-05	-5.0199	9.42E-07	***
Cap Ade	0.139140	3.53E-02	3.945	0.0001019	***
Cost Ratio	-0.004209	7.28E-04	-5.7813	2.05E-08	***
Size	-0.029163	3.44E-03	-8.4703	1.62E-15	***
ROENor	0.005879	2.50E-03	2.3476	0.0196204	*
NPL Ratio	0.097825	1.47E-02	6.6746	1.41E-10	***

Total Sum of Squares: 0.04779
Residual Sum of Squares: 0.02494
R-Squared: 0.47814
Adj. R-Squared: 0.40054
F-statistic: 24.6466 on 10 and 269 DF, p-value: < 2.22e-16
Signif. codes: 0 '***' 0.001 '**' 0.01 '*' 0.05 '.' 0.1 ' ' 1

Finally, using the variation of the model that also has the NPL logarithm as independent variable, the Random-effect model is more performing. The result is very similar, and the coefficient associated with NPL appears to be statistically very significant in explaining the variance of the solvency ratio based on t-statistics (5.4202) and p-value (5.95E-08) (see Table 6.8).

The coefficient in question has a positive sign, precisely 0.006(***) (RQ3).

The R^2 coefficient of determination (0.4164) in regression indicates that the model can explain 41.64% of the solvency ratio variance.

5 Conclusion, Main Implication, and Future Developments

The study evaluates the relationship between the ESG variables of the Refinitiv database and the performance of the European banking sector for the period 2012–2021. Few previous studies have analyzed the

Table 6.8 Effects of NPL & ESG on solvency ratio

Variables	Estimate	Std. error	t-value	Pr(>|t|)	Signif. code
(Intercept)	0.491370	6.03E-02	8.1444	3.81E-16	***
NPL log	0.006707	1.24E-03	5.4202	5.95E-08	***
ESG Score	0.172410	7.71E-02	2.2363	0.025335	*
ESGENV	-0.038879	1.28E-02	-3.0363	0.002395	**
ESGCG	-0.064175	2.86E-02	-2.2456	0.024728	*
ESGSO	-0.065586	4.25E-02	-1.5433	0.122764	
ROE	-0.000313	6.17E-05	-5.073	3.92E-07	***
Cap Ade	0.188310	3.59E-02	5.2528	1.50E-07	***
Cost Ratio	-0.004446	7.35E-04	-6.0511	1.44E-09	***
Size	-0.027020	3.27E-03	-8.2648	2.20E-16	***
ROENor	0.005884	2.53E-03	2.3273	0.019951	*

Total Sum of Squares: 0.048614
Residual Sum of Squares: 0.028369
R-Squared: 0.41646
Adj. R-Squared: 0.39694
Chisq: 213.389 on 10 DF, p-value: < 2.22e-16
Signif. codes: 0 '***' 0.001 '**' 0.01 '*' 0.05 '.' 0.1 ' ' 1

influence of ESG activities on financial performance and creditworthiness indicators (Xie et al., 2019; Gümüş et al., 2018; Naili & Lahrichi, 2020). In this regard, the work can make an innovative contribution to the existing literature as it analyzes the relationship between ESG factors and CR metrics, the latter measured by the CDS spread.

This relationship in turn is observed by relating it to NPL volume and solvency ratio, considered across all dimensions, such as capitalization, profitability, efficiency, and liquidity. The effects of this dual relationship were examined using a data panel built on a sample of listed European banks, which assigns an ESG score based on sustainable activities, resource intensity, share capital, and governance.

From the regression analysis, which answers the first research question, a positive relationship emerges between a better ESG performance and a solid credit risk profile that banks with better ESG performance are associated with better credit risk performance.

Regarding the second and third research questions, the models show a positive relationship between better ESG performance and the likelihood of higher profitability and creditworthiness metrics.

The results of the analyses support research questions RQ1, RQ2, and RQ3 by highlighting a positive relationship of ESG performance with a robust credit risk profile and increased profitability and creditworthiness of institutions. A possible explanation for this could be found in the greater prudence in carrying out banking activities due to the banks' commitment to environmental, social, and corporate governance practices; this virtuous attitude could in turn be a harbinger of more stable and profitable relationships.

These observations lead to several reflections: (i) attention to ESG issues is important in the banking sector and supports the EBA's proposal to include ESG activities in supervisory checks (EBA, 2020); (ii) the integration of sustainability practices into banks' internal processes should be a driving force for actions inspired by the principle of sound management (Faiella & Malvolti, 2020).

Despite the many implications just highlighted, the results suggest that the greatest benefits to the levels of profitability and solvency of banks, following the adoption of sustainability practices, can be felt more in the long term.

In other words, this study is needed now because it sheds light that the containment of CR can be achieved through a greater commitment by banks on sustainability issues. As emerges from the descriptive analysis, better overall loan portfolio quality corresponds to higher ESG_{comb} levels; this aspect should not be underestimated because the European banks still need to dispose a large amount of NPLs in the balance sheet. This is also an incentive for authorities, who must direct their regulatory policies towards greater attention to ESG issues. It is evident that a contraction of NPLs produces a positive impact on FP and SLV ratio levels and contributes to the stability of a bank. The latter aspect should not be understating, since greater bank stability leads to a strengthening of the conditions of financial resilience, in a context, such as the current one, characterized by the presence of negative contingent factors (e.g., the COVID-19 pandemic, the Russia–Ukraine war, and so on). These factors inevitably give rise to strong pressures deriving from systemic instability.

However, it is important to remember that throughout history, crises have been pivotal in developing societies (Vrontis et al., 2022; Thrassou et al., 2022).

This study has some limitations. One limitation could be the small number of banks in our sample; even if this (the sample) is in any case able to provide robust results for the analysis in question. Another limitation is linked to the possibility that other variables (typically those that are exogenous to the banking activity) may influence the relationships between the ESGr–NPL ratio–SLV ratio dimensions.

Possible future developments of the research could concern analyses of ESG policies on various dimensions of financial metrics, also extending the field of investigation to other contexts, such as that of emerging markets. For instance, if employees involved in the customer creditworthiness assessment process could affect overall portfolio CR, an analysis of their more advanced professional training could be conducted. This would limit the analysis to the rewarding aspects of the Social and Governance Pillars.

References

Albertini, E. (2013). Does environmental management improve financial performance? A meta-analytical review. *Organization & Environment, 26*(4), 431–457.

Anginer, D., Demirguc-Kunt, A., Huizinga, H., & Ma, K. (2018). Corporate governance of banks and financial stability. *Journalof Financial Economics, 130*(2), 327–346.

Attig, N., El Ghoul, S., Guedhami, O., & Suh, J. (2013). Corporate social responsibility and credit ratings. *Journal of Business Ethics, 117*(4), 679–694.

Azmi, W., Hassan, M. K., Houston, R., & Karim, M. S. (2021). ESG activities and banking performance: International evidence from emerging economies. *Journal of International Financial Markets, Institutions and Money, 70*, 101277.

Bank of England. (2021, June). *Guidance for participants of the 2021 Biennial Exploratory Scenario: Financial risks from climate change.*

Bătae, O. M., Dragomir, V. D., & Feleagă, L. (2020). Environmental, social, governance (ESG), and financial performance of European banks. *Accounting and Management Information Systems, 19*(3), 480–501.

Berger, A. N., Imbierowicz, B. R., & Rauch, C. (2016). The roles of corporate governance in bank failures during the recent financial crisis. *Journal of Money, Credit and Banking, 48*(4), 729–770.

Birindelli, G., Bonanno, G., Dell'Atti, S., & Iannuzzi, A. P. (2022). Climate change commitment, credit risk and the country's environmental performance: Empirical evidence from a sample of international banks. *Business Strategy and the Environment, 31*(4), 1641–1655.

Bouslah, K., Kryzanowski, L., & M'Zali, B. (2018). Social performance and firm risk: Impact of the financial crisis. *Journal of Business Ethics, 149*, 643–669.

Bryant, A., Griffin, J. J., & Perry, V. G. (2020). Mitigating climate change: A role for regulations and risk-taking. *Business Strategy and the Environment, 29*(2), 605–618.

Buallay, M. A. (2019). Is sustainability reporting (ESG) associated with performance? Evidence from the European banking sector. *Management of Environmental Quality: An International Journal, 30*(1), 98–115.

Buallay, M. A., Al Marri, M., Nasrallah, N., Hamdan, A., Barone, E., & Zureigat, Q. (2021). Sustainability reporting in banking and financial services sector: A regional analysis. *Journal of Sustainable Finance & Investment, 13*, 1–26.

Cheng, B., Ioannou, I., & Serafeim, G. (2014). Corporate social responsibility and access to finance. *Strategic Management Journal, 35*(1), 1–23.

Chiaramonte, L., Dreassi, A., Girardone, C., & Piserà, S. (2022). Do ESG strategies enhance bank stability during financial turmoil? Evidence from Europe. *The European Journal of Finance, 28*(12), 1173–1211.

Cornett, M. M., Erhemjamts, O., & Tehranian, H. (2016). Greed or good deeds: An examination of the relation between corporate social responsibility and the financial performance of US commercial banks around the financial crisis. *Journal of Banking & Finance, 70*, 137–159.

Cui, Y., Geobey, S., Weber, O., & Haiying, L. (2018). The impact of green lending on credit risk in China. *Sustainability, 10*(6), 1–16.

Di Tommaso, C., & Thornton, J. (2020). Do ESG scores effect bank risk taking and value? Evidence from European banks. *Corporate Social Responsibility and Environmental Management, 27*(5), 2286–2298.

Dowell, G., Stuart, H., & Yeung, B. (2000). Do corporate global environmental standards create or destroy market value? *Management Science, 46*(8), 1059–1074.

Drago, D., Carnevale, C., & Gallo, R. (2019). Do corporate social responsibility ratings affect credit default swap spreads? *Corporate Social Responsibility and Environmental Management, 26*(4), 644–652.

El Ghoul, S. E., Guedhami, O., Kwok, C. C. Y., & Mishra, D. R. (2011). Does corporate social responsibility affect the cost of capital? *Journal of Banking and Finance, 35*(9), 2388–2406.

European Banking Authority. (2020, October 30). Discussion Paper on management and supervision of ESG risks for credit institutions and investment firms. *EBA/DP/2020/03*.

European Central Bank. (2020, November 27). Supervisory expectations relating to risk management and disclosure. *Guide on climate-related and environmental risks*.

Faiella, I., & Malvolti, F. (2020, February). The climate risk for finance in Italy. *Occasional paper Bank of Italy*, N. 545.

Finger, M., Gavious, I., & Manos, R. (2018). Environmental risk management and financial performance in the banking industry: A cross-country comparison. *Journal of International Financial Markets, Institutions and Money, 52*, 240–261.

Gangi, F., Meles, A., D'Angelo, E., & Daniele, L. M. (2019). Sustainable development and corporate governance in the financial system: Are environmentally friendly banks less risky? *Corporate Social Responsibility and Environmental Management, 26*(3), 529–547.

García-Sánchez, I. M., & García-Meca, E. (2017). CSR engagement and earnings quality in banks. The moderating role of institutional factors. *Corporate Social Responsibility and Environmental Management, 24*(2), 145–158.

Gümüş, N., Yanıkkaya, H., & Pabuççu, Y. U. (2018). How profitability differs between conventional and Islamic banks: A dynamic panel data approach. *Pacific-Basin Finance Journal, 48*, 99–111.

Konar, S., & Cohen, M. A. (2001). Does the market value environmental performance? *Review of Economics and Statistics, 83*(2), 281–289.

Liang, H., & Renneboog, L. (2017). On the foundations of corporate social responsibility. *The Journal of Finance, LXXII*(2), 853–910.

Lind, D. A., Marchal, W. G., & Wathen, S. A. (2017). *Technical statistics in business and Economics*. Milano: McGraw-Hill Education.

Luo, X., & Bhattacharya, C. B. (2006). Corporate social responsibility, customer satisfaction, and market value. *Journal of Marketing, 70*, 1–18.

Masulis, R. W., & Reza, S. V. (2015). Agency problems of corporate philanthropy. *Review of Financial Studies, 28*, 592–636.

Mate, F. B., Boboc, C., & Ghitá, S. (2021). The relationship between corporate social responsibility and financial performance in romanian companies. *Economic Computation & Economic Cybernetics Studies & Research, 55*(3), 297–314.

Matuszak, Ł., & Różańska, E. (2017). CSR disclosure in Polish-listed companies in the light of Directive 2014/95/EU requirements: Empirical evidence. *Sustainability, 9*(12), 2304.

Miralles-Quirós, M. M., Miralles-Quirós, J. L., & Redondo Hernández, J. (2019). ESG performance and shareholder value creation in the banking industry: International differences. *Sustainability, 11*(5), 1404.

Naili, M., & Lahrichi, Y. (2020). The determinants of banks' credit risk: Review of the literature and future research agenda. *International Journal of Finance and Economics, 27*(1), 334–360.

Nizam, E., Dewandaru, A. N. G., Nagayev, R., & Nkoba, M. A. (2019). The impact of social and environmental sustainability on financial performance: A global analysis of the banking sector. *Journal of Multinational Financial Management, 49*(C), 35–53.

Ren, C., Ting, I. W. K., Lu, W. M., & Kweh, Q. L. (2022). Nonlinear effects of ESG on energy-adjusted firm efficiency: Evidence from the stakeholder engagement of apple incorporated. *Corporate Social Responsibility and Environmental Management, 29*(5), 1231–1246.

Schultz, F., Castelló, I., & Morsing, M. (2013). The construction of corporate social responsibility in network societies: A communication view. *Journal of Business Ethics, 115*(4), 681–692.

Servaes, H., & Tamayo, A. (2013). The impact of corporate social responsibility on firm value: The role of customer awareness. *Management Science, 59*(5), 1045–1061.

Shen, C. H., Wu, M. W., Chen, T. H., & Fang, H. (2016). To engage or not to engage in corporate social responsibility: Empirical evidence from global banking sector. *Economic Modelling, 55*, 207–225.

Stiroh, K. J. (2020). *The Basel Committee's initiatives on climate-related financial risks. Panel session on "New regulatory and policy landscape for sustainable finance"*, 2020 IIF Annual Membership Meeting, 14 October.

Thrassou, A., Uzunboylu, N., Efthymiou, L., Vrontis, D., Weber, Y., Shams, R., & Tsoukatos, E. (2022). Editorial introduction: Business under crises: Organizational adaptations. In D. Vrontis, A. Thrassou, Y. Weber, S. M. R. Shams, E. Tsoukatos, & L. Efthymiou (Eds.), *Business under crisis, Volume II* (Palgrave Studies in Cross-disciplinary Business Research, In Association with EuroMed Academy of Business). Palgrave Macmillan. https://doi.org/10.1007/978-3-030-76575-0_1

Trigo, A., Marta-Costa, A., & Fragoso, R. (2022). Sustainability assessment: A tool to build resilience in the face of future crisis. In D. Vrontis, A. Thrassou, Y. Weber, S. M. R. Shams, E. Tsoukatos, & L. Efthymiou (Eds.), *Business under crisis, Volume III* (Palgrave Studies in Cross-disciplinary Business Research, In Association with EuroMed Academy of Business) (pp. 19–45). Palgrave Macmillan.

Vrontis, D., Thrassou, A., Efthymiou, L., Uzunboylu, N., Weber, Y., Shams, S. M. R., & Tsoukatos, E. (2022). Editorial introduction: Business under crisis—Avenues for innovation, entrepreneurship and sustainability. In D. Vrontis, A. Thrassou, Y. Weber, S. M. R. Shams, E. Tsoukatos, & L. Efthymiou (Eds.), *Business under crisis, Volume III* (Palgrave Studies in Cross-disciplinary Business Research, In Association with EuroMed Academy of Business) (pp. 1–17). Palgrave Macmillan.

Widyawati, L. (2020). A systematic literature review of socially responsible investment and environmental social governance metrics. *Business Strategy and the Environment, 29*(2), 619–637.

Wu, M. W., & Shen, C. H. (2013). Corporate social responsibility in thebanking industry: Motives and financial performance. *Journal of Banking & Finance, 37*(1), 3529–3547.

Xie, J., Nozawa, W., Yagi, M., Fujii, H., & Managi, S. (2019). Do environmental, social, and governance activities improve corporate financial performance? *Business Strategy and the Environment, 28*(2), 286–300.

Zhang, D., Cai, J., Dickinson, D. G., & Kutan, A. M. (2016). Non-performing loans, moral hazard and regulation of the Chinese commercial banking system. *Journal of Banking & Finance, 63*, 48–60.

7

Corporate Environmental Performance and Bond Ratings: European Evidence

Panagiotis E. Dimitropoulos and Konstantinos Koronios

1 Introduction

Corporate sustainability has been at the forefront of academic research and business conduct worldwide, where more and more corporations within various sectors devote significant funds and effort to incorporate social and environmental-related strategies and policies (Gillan et al., 2021). Extant empirical evidence documents that the disclosure of

P. E. Dimitropoulos (✉)
Department of Accounting and Finance, University of Peloponnese, Kalamata, Greece

School of Social Sciences, Hellenic Open University, Patras, Greece
e-mail: dimitrop@go.uop.gr

K. Koronios
Department of Physical Therapy, University of Peloponnese, Sparta, Greece
e-mail: konskoron@hotmal.com

D. Vrontis et al. (eds.), *Business for Sustainability, Volume I*, Palgrave Studies in Cross-disciplinary Business Research, In Association with EuroMed Academy of Business, https://doi.org/10.1007/978-3-031-37361-9_7

environmental-related information and the dissemination of relevant sustainability reports are useful sources of information and can deliver important benefits for firms and investors. Among those benefits is the enhancement of risk perception and evaluation by investors and market participants (Migliorelli & Marini, 2020). According to Migliorelli (2020), environmental degradation also has significant side effects for banks and insurance companies since destruction of production facilities and even inability of customers to repay existing debt obligations can hamper the financial stability of the money and insurance markets.

Elaborating this issue further, environmental-related risks are not considered as primary risk factors, but they can exacerbate other forms of economic risks. For example, floods and other extreme weather conditions could have detrimental effects on agricultural production, industrial assets destruction, and even operation (and production) process disruptions. Those cases could be detrimental to firms' financial performance and survivorship. So environmental-related risks could be considered by banks and investors as a source for credit risk and underestimating such risks and their impact on firms' survivorship could lead to flaws in risk assessment and thus a limited capacity of firms to attract necessary funds from money and capital markets (Migliorelli, 2020). According to Dimitropoulos and Koronios (2021), sustainability performance (and specifically environmental performance) improves firms' reputational capital yielding an "insurance-type of protection" mitigating the stakeholders' perception of firm risk. Also, the development of the so-called green bond market posits the fact that stakeholders and investors pay more attention to firms' environmental performance, and corporate lending is closely tied to this matter (Chabowski et al., 2019).

Several banks in the EU, such as Barclays (2021) and HSBC (2021), have already adopted sustainability and environmental risk policies for the evaluation of their client's creditworthiness and risk exposure. Also, within the Eurozone, the European Securities and Markets Authority (ESMA, 2019) has published technical guidance on assessing environmental reports and performance on credit ratings. Thus, credit rating agencies are using those reports along with environmentally related information on their assessments of credit spreads and ratings (Barth et al., 2022). Migliorelli and Marini (2020) argue that an improved comprehension of sustainability-related risk can contribute to lower cost of capital and even improved credit ratings for firms' creditworthiness under lending evaluation processes (Dimitropoulos, 2022). It is evident that banking institutions and other financial firms are already considering environmental and sustainability risks on their credit assessments since they are a new form of financial risk. Empirical evidence by Oikonomou et al. (2014), Kim et al. (2013), and Cheng et al. (2014) document that socially responsible firms are associated with lower cost of debt capital, lower bond spreads, and enhanced credit ratings. According to Schröder (2014), the positive impact of social and environmental performance on risk assessment is attributed to the lower susceptibility of environmentally responsible firms to extreme risks, a fact that leads to lower borrowing costs and improved creditworthiness and lending ability.

Theoretically, there are two main views on how sustainability performance impacts corporate risk assessment. Agency theory postulates that CSR and environmental activities are a misappropriation of corporate resources in order for managers to extract private benefits. This fact works at the expense of shareholders, leading to lower firm values and higher borrowing costs (Chakraborty et al., 2019). On the contrary, stakeholder theory perceives sustainability activities as value enhancing since they can generate "relational wealth" or the so-called moral capital through enhanced relationships with stakeholders. This leads to enhanced firm value and improved assessment of credit risk by managing both investing and non-investing stakeholders (Godfrey, 2005; Godfrey et al., 2009).

The scope of this chapter is to disentangle the contradictory evidence in the literature and further extend the empirical evidence on environmental performance on the assessment of credit risk and specifically bond credit ratings within the EU. This study approaches corporate environmental performance (CEP) by considering three basic dimensions, namely emission reduction policies, environmental innovation activities, and resource use efficiency on firms' creditworthiness, measured through bond credit ratings. The chapter quantitatively analyzes a sample of 3329 unique listed firms from 24 EU countries, which have made bond offerings to their markets over the period 2003–2020 and have been rated by either Standard and Poor's or/and Moody's. Empirical evidence documented a positive association of enhanced environmental performance on the ratings of bonds, suggesting that environmentally responsible firms are awarded higher credit ratings and thus are considered more creditworthy by the rating agencies.

This study contributes to the existing literature on several aspects. Firstly, we respond to a call from Schröder (2014) who asks for a focus on international studies using a broad range of data from different countries. This chapter tries to fill this gap in the literature by selecting a multi-country sample from the EU, thus providing more robust evidence relevant to previous studies focusing only on a single market. Secondly, the link between environmental performance and financial risks and credit ratings especially has been an under-researched topic within the EU markets. Our study tries to provide up-to-date evidence on the matter and enhance our understanding of CEP on bond ratings (Chabowski et al., 2019; Migliorelli, 2020). Thirdly, according to Dimitropoulos and Koronios (2021), CEP is a multi-dimensional issue and extant studies on the literature are focused only on single pillars of CEP (such as CO_2 emissions, pollution activities, water usage etc.). Thus, this chapter advances the previous studies on the filed by creating an aggregate CEP measure by using different dimensions of environmental performance, thus yielding more robust evidence on the examined topic. Finally, following the propositions by Moser and Martin (2012) and Chiang et al. (2017), we combine the topics of corporate environmental performance from the business literature with bond ratings from corporate finance literature and we theoretically discuss the implications from incorporating the stakeholder view of the firm on evaluating firms' creditworthiness via credit ratings.

The rest of the chapter is organized as follows: The second section discusses the theoretical background and the literature review of the study, offering competent research hypotheses. Then, Sect. 3 presents the data selection procedure and the research design of the study. The empirical results would then be presented in Sect. 4 along with sensitivity analysis. Finally, Sect. 5 would conclude the chapter with a discussion of the main findings, along with the implications, limitations, and potential avenues for future research.

2 Literature Review and Hypothesis Development

Bond ratings represent an evaluation of the probability of the issuer to repay interest and principal over a specific period. This repayment ability could be affected by several factors, including firms' capital structure, profitability, cash flows, the sector that operates, and even adverse economic events (Hu et al., 2021). Over the years, researchers have pointed out that financial reports and the quality of such information is also a significant determinant of bond ratings since high-quality financial reports reduce information asymmetries and allow investors to efficiently assess risks and allocate resources (Raman, 1981). Nevertheless, fairly recently there has been an increased research effort to examine the association of non-financial information on the bond ratings specifically and the lending costs in general. Among non-financial information, the sustainability performance of corporations is the most important feature (including social and environmental activities), focusing on the protection of the environment (via less carbon emissions and pollution reduction) and adhering to social inequalities and problems (Bauer & Hann, 2010; Seltzer et al., 2022; Oikonomou et al., 2014; Barth et al., 2022; Hsu & Chen, 2015; Gong et al., 2018; Thrassou et al., 2022a, 2022b).

According to Dimitropoulos and Koronios (2021), Chakraborty et al. (2019), and Hu et al. (2021), there are two competing theoretical lenses under which the impact of sustainability and environmental-related information differs on the assessment of firms' credit risk. The stakeholder theory is the most dominant on this topic, arguing that the enhanced environmental performance reduces information asymmetries between firms and lenders, leading to lower lending costs and an improved assessment of firms' credit risk. Dimitropoulos and Koronios (2021) point that CEP makes the firm more appealing to creditors and investors (providing an "insurance protection" to stakeholders) by reducing their perception of future uncertainty around firms' investments and prospects through the publication of high-quality accounting information. Also, Chabowski et al. (2019) argue that corporate environmental efficiency improves bond ratings for two main reasons. Firstly, pollution reduction enhances operating performance and profitability, and this is portrayed on the bond rating process. Secondly, the inability of firms to address stakeholders' environmental concerns may signal the public managers' inability or unwillingness to deal with other important issues. Thus, those firms are perceived as poorly managed and less trustworthy, leading to higher credit spreads and lower ratings.

There is an abundance of empirical evidence corroborating the theoretical arguments of the stakeholder theory. Stellner et al. (2015) documented that superior corporate social performance is considered by lenders as risk-reducing activities leading to improved bond credit ratings and yield spreads. Similarly, Jiraporn et al. (2014) and Chiang et al. (2017) considered the impact of irresponsible activities on bond ratings, especially for those firms that were near a broad rating change. Chiang et al. (2017) concluded that firms reduce their irresponsible social activities when they are close to a bond rating change. Corroborative evidence on the positive impact of environmental performance on bond credit ratings is also provided by Chabowski et al. (2019) and Hu et al. (2021) in the US and Chinese market respectively.

However, agency theory offers an opposing view on this matter, arguing that environmental responsibility activities are a waste of valuable corporate resources leading to more uncertainty regarding future profits and cash flows. Also, Hu et al. (2021) argue that the potential benefits of CEP are received by the managers, yet the costs are borne by the shareholders. Thus, managers may use environmental responsibility activities as a tool for improving their own reputation and extract private interests. This leads to unnecessary firm costs and risks which may be incorporated on the bond rating evaluations. Empirical evidence by Nguyen and Nguyen (2015) and Cespa and Cestone (2007) document that firms with systematic engagement on environmental investments are associated with higher managerial entrenchment and thus enhanced systematic risk. Therefore, the positive association between environmental responsibility and systematic risk could be incorporated into the credit rating evaluation process, leading to lower bond credit ratings. In conclusion, agency theory posits a negative impact of environmental performance on firm's creditworthiness, since sustainability performing firms are left at a competitive disadvantage due to the self-interest behavior of managers (Hu et al., 2021). Therefore, due to the contradictory theoretical views on the literature, we propose the following opposing research hypotheses as follows:

H_0*: *Corporate environmental performance impacts negatively on bond credit ratings.

H_A*: *Corporate environmental performance impacts positively on bond credit ratings.

3 Data Selection and Research Design

The empirical analysis of this chapter is based on a sample of listed corporations from 24 EU-member countries that have made a public bond offering over the period 2003–2020. We collected bond ratings, environmental performance, and financial data from Datastream database. The sample collection procedure started by including all corporations that have issued a public bond offering and have been rated by either Standard and Poor's (S&P) or Moody's. Next, we matched those ratings with environmental performance scores provided by Datastream during the sample period. For comparability reasons, we chose firms that close their fiscal year on December. We also excluded banks and other financial institutions from the sample. Finally, we winsorized the upper and lower one per cent of the sample distribution for limiting the effect of significant outliers on the sample. This procedure produced a final sample of 4177 bond issues from 3329 unique firms.

For testing the validity of the research hypothesis, we followed previous studies by Chabowski et al. (2019), Chiang et al. (2017), and Hu et al. (2021) and transformed the bond credit ratings ranging from the highest quality (AAA) to lowest quality (D) into an ordered variable ranging from unity (1) for the AAA bonds to 20 for the D rating bonds. So smaller values of this variable (BOND_R) signify enhanced creditworthiness. Environmental performance is estimated as each firm's annual average emissions score, environmental innovation score, and resource use score, as published by Datastream's ESG data. These scores range between zero (0) and 100 with higher values signifying higher environmental performance. In our case, we created a dummy variable (HIGH_CEP) which receives unity (1) if the firm has an annual CEP score above the third quartile for each sample year, and zero (0) otherwise. Consequently, BOND_R is the dependent variable on a panel-ordered regression model, using random effects with robust standard errors. The functional form of this model is operationalized as follows:

$$\begin{aligned} BOND\_R_{it} &= \alpha_1 HIGH\_CEP_{it} + \alpha_2 SIZE_{it} + \alpha_3 LEV_{it} + \alpha_4 ROA_{it} \\ &+ \alpha_5 GROWTH_{it} + \alpha_6 CFO_{it} + \alpha_7 PPE_{it} + \alpha_8 LOSS_{it} + u_{it} \end{aligned} \quad (7.1)$$

where:

BOND_R:	Ordered variable ranging from (1) for AAA bonds to (20) for D bonds.
HIGH_CEP:	Dummy variable receiving (1) if a firm has a CEP score above the third quartile for each year and zero (0) otherwise.
SIZE:	Natural logarithm of total assets.
LEV:	The ratio of total debt to total assets.
ROA:	Return on assets, calculated as operating income divided by total assets.
GROWTH:	The annual percentage change in sales revenues.
CFO:	The ratio of operating cash flows to total assets.
PPE:	The ratio of property, plant, and equipment to total assets.
LOSS:	Dummy variable that is coded (1) if the net profit is negative in the current year, and (0) otherwise.
u	is the disturbance term.

If stakeholder theory is valid and environmental performance improves the information environment of firms, this is expected to impact positively on firms' creditworthiness, leading to improved credit ratings. Thus, a negative α_1 coefficient is expected, suggesting that enhanced CEP performance is associated with a lower BOND_R score, hence improved credit ratings.

Furthermore, we controlled for additional variables that previous studies pointed as significant determinants of credit ratings (Chabowski et al., 2019; Hu et al., 2021; Chiang et al., 2017; Dimitropoulos & Koronios, 2021). SIZE is the natural logarithm of total assets capturing firm size. According to Hu et al. (2021), larger firms face fewer information asymmetries between their investors and lenders, so they could receive improved credit ratings and lower borrowing costs. Thus, a negative coefficient is expected for the SIZE variable. LEV is financial leverage estimated as the ratio of total debt to total assets. Highly leveraged firms are associated with higher systematic risk (Dimitropoulos & Koronios, 2021), so this is expected to be portrayed through lower credit ratings. Thus, a positive coefficient is expected in this variable. ROA is the ratio of return on assets measuring profitability. Profitable firms face lower debt costs and so they should be awarded higher credit ratings, leading to a negative coefficient (Chabowski et al., 2019).

GROWTH captures firms' growth opportunities and is estimated as the annual percentage change in sales revenues. Also, CFO is the ratio of operating cash flows to total assets. According to Dimitropoulos and Koronios (2021), firms with growth opportunities and enhanced operating cash flows face less uncertainty about their future cash flows and this can be associated with lower cost of debt and improved credit ratings, so a negative coefficient is expected for both GROWTH and CFO variables. Finally, we control for firms' tangibility measured by the ratio of property, plant, and equipment (PPE) to total assets, and a dummy variable (LOSS) receiving unity (1) if net income is negative in a given year and zero (0) otherwise. Firms with accounting losses are perceived as less creditworthy, thus a positive coefficient is expected on the LOSS variable. On the contrary, higher tangibility is associated with improved borrowing costs and lower spreads (since tangible assets are useful as collateral reducing loan repayment uncertainty), and consequently to improved credit ratings. So, a negative coefficient is expected for the PPE variable.

4 Empirical Results

Table 7.1 presents the descriptive statistics of the variables utilized in the regression model. First of all, the mean of overall environmental performance (AV_CEP) is 64.59 (with a standard deviation of 21.16), indicating that the sample firms have a satisfactory environmental performance score, comprised of the emission, resource use, and environmental innovation sub-scores. Also, the dummy variable HIGH_CEP has an average of 0.86, indicating that the vast majority of the sample firms have an average CEP score above the sample's third quartile, verifying the enhanced environmental performance of the EU firms (Dimitropoulos & Koronios, 2021). The average BOND_R is 8.78, which shows that the average credit ranking among the sample firms is close to BBB+. The standard deviation of credit ranking is 0.34, suggesting that there are differences on the deviation of corporate credit ratings (Hu et al., 2021).

Turning to the control variables, sample firms are highly profitable (mean ROA 21.28) and present significant growth opportunities (mean GROWTH at 589.3). Their assets are financed partly by debt (average LEV is 0.46) and their average fixed assets comprise 59 per cent of their total assets (PPE). Nevertheless, the sample firms produced very small positive operating cash flows with an average CFO of around 3 per cent of total assets. Finally, 23 per cent of the sample firms on average reported a negative income figure during the sample period.

Table 7.1 Descriptive statistics of sample variables

	Mean	Std. Dev.	Min.	Max.
BOND_R	8.78	3.58	1.00	20.00
AV_CEP	64.59	21.16	3.16	99.42
HIGH_CEP	0.86	0.34	0	1
SIZE	20.49	2.84	2.30	30.31
LEV	0.46	0.43	0.01	0.69
ROA	21.28	48.25	-27.86	174.17
GROWTH	589.3	1417.4	-697.11	4009.07
CFO	0.03	5.04	-29.42	38.94
PPE	0.59	0.24	0.01	0.99
LOSS	0.23	0.42	0	1

The Pearson correlation coefficients of the sample variables are presented in Table 7.2, and since all correlations are lower than 0.8, multicollinearity is not a serious problem in our sample. We can see that bond ratings (BOND_R) are negatively and significantly correlated with HIGH_CEP, suggesting that firms with enhanced environmental performance are associated with lower values of the BOND_R variable, thus with improved credit ratings (Chiang et al., 2017). This provides initial support for H_A. In addition, bond credit ratings are negatively correlated with SIZE and ROA, suggesting that larger and more profitable firms are perceived by credit rating agencies as more creditworthy, so they are assigned higher ratings. Finally, firms with enhanced environmental performance are smaller in size, less profitable, more leveraged, and have higher tangibility.

Table 7.3 illustrates the results of the order logistic regression mode (1) using random effects with robust standard errors. The main variable of interest, HIGH_CEP produced a negative and statistically significant coefficient (at the one per cent significance level) of -0.161. This result led us to accept hypothesis H_A, suggesting that firms' enhanced environmental performance leads to improved credit ratings. This finding corroborates the stakeholder theory arguing that the enhanced environmental performance reduces information asymmetries between firms and lenders leading to lower lending costs and an improved assessment of firms' credit risk. Our result verifies pre-existing empirical evidence by Chabowski

Table 7.2 Pearson correlation coefficients of sample variables

Variables	1	2	3	4	5	6	7	8	9
1. BOND_R	1								
2. HIGH_CEP	**-0.05**	1							
3. SIZE	**-0.03**	**-0.05**	1						
4. LEV	-0.01	**0.01**	**-0.05**	1					
5. ROA	**-0.03**	-0.01	**0.13**	**-0.07**	1				
6. GROWTH	-0.00	0.00	0.00	-0.01	-0.00	1			
7. CFO	0.01	-0.01	**0.02**	**-0.73**	**0.06**	0.01	1		
8. PPE	-0.01	**0.02**	**0.28**	**-0.03**	**0.02**	0.00	**0.01**	1	
9.LOSS	0.01	**0.03**	**-0.24**	**0.01**	**-0.04**	0.00	**-0.02**	**0.04**	1

Note: Correlation coefficients in bold indicate statistical significance at the 5% significance level at least (two-tailed test)

Table 7.3 Ordered Logistic Regression results (random effects with robust standard errors)

Variables	Coeff.	*z*-stat	*p*-value
HIGH_CEP	-0.161***	-2.81	0.005
SIZE	-0.008	-0.64	0.525
LEV	0.001***	3.02	0.002
ROA	-0.002**	-2.23	0.026
GROWTH	-0.001**	-2.47	0.013
CFO	-0.007	-0.62	0.535
PPE	-0.066	-0.53	0.597
LOSS	0.076	1.09	0.274
No. of obs.		4177	
Wald Chi-square		250.68***	
Prob > Chi-square		0.000	

Note: Dependent variable: BOND_R. *** indicates significance at the 0.01 level (2-tailed), ** indicates significance at the 0.05 level (2-tailed)

et al. (2019), Hu et al. (2021), and Chiang et al. (2017) that superior corporate social performance is considered by lenders as risk-reducing activities, leading to improved bond credit ratings.

Moving on to the control variables, we can see that only LEV, ROA, and GROWTH produced statistically significant coefficients with the expected sign. Specifically, firms with increased leverage are perceived as less creditworthy; thus, their bond issues are assigned lower credit ratings. On the contrary, highly profitable and growth firms receive higher ratings from credit agencies because they face lower debt costs due to their reduced uncertainty. The evidence again corroborates the findings by Chabowski et al. (2019) and Hu et al. (2021) in the US and Chinese markets, respectively.

Moreover, we performed several sensitivity tests (untabulated) for checking the robustness of the findings in Table 7.3. Firstly, following the works by Dimitropoulos and Koronios (2021) and Cai et al. (2016), we (a) replaced the HIGH_CEP dummy variable on model (1) with the actual environmental performance score and (b) we re-estimated model (1) HIGH_CEP dummy variable based on the estimation of the principal component of the three sub-scores. Thus, we constructed the CEP_PC variable which equals the first principal component from the emission, environmental innovation, and resource use sub-scores. The principal component was determined using eigenvalues greater than 1.0. We used the Varimax rotation for extracting the component. Empirical results remained qualitatively unchanged relative to those presented in Table 7.3. Additional sensitivity tests were performed after changing the definition of the control variables by estimating LEV as the ratio of long-term debt to total assets, GROWTH as the ratio of book value to market value of equity (BV/MV), and ROA was replaced by ROE but the results remain unchanged after these definitional changes (Dimitropoulos & Koronios, 2021).

Finally, we controlled for the impact of potential endogeneity on the regression model (due to reverse causality and omitted variables) which could affect the environmental performance and credit rating of firms. Following the work by Chiang et al. (2017) and Chabowski et al. (2019), we estimated a two-stage least square regression (2SLS) using the average CEP value for firms in the same industry as the instrument. So, CEP_instr (estimated based on the first 2-digit SIC code) was used as the instrument for first-stage regression and estimated the instrumented CEP performance (CEP_instr) which was included in the second-stage regression. According to Chabowski et al. (2019), CEP_instr is a valid instrument for this case since the industry's average CEP performance is related to each firm's CEP performance yet is unrelated to each firm's credit rating. Empirical evidence from the second-stage regression indicated that enhanced CEP performance is positively impacting credit ratings, so our initial evidence is unaffected by simultaneous bias caused by endogeneity.

5 Conclusions

The disclosure and dissemination of environmental-related information and sustainability reports are useful sources of information for assessing firms' risk exposure (Dimitropoulos & Koronios, 2021). The enhanced risk perception by investors and market participants is being considered as an important benefit of environmental responsibility (Migliorelli & Marini, 2020). According to Migliorelli (2020), environmental performance has also been considered by banking institutions in assessing the risk of their clients or their ability to repay existing debt obligations. Over the years, environmental-related risks have been considered as a primary risk factor that can exacerbate other forms of economic risks, including firms' creditworthiness and viability.

The scope of this chapter is to provide ample empirical evidence on how and whether corporate environmental performance impacts on firms' credit risk and specifically bond credit ratings within the EU. This study approached corporate environmental performance (CEP) based on three environmental responsibility dimensions, namely emission reduction policies, environmental innovation activities, and resource use efficiency, on firms' creditworthiness, measured through bonds credit ratings. The chapter quantitatively analyzes a sample of 3329 unique listed firms from 24 EU countries, which have made bond offerings to their markets over the period 2003–2020 and have been rated by either Standard and Poor's or/and Moody's. Empirical evidence documented a positive association of enhanced CEP performance on the ratings of bonds suggesting that environmentally responsible firms are awarded higher credit ratings, and thus are considered as more creditworthy by rating agencies.

The empirical evidence of this study offers useful policy implications for researchers, managers, and investors (bondholders). Firstly, our evidence yield supports the stakeholder theory since we document that enhanced environmental performance reduces information asymmetries between bond issuers and rating agencies, leading to improvements in credit ratings. Thus, environmental performance is an important risk-related determinant which needs to be considered by banks and risk analysts in assessing firms' creditworthiness. Secondly, our evidence corroborates arguments in the literature (Chabowski et al., 2019; Hu et al., 2021; Chakraborty et al., 2019) that corporate creditworthiness is affected by the firms' business and information environment, suggesting that environmental responsibility activities and strategies could be used as a communication tool towards market participants, investors, and lenders. In other words, environmental performance could be used by potential bondholders as a valuable supplemental source of information for assessing firm risk exposure and future uncertainty. Thus, bond investors should use such information and invest in bonds of firms with enhanced environmental performance. Finally, managers should have in mind that investments in environmental-related strategies is not a waste of a firm's valuable resources. Efforts to improve firm's environmental footprint and the efficient communication of this performance could yield significant competitive advantages, including enhanced creditworthiness and the ability to raise necessary funds from money markets.

Nevertheless, the current study does not come without limitations. Our sample is restricted within the EU; thus, our evidence may not be generalizable to other international markets. So future research can replicate this study within other developed and even developing markets. Also, the examination period is focused before the recent pandemic, so our evidence is restricted within a period of rather stable credit markets. Future research could examine how the economic crisis created by the extensive international lockdowns and disruption of economic activity could alter or even improve the association between environmental performance and credit ratings under adverse economic conditions. Finally, the study is using the assigned ratings published by two major rating agencies when firms issue bonds and not the ratings assigned to firms after the initial bond offering. Also, we have not considered the case of credit rating changes (upgrading or downgrading) and how continuous environmental and social performance (score changes) contributes on ratings upgrades. Future research could address both issues and reach more decisive conclusions on the contribution of sustainability performance on firms' creditworthiness.

References

Barclays Bank Ireland PLC. (2021, March). *Summary of sustainability risk policy*. Dublin, Ireland.

Barth, F., Hübel, B., & Scholz, H. (2022). ESG and corporate credit spreads. *The Journal of Risk Finance, 23*(2), 169–190.

Bauer, R., & Hann, D. (2010). *Corporate environmental management and credit risk*. Working Paper. SSRN: http://ssrn.com/abstract=1660470.

Cai, L., J. Cui, and H. Jo. (2016). Corporate environmental responsibility and firm risk. *Journal of Business Ethics, 139*, 563–594.
Cespa, G., & Cestone, G. (2007). Corporate social responsibility and managerial entrenchment. *Journal of Economics and Management Strategy, 16*(3), 741–771.
Chabowski, B., Chiang, W. C., Deng, K., & Sun, L. (2019). Environmental inefficiency and bond credit rating. *Journal of Economics and Business, 101*, 17–37.
Chakraborty, A., Gao, L. S., & Sheikh, S. (2019). Managerial risk taking incentives, corporate social responsibility and firm risk. *Journal of Economics and Business, 101*, 58–72.
Cheng, B., Ioannou, I., & Serafeim, G. (2014). Corporate social responsibility and access to finance. *Strategic Management Journal, 35*(1), 1–23.
Chiang, W. C., Shang, J., & Sun, L. (2017). Broad bond rating change and irresponsible corporate social responsibility activities. *Advances in Accounting, 39*, 32–46.
Dimitropoulos, P., & Koronios, K. (2021). *Corporate environmental responsibility, accounting and corporate finance in the EU. Springer Nature, Cham, Switzerland.* https://doi.org/10.1007/978-3-030-72773-4_8
Dimitropoulos, P. E. (2022). A review of internet financing through peer-to-peer lending: A cross-country comparative analysis. In A. Thrassou, D. Vrontis, L. Efthymiou, Y. Weber, S. M. R. Shams, & E. Tsoukatos (Eds.), *Business advancement through technology volume I. Palgrave studies in cross-disciplinary business research, in association with EuroMed academy of business.* Palgrave Macmillan. https://doi.org/10.1007/978-3-031-07769-2_4
European Securities and Markets Authority (ESMA). (2019). *Final report-Guidelines on disclosure requirements applicable to credit ratings*. ESMA 33-9-320.
Gillan, S. L., Koch, A., & Starks, L. T. (2021). Firms and social responsibility: A review of ESG and CSR research in corporate finance. *Journal of Corporate Finance, 66*, 101889.
Godfrey, P. C. (2005). The relationship between corporate philanthropy and shareholder wealth: A risk management perspective. *Academy of Management Review, 30*(4), 777–798.
Godfrey, P. C., Merrill, C. B., & Hansen, J. M. (2009). The relationship between corporate social responsibility and shareholder value: An empirical test of the risk management hypothesis. *Strategic Management Journal, 30*(4), 425–445.

Gong, G., Xu, S., & Gong, X. (2018). On the value of corporate social responsibility disclosure: An empirical investigation of corporate bond issues in China. *Journal of Business Ethics, 150*, 227–258.

HSBC. (2021, February). *Introduction to HSBC's sustainability risk policies.*

Hsu, F. J., & Chen, Y. C. (2015). Is a firm's financial risk associated with corporate social responsibility? *Management Decision, 53*(9), 2175–2199.

Hu, J., Long, W., Wang, Y., & Zhou, L. (2021). Do participants in the bond market care about corporate social responsibility? Evidence from China. *International Journal of Emerging Markets.* https://doi.org/10.1108/IJOEM-01-2021-0156

Jiraporn, P., Jiraporn, N., Boeprasert, A., & Chang, K. (2014). Does corporate social responsibility (CSR) improve credit ratings? Evidence from geographic identification. *Financial Management, 43*(3), 505–531.

Kim, M., Surroca, J., & Tribó, J. (2013). The impact ethical behavior on syndicated loan rates. *Journal of Banking and Finance, 38*, 122–144.

Migliorelli, M. (2020). The sustainability–financial risk nexus. In M. Migliorelli & P. Dessertine (Eds.), *Sustainability and financial risks* (Palgrave Studies in Impact Finance). Palgrave Macmillan. https://doi.org/10.1007/978-3-030-54530-7_1

Migliorelli, M., & Marini, V. (2020). Sustainability-related risks, risk management frameworks and non-financial disclosure. In M. Migliorelli & P. Dessertine (Eds.), *Sustainability and financial risks* (Palgrave Studies in Impact Finance). Palgrave Macmillan. https://doi.org/10.1007/978-3-030-54530-7_4

Moser, D., & Martin, P. (2012). A broader perspective on corporate social responsibility research in accounting. *The Accounting Review, 87*(3), 797–806.

Nguyen, P., & Nguyen, A. (2015). The effect of corporate social responsibility on firm risk. *Social Responsibility Journal, 11*(2), 324–339.

Oikonomou, I., Brooks, C., & Pavelin, S. (2014). The effects of corporate social performance on the cost of corporate debt and credit ratings. *The Financial Review, 49*, 49–75.

Raman, K. K. (1981). Financial reporting and municipal bond rating changes. *The Accounting Review, 56*(4), 910–926.

Schröder, M. (2014). Financial effects of corporate social responsibility: A literature review. *Journal of Sustainable Finance & Investment, 4*(4), 337–350.

Seltzer, L. H., Starks, L., & Zhu, Q. (2022). *Climate regulatory risk and corporate bonds*. NBER Working Paper No. 29994, http://www.nber.org/papers/w29994

Stellner, C., Klein, C., & Zwergel, B. (2015). Corporate social responsibility and Eurozone corporate bonds: The moderating role of country sustainability. *Journal of Banking and Finance, 59*, 538–549.

Thrassou, A., Efthymiou, L., Vrontis, D., Weber, Y., Shams, S. M. R., & Tsoukatos, E. (2022a). Editorial introduction: Crisis in context. In D. Vrontis, A. Thrassou, Y. Weber, S. M. R. Shams, E. Tsoukatos, & L. Efthymiou (Eds.), *Business under crisis volume I. Palgrave studies in cross-disciplinary business research, in association with EuroMed academy of business*. Palgrave Macmillan. https://doi.org/10.1007/978-3-030-76567-5_1

Thrassou, A., Uzunboylu, N., Efthymiou, L., Vrontis, D., Weber, Y., Shams, S. M. R., & Tsoukatos, E. (2022b). Editorial introduction: Business under crises: Organizational adaptations. In D. Vrontis, A. Thrassou, Y. Weber, S. M. R. Shams, E. Tsoukatos, & L. Efthymiou (Eds.), *Business under crisis, volume II. Palgrave studies in cross-disciplinary business research, in association with EuroMed academy of business*. Palgrave Macmillan. https://doi.org/10.1007/978-3-030-76575-0_1

8

Are Football Societies Aware of the Relevance of Diversity in Good Governance? The Case of "Pink Quota"

Nicola Davola and Francesca Vicentini

1 Introduction

The need to include diversity is becoming a business imperative to make sustainable long-term strategic plans. According to the principle, "comply and explain" therefore, business and financial companies are investing in it at all levels. Moreover, a significant number of business and sport companies are bound by law to comply with gender inclusion rules, the so-called pink quotas (in Italy Legge Golfo-Mosca, 1998).

Since companies are an expression of their own culture, the concept and the implementation of inclusivity could be not the same for all: sector characteristics, past history and potentialities should always be considered. Moreover, the efficacy of a process of inclusion strictly depends on how the involved participants perceive their roles and duties.

N. Davola (✉) • F. Vicentini
University of Rome "Foro Italico" (IUSM), Rome, Italy
e-mail: n.davola@studenti.uniroma4.it; francesca.vicentini@uniroma4.it

D. Vrontis et al. (eds.), *Business for Sustainability, Volume I*, Palgrave Studies in Cross-disciplinary Business Research, In Association with EuroMed Academy of Business, https://doi.org/10.1007/978-3-031-37361-9_8

The aim of this study is to analyse the actual impact of the "pink quota" on strategic behaviour, feelings of inclusiveness and participation and perceived company image in three different Italian sectors: football, represented by Roma Calcio Spa; energy production, represented by ENEL Spa and financial services, represented by Generali Spa.

It was carried out through a questionnaire administered to all board of director members (both male and female) of those companies. The questionnaire is divided into three parts: I-Demographics, II-Self-assessed individual characteristics and III-individual perception of the "pink quota" effects. The combination of this information demonstrates whether the presence of women on boards of directors is accepted and implemented in different ways in different sectors, how they feel and how they are embodied in the process of decision and procedures, how much they could contribute to them and how much they could introduce patterns of behaviour that differ from the more standard way to cope both with owners and stakeholders. More generally, this will allow us to understand whether company characteristics could be drivers of gender diversity.

We hope to be able to answer the basic question: are pink quotas perceived by boards of directors as a means to improve their effectiveness, also thanks to the acceptance of the contribution of diversity? This could occur differently in different sectors of activity.

We expected to find through the answers to the questionnaire the effect of gender differentiation in boards of directors mainly on behaviours rather than on company outcomes. In the light of the literature, we assume that the "pink quota" increases cooperation, communication and trust among the members of the investigated boards and reinforces the sense of belonging and participation of their members. This could, in turn, affect the external image of a firm and therefore, potentially, its financial performance (investors are more likely to invest in it). However, we do not expect a significant alteration in the economic performance and corporate strategies.

Given that our focus remains on how these effects could work differently in different sectors, with a particular focus on the capability of a football firm (as representative of an economically important sport) for inclusion compared to the others, industry and finance sectors, based on the intrinsic characteristics of their core business. This will give some insight to complete our final aim of evaluating how useful and profitable it may be for a professional football company to invest in female football (at all levels from players to coaches to technical and managerial directors).

In the following, we present in Sect. 2 our motivation for the study and how they stand on the existing literature; in Sect. 3, the main hypotheses of the research and the methodology applied to investigate our research question; in Sect. 4, the more significant results from the survey and in Sect. 5 our main conclusions.

2 Motivation and Contribution to the Literature

Imposing a greater level of heterogeneity in boards of directors means introducing people who bring with them all the weight of their characteristics and differences in the decision-making process, and that should improve the result of a company (Wu et al., 2022); (Rosenblum and Roithmayr, 2014). This should finally lead to better company performance and to a greater correspondence of management to the society in which firms are embedded. Recently, much importance and debate are being devoted to the inclusion of women on boards of directors and its actual relevance and consequences (Olthuis, B. R., & van den Oever, K. F. (2020)).

In management literature, three main arguments are identified to promote gender diversity in corporate boards: equality, economics and better business. The first is to signal an acceptance of social values such as having an equal amount of power. The second is linked to the fact that corporations with female directors on their boards perform better economically (McCunliffe and Savio, 2015). However, the improvement in economic performance could be due not to the quota itself but to the expectations related to a general change in leadership, so is related more to a different image of the firm. The third argument is related to the possibility that the presence of women encourages better corporate business practices: reducing groupthink, making the board more cohesive and, therefore, more effective (Xue et al., 2022).

As a matter of fact, women have proved to be less risk prone in many situations (Choudhury, 2014; Eckel & Grossman, 2008); they exhibit a higher propensity to cooperate in groups (Charness & Rustichini, 2011) and to contribute to joint projects and fair division (Andreoni & Vesterlund, 2001). The literature on gender-based differences highlights the agentic characteristics (assertiveness, competitivity, self-confidence, aggressivity and ambition) typical of men compared to communal characteristics (concern about others, sympathy, kindness, nurturing and contribution to problem-solving situation) of women (Eagly et al., 2003).

Corporate literature points out that women on boards may take a more active role in monitoring, contribute higher accuracy and efficiency to corporate bodies as well as have higher attendance rates at board meetings than men, which leads to a reduction in male absenteeism (Adams & Ferreira, 2009). Campbell and Minguez-Vera (2008) found that a rise in the percentage of females on boards leads to an increase in company value. Finegold et al. (2007) state that gender diversity better meets the so-called Stakeholder Model, which requires companies to maximize the well-being of all stakeholders. Positive correlations between the ratio of women on boards and company financial performance are also highlighted by Farrell et al. (2008). Their contribution to board decision-making relates to monitoring, strategy development, and engagement with stakeholder issues (Choudhury, 2014) and has "a positive impact on financial reporting, auditing, and internal controls" (McCauliff & Savio, 2015). Moreover, it seems that shareholders want to improve gender diversity, considering it a signal of good governance and consequently, of good economic and financial performance (Terjesen et al., 2009; Yang et al., 2019) in the case of football companies in Italy (Trequattrini et al., 2022). However, the effects of gender diversity on the performance of organizations remain highly controversial (Carteretal, 2010). In particular, referring to the football setting, Varriale et al. (2019) affirm: "Most scholars often conceive diversity as a 'double edge sword' because of its both positive and negative effect on team functioning and performance within organization".

Many social scientists affirm that in top-level management situations, gender differences are minimized, and consequently, men and women who occupy the same leadership role will behave very similarly (Kanter, 1977) whereas others (Eagly & Johannesen-Schmidt, 2001) assert that gender could exert some influence causing men and women to behave differently in the same organizational role. Yukl (2002) synthesized this opposite evidence with the conclusion that even if there are no significant differences in the effectiveness of boards between male and female leaders, for some types of behaviour, gender-related differences still exist. Peterson and Philpot (2007) using commitment assignments and director background of top board committees find that female directors are less likely than male directors to sit on executive committees and more likely to sit on public affairs committees. Nevertheless, it is stated that, in general, women on boards are more successful when their decision-making is based on an understanding of the community that they serve, increasing trust in board activities. The visibility of women in leadership roles in clubs is also important to encourage other women to engage with them.

The first important step in the direction of a greater level of inclusivity in all economic activities is that recently the European Union has been pushing for EU community-wide gender quotas and EU courts have stressed the principle of gender diversity. In 1998, Italian Law imposed for Spa. the presence of at least 30% of women on the boards of directors, the so-called pink quota. In 2003, Norway was the first country to require state-owned companies to have at least 40% representation of each gender on their boards. Many European member states followed this, enacting gender quotas (France in 2011, 2016; UK in 2018; Australia in 2019).

Many football clubs in several countries are and will be obliged to comply with gender quotas. Nowadays, however, still two-thirds of clubs have all-male boards: two-thirds of football clubs in England and Wales had all-male boards with 40% of Premier League and 83% of the EFL Championship clubs having all-male boards. The representation of women in football boards is between 4.2% and 11.3%, depending on the league, and women in leadership roles have often been limited to a select few roles on board matters (Konrad et al., 2008). Also, Italian football is characterized by being an "almost exclusive context for men" (Trequattrini et al., 2022).

But even if this gap is reduced and possibly eliminated, a question still arises: is the selection of women directors based on their capabilities? Are there differences in their selection and involvement in the board in football compared to other sectors of economic activities? How much can they contribute to management? How do they feel part of the team? What is the difference in the way they evaluate company characteristics?

When analysing diversity and inclusion in boards of directors, the gender gap represents an important part, but it is only a part of the problem, especially as far as top positions are concerned (the so-called *glass ceiling*). Moreover, when looking at differences in the possibility of reaching such positions and being determinant in decision-making, not only do demographics and observables matter, but also more difficult aspects such as education, experience, competence and social networks to which each one belongs (Nielsen and Huse, 2010; Mahadeao et al., 2012; Galia and Zenou, 2012). Even if there is a positive relationship between cohesion and performance, this could not be assured only by "pink quotas" introducing the benefits of diversity. It is important that diversity really affects the ordinary and extraordinary processes through which the board of directors contributes to company activities. Nekhili and Gatfaoui (2013) highlighted that either it is possible that women are relegated to "ancillary tasks" (Kesner, 1988; Peterson and Philpot, 2007), or the division of tasks on the basis of respective characteristics might not be applied and the process of selection of the board could remain related to rules, behaviours, and mentality of the "male club" (Burke & MacKay, 1997) ending up selecting female "clones" of males, therefore reinforcing and not completing the dominant governance.

This could occur differently in different sectors of activity, an issue that must also be deeply investigated. This issue involves topics such as different task-related capabilities and differences in leadership styles in groups.

Continuing along these lines, it is interesting to highlight that the differences between men and women are not only in the characteristics or selection process but also involve the roles that women cover in business, as pointed out in some studies (Bertrand, M. & Hallock, K. F. 2001. The gap between men and women is high in top positions, especially in terms of wage differences. Using the ExecuComp data set, which contains information on the five highest-paid executives in each of many US firms for the years 1992–1997, the authors examine the gender compensation gap among high-level executives. Women, representing approximately 2.5% of the sample, earned about 45% less than men. As much as 75% of this gap can be explained by the fact that women managed smaller companies and were less likely to be CEO, Chair, or company President. The complexity of the selection process still makes it more difficult for a woman to be a board nominee (Brière et al., 2010).

The perceptions surrounding decisions for board member selection can also be an issue for board diversity (Terjesen et al., 2009), such as beliefs that women have a "woman's agenda" or are unqualified (Burke & MacKay, 1997), or fear of appointing women not currently holding a directorship that is less obvious for men in the same situation (Peterson and Philpot, 2007).

The theory of group effectiveness (Gist et al., 1987) postulates that the role of the "pink quota" in boards of directors should be a relevant moderator of team behaviour and effectiveness. However, the literature on the effects of the introduction of a certain number of women to boards of directors on company financial performance is still not unanimous (Adams & Ferreira, 2004; Carter et al., 2003 as examples).

But is this different in different sectors? Are some environments more friendly than others in introducing effective diversity in management policies? Could this reinforce the link between economic activity and the company impacts?

When we refer to sports, we have the impression that inclusion and diversity in boards of directors could account for, and even work better, but in a different way compared to other economic sectors. In fact, since making financial and administrative decisions on boards of directors involves also being aware of actual gender differences and dangerous stereotypes, we believe that in sports these aspects could more easily be identified. So, the analysis of diversity and inclusion in sports boards of directors could represent a useful test both from an economic and social point of view. This process should lead, in fact, to economic advantages that stem not only from a market selling of "reverse discrimination" but are also grounded in its social impact.

We focus on football since it is undeniable that it represents the most popular sport worldwide, especially in Europe and South America, but also because over the past years, it has experienced a number of crucial changes that have increased its business orientation (Callejo & Forcadell, 2006).

In Italy, female football became professional only in 2022. However, the average pay of a female player in Serie A is around € 40, 000, still far from the pay of a male player in Serie A (Archer & Prange 2019). Also, a strong "participation gap" is shown by the analysis by Thibault et al. (2010) of the lack of women in leadership positions in football companies, as reported by Varriale et al. (2019).

3 Methodology

To assess how much of the gender gap is explained by differences in performance and experience rather than in some a priori beliefs that confine female leadership members to residual roles in defining business and strategies and benefitting from the related earnings, we developed a purpose-built questionnaire.

The questionnaire was administered to all participants (males and females) of the three considered boards of directors (9 subjects each, of which 4 women respectively in Enel, Roma, Generali, for a total of 27 questionnaires).

To investigate the actual and potential strategic behaviour and the leadership position effect of women on football boards of directors compared with those of men sitting on the same board of directors and of females and males on the boards of directors of the other two firms, we submitted a set of questions to our participants regarding beliefs and perceptions of the presence of females on their own board of directors.

In particular, the questionnaire was divided into three parts: PART 1 included basic demographics (gender, education, cultural origin); PART 2 included self-assessed perceptions of respective roles, personality traits, risk aversion, and perceived inclusiveness in their own board (Gachter et al., 2015); PART 3 investigated opinions, of both male and female members, of how female participation in the board of directors is perceived to affect decisions and beliefs of the board and company performance.

In particular, related to the collected information on the level of inclusiveness and belonging that board members feel they have, this indicator could represent a measure of their relative position inside the board of directors. Participants should indicate their sense of belonging to their board by choosing one of the intersections between two circles representing respectively themselves and others (numbered from 1 to 7) to fit their sense of embeddedness (from 1 completely apart to 7 almost totally overlapping) (Gachter et al., 2015).

For the assessment of individual personality traits, we presented questions to our participants inspired by the Big Five by Costa and McCrae (1992), related to the basic characteristics of Extraversion, Agreeableness, Conscientiousness, Emotional Stability, and Openness to Experience. This allowed us to weigh the reported feelings of belonging through some relevant characteristics that could increase or decrease the possibility of including and being included.

In PART 3, we focused on questions about the perceived effects of "pink quota" in relation to good governance, characteristics of the sector of activity, modification in the internal and external operativity of the board of directors (conflict in the process of decision-making, competence and capability exerted, level of attendance, participation and punctuality in board meetings, relationship with the company management, internal and external communication, consulting activities and economic performance).

4 Results

We report hereafter a summary of the main results of the survey. We selected among others, results that better allow us to answer our main research question: are "quote rosa" leading to the diversity in boards of directors that could improve their contribution to company performance? What is the level of inclusion and respect for diversity on boards? And how are they perceived by different genders and in different sectors? Are there some differences that could enforce, especially in some sectors, female contribution to leadership activities?

1. *How do women and men feel embedded in their own board?*

We report the answer to the "inclusiveness test" that measures the sense of belonging among both women and men in the three boards of directors.

We find that most of the answers of woman participants lie between 4 and 5 while for men the most frequent answer is 6. This means that, even if nicely embedded in boards of directors, women feel more apart than men. In the financial sector (Generali), we find the greatest difference in the self-assessed rate of inclusion between men and women (100% for males and 50% for female directors). While more than 80% in Enel, 50% in Roma and 100% in Generali of the men feel they are well involved in their respective boards, only 70% in Roma, 50% in Enel and in Generali of women report to perceive themselves well embedded in their own board (see Fig. 8.1).

Most importantly, collected answers show a greater capability of inclusiveness in Roma Spa. compared to the other two companies.

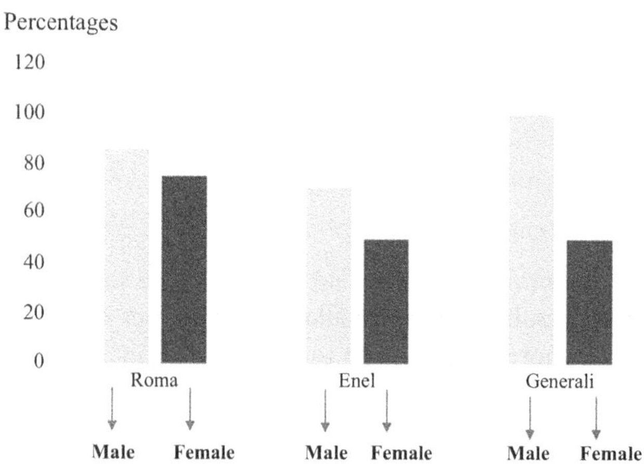

Fig. 8.1 Inclusiveness

Result 1 *Women introduced in Board of Directors as "pink quota" feel less integrated in their boards than men in all sectors. However, in football their level of embeddedness is higher than in the other sectors (which is the least in the financial company).*

2. *How are women perceived to affect board performance?*

Our data show that women are in general perceived to influence the activity of their board. However, while it seems that they are considered neither particularly influencing on the overall capabilities and general conflictual attitudes of their boards, nor to have a particular impact on the relationship with the management, most of the participants stress the relevance of women's role on boards of directors in terms of capacity to improve communication on the board in all the three sectors both by the men and women surveyed. Moreover, general agreement is found in their capability to improve the external image of the firm and therefore possibly its future economic and financial performance (see Figs. 8.2 and 8.3).

Collected answers show that the performance of Board of Directors (BoD) is affected by the inclusion of women among their own members essentially through:

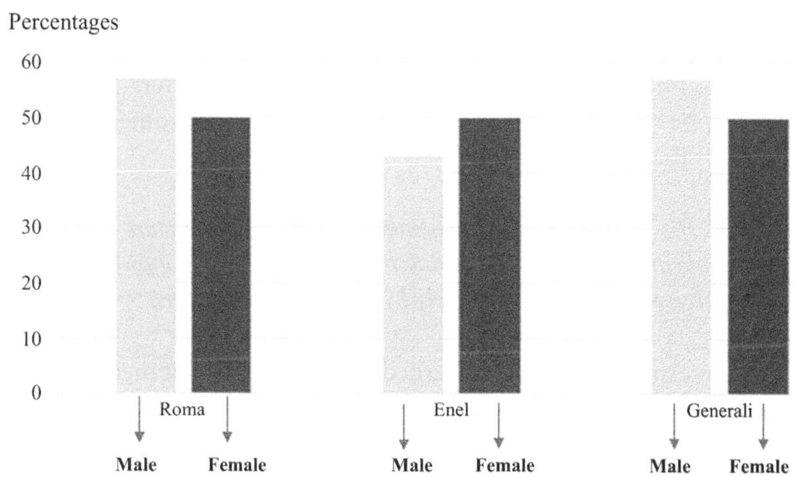

Fig. 8.2 Communication

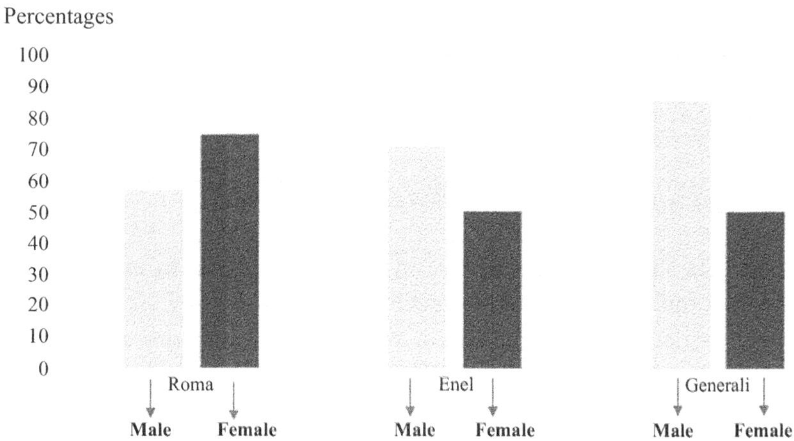

Fig. 8.3 External Image (here)

1. Increasing participation and encouraging the flow of information inside the Board of Directors (BoD).
2. Improving the image of the firms among the public and the stakeholders and the level of perceived competence of the board of directors.

As far as communication is concerned, 55% of men in Roma, more than 40% in Enel and nearly 60% in Generali think that the "pink quota" increases communication among the respective boards while 50% of women think the same in all the sectors. It seems that, where the core business is more technical, communicating more matters more. But could this be related to the well-known stereotype that women are more loquacious than men?

Result 2 *The presence of female members in board of directors is perceived by both male and female as improving both communication inside the board and the perceived image of the society by external stakeholders.*

As far as external image is concerned, more than 50% of men in Roma, 70% in Enel and more than 80% in Generali think that their presence in Board of Directors improved the external image of their firm.

This signals that in football, men are less confident on the image contribution of having a greater level of gender diversity in their leadership (showing maybe a mentality slightly lagging behind), while in the other two productive sectors, they seem more aware of the relevance of women's presence on their boards for the brand image. On the other hand, the fact that women are more confident in their capability to contribute to the firm's image in the football sector than in the other two firms is evidence of their enthusiasm for participation and of the possibility to enlarge the space and role of women in football leadership.

Overall, it seems that gender in football leadership is still under construction, allowing space for a wider vision and opportunities both for women and football businesses.

5 Conclusion

The analysis of the perception of inclusiveness and of the actual capability to affect decisions and consequences in boards of directors, especially when we believe that diversity matters, is a way to contribute to the debate on the role and the access of women in leadership positions. The contribution of differences relies in fact on the maintenance of such diversities and on the possibility of letting them operate and spread out.

This could have beneficial effects on long-term sustainability for companies (Ain et al., 2021). Given the different approaches which naturally characterize women in taking decisions which take into account different aspects of social interactions, their presence and involved participation in the board of directors could then lead to a different development of expertise and a greater heterogeneity of approaches to management (Ruel et al., 2020). This in turn will introduce government practices that better fill the gap between ethics and profitability and between voluntary contribution to group public goods and individual self-serving interests, especially in stressful situations (Schinzel, 2022, Thrassou et al., 2022a, 2022b).

Nowadays, the reputation of a company includes the implementation of politically correct behaviours that could be highly appealing for marketing purposes with beneficial consequences related to accrued demand

and revenues in any kind of economic activity. Social responsibility is becoming in fact not only an imperative to which all companies, including sports societies, should obey, either for moral adhesion or pressure from other stakeholders (Bradish & Cronin, 2009) but could be also an opportunity to increase revenues, improve the image of a brand and facilitate fundraising (Katz-Bénichou, 2004; Tribou & Augé, 2006).

This study focusses on the role of pink quotas in introducing heterogeneity in approaches and cultural backgrounds through the elicitation of the beliefs that it generates in all boards of director participants (males and females). We reached our goal through the submission of a purpose-built questionnaire to all participants of the board of directors of three big Italian companies in the sectors of production (ENEL), services (ASSICURAZIONI GENERALI), and sports (ROMA CALCIO).

Results from our survey confirm some but not all of our hypotheses. We find that female participation on boards of directors is generally perceived as improving communication, attendance, respect of rules and the external image of the firm. No answers stressed the crucial role of female participation in the outcomes and strategies of the firm.

No significant differences emerge between football firms and industrial firms; nevertheless, we discover that women in leadership positions feel a stronger sense of belonging to the group of directors in Roma than in Enel and Generali. In all the three firms, their feeling of belonging to the group was however lower than men's.

In general, we find that the presence of female members on boards of directors is perceived, by both male and female participants, to improve both communication inside the board and the image of the company held by external stakeholders.

Overall results show that the impact of "quote rosa" is mainly behavioural and consistent with the evidence showed by the experimental literature.

Nevertheless, we find interesting sector differences that seem to show how in football there is still room and scope to increase women participation and to benefit from it. Moreover, since females see themselves more integrated in the football board of directors, this could signal sports in general, and football in particular, as a strong vehicle of gender inclusion.

So, the main contribution of this study is to add some light on the relevance of behavioural aspects underlying the introduction of gender diversity in leadership management motivated by the feelings not only to be accepted but to be part of. Moreover, our findings support the impression that sports could highly contribute to spread out the mentality of inclusion of diversity in leadership decision-making.

However, given the limited number of observations collected, we are aware of the limitation of the significance of our analysis. In future research, we are planning to extend it to involve a greater number of firms and sectors, especially in football, to increase the robustness of our results.

References

Adams, R. B., & Ferreira, D. (2004). Gender diversity in the boardroom. *European Corporate Governance Institute, Finance Working paper, 57*, 30.

Adams, R. B., & Ferreira, D. (2009). Women in the boardroom and their impact on governance and performance. *Journal of Financial Economics, 94*(2), 291–309.

Ain, Q. U., Yuan, X., Javaid, H. M., & Naeem, M. (2021). Board gender diversity and sustainable growth rate: Chinese evidence. *Economic Research-Ekonomska Istraživanja*, 1–21.

Andreoni, J., & Vesterlund, L. (2001). Which is the fair sex? Gender differences in altruism. *The Quarterly Journal of Economics, 116*(1), 293–312.

Archer, A., & Prange, M. (2019). 'Equal play, equal pay': Moral grounds for equal pay in football. *Journal of the Philosophy of Sport, 46*(3), 416–436.

Bertrand, M., & Hallock, K. F. (2001). The gender gap in top corporate jobs. *ILR Review, 55*(1), 3–21.

Bradish, C., & Cronin, J. J. (2009). Corporate social responsibility in sport. *Journal of Sport Management, 23*(6), 691–697.

Brière, S., Rinfret, N., & Québec, Q. C. (2010). la réalité des femmes sur les conseils d'administration suite à l'adoption de la loi québécoise sur la gouvernance des sociétés d'état: obstacles et accès. *Innovation Journal, 15*(1), 2–29.

Burke, D. M., & MacKay, D. G. (1997). Memory, language, and ageing. *Philosophical Transactions of the Royal Society of London. Series B: Biological Sciences, 352*(1363), 1845–1856.

Callejo, M. B., & Forcadell, F. J. (2006). Real Madrid football club: A new model of business organization for sports clubs in Spain. *Global Business and Organizational Excellence, 26*(1), 51–64.
Campbell, K., & Mínguez-Vera, A. (2008). Gender diversity in the boardroom and firm financial performance. *Journal of Business Ethics, 83*(3), 435–451.
Carter, D. A., Simkins, B. J., & Simpson, W. G. (2003). Corporate governance, board diversity, and firm value. *Financial Review, 38*(1), 33–53.
Charness, G., & Rustichini, A. (2011). Gender differences in cooperation with group membership. *Games and Economic Behavior, 72*(1), 77–85.
Choudhury, B. (2014). New rationales for Women on Boards. *Oxford Journal of Legal Studies, 34*, 511–513.
Costa Jr, P. T., & McCrae, R. R. (1992). Four ways five factors are basic. *Personality and Individual Differences, 13*(6), 653–665.
Eagly, A. H., & Johannesen-Schmidt, M. C. (2001). The leadership styles of women and men. *Journal of Social Issues, 57*(4), 781–797.
Eagly, A. H., Johannesen-Schmidt, M. C., & Van Engen, M. L. (2003). Transformational, transactional, and laissez-faire leadership styles: A meta-analysis comparing women and men. *Psychological Bulletin, 129*(4), 569.
Eckel, C. C., & Grossman, P. J. (2008). Men, women and risk aversion: Experimental evidence. *Handbook of Experimental Economics Results, 1*, 1061–1073.
Farrell, K. A., Friesen, G. C., & Hersch, P. L. (2008). How do firms adjust director compensation? *Journal of Corporate Finance, 14*(2), 153–162.
Finegold, D., Benson, G. S., & Hecht, D. (2007). Corporate boards and company performance: Review of research in light of recent reforms. *Corporate Governance: An International Review, 15*(5), 865–878.
Gächter, S., Starmer, C., & Tufano, F. (2015). Measuring the closeness of relationships: A comprehensive evaluation of the 'inclusion of the other in the self' scale. *PloS one, 10*(6), e0129478.
Galia, F., & Zenou, E. (2012). Board composition and forms of innovation: Does diversity make a difference? *European Journal of International Management, 6*(6), 630–650.
Gist, M. E., Locke, E. A., & Taylor, M. S. (1987). Organizational behavior: Group structure, process, and effectiveness. *Journal of Management, 13*(2), 237–257.
Kanter, R. M. (1977). Some effects of proportions on group life. In *The gender gap in psychotherapy* (pp. 53–78). Springer.

Katz-Bénichou, G. (2004). L'éthique sportive est-elle un instrument de marketing? *Revue française de gestion, 150*(3), 177–192.

Kesner, I. F. (1988). Directors' characteristics and committee membership: An investigation of type, occupation, tenure, and gender. *Academy of Management Journal, 31*(1), 66–84.

Konrad, A. M., Kramer, V., & Erkut, S. (2008). The impact of three or more women on corporate boards. *Organizational Dynamics, 37*(2), 145–164.

Legge Golfo-Mosca. (1998). Tuif, Decreto legislativo 24 febbraio 1998.

Mahadeo, J. D., Soobaroyen, T., & Hanuman, V. O. (2012). Board composition and financial performance: Uncovering the effects of diversity in an emerging economy. *Journal of Business Ethics, 105*, 375–388.

McCauliff, C., & Savio, C. A. (2015). Gender considerations on the boards of European Union companies: Lesson for US corporations or cautionary tale? *Georgetown Journal of Gender and the Law, 16*, 505.

Nekhili, M., & Gatfaoui, H. (2013). Are demographic attributes and firm characteristics drivers of gender diversity? Investigating women's positions on French boards of directors. *Journal of Business Ethics, 118*(2), 227–249.

Nielsen, S., & Huse, M. (2010). The contribution of women on boards of directors: Going beyond the surface. *Corporate governance: An International Review, 18*(2), 136–148.

Olthuis, B. R., & van den Oever, K. F. (2020). The board of directors and CSR: How does ideological diversity on the board impact CSR? *Journal of Cleaner Production, 251*, 119532.

Peterson, C. A., & Philpot, J. (2007). Women's roles on US Fortune 500 boards: Director expertise and committee memberships. *Journal of Business Ethics, 72*(2), 177–196.

Rosenblum, D., & Roithmayr, D. (2014). More than a woman: Insights into corporate governance after the French sex quota. *The Indiana Law Review, 48*, 889.

Ruel, S., Fritz, M., & Subramanian, N. (2020). Gender diversity for sustainability management: Developing a research agenda from a supply chain perspective. *Logistique & Management, 28*(3–4), 224–239.

Schinzel, U. (2022). Business under crisis: Talent management and responsible leadership in Luxembourg in Pandemic Times. In D. Vrontis, A. Thrassou, Y. Weber, S. M. R. Shams, E. Tsoukatos, & L. Efthymiou (Eds.), *Business under crisis Volume I. Palgrave studies in cross-disciplinary business research, in association with EuroMed academy of business*. Palgrave Macmillan. https://doi.org/10.1007/978-3-030-76567-5_10

Terjesen, S., Sealy, R., & Singh, V. (2009). Women directors on corporate boards: A review and research agenda. *Corporate Governance: An International Review, 17*(3), 320–337.

Thibault, V., Guillaume, M., Berthelot, G., El Helou, N., Schaal, K., Quinquis, L., ... & Toussaint, J. F. (2010). Women and men in sport performance: the gender gap has not evolved since 1983. *Journal of Sports Science & Medicine, 9*(2), 214.

Thrassou, A., Efthymiou, L., Vrontis, D., Weber, Y., Shams, S. M. R., & Tsoukatos, E. (2022a). Editorial introduction: Crisis in context. In D. Vrontis, A. Thrassou, Y. Weber, S. M. R. Shams, E. Tsoukatos, & L. Efthymiou (Eds.), *Business under crisis volume I. Palgrave studies in cross-disciplinary business research, in association with EuroMed academy of business*. Palgrave Macmillan. https://doi.org/10.1007/978-3-030-76567-5_1

Thrassou, A., Uzunboylu, N., Efthymiou, L., Vrontis, D., Weber, Y., Shams, S. M. R., & Tsoukatos, E. (2022b). Editorial introduction: Business under crises: Organizational adaptations. In D. Vrontis, A. Thrassou, Y. Weber, S. M. R. Shams, E. Tsoukatos, & L. Efthymiou (Eds.), *Business under crisis, volume II. Palgrave studies in cross-disciplinary business research, in association with EuroMed academy of business*. Palgrave Macmillan. https://doi.org/10.1007/978-3-030-76575-0_1

Trequattrini, R., Cuozzo, B., Petrecca, F., & Manzari, A. (2022). Corporate governance and gender issues: The case of professional football companies in Italy. In *Organizational resilience and female entrepreneurship during crises* (pp. 123–135). Springer.

Tribou, G., & Augé, B. (2006). *Management du Sport. Marketing et Gestion des Clubs Sportifs*. Dunod.

Varriale, L., Briganti, P., Tafuri, D., & Ferrara, M. (2019). Gender diversity in the football setting: The contribution of organizational studies. *Sport Science, 12*(*1*), 82–89.

Wu, J., Richard, O. C., Triana, M. D. C., & Zhang, X. (2022). The performance impact of gender diversity in the top management team and board of directors: A multiteam systems approach. *Human Resource Management, 61*(2), 157–180.

Xue, K., Wu, L., Fu, S., & Wang, H. (2022). *Shareholder heterogeneity, the board decision-making process and Ambidextrous Corporate Innovation*. Available at SSRN 4022107.

Yang, P., Riepe, J., Moser, K., Pull, K., & Terjesen, S. (2019). Women directors, firm performance, and firm risk: A causal perspective. *The Leadership Quarterly, 30*(5), 101297.

Yukl, G., Gordon, A., & Taber, T. (2002). A hierarchical taxonomy of leadership behavior: Integrating a half century of behavior research. *Journal of Leadership & Organizational Studies, 9*(1), 15–32.

9

How Do Companies Conceive Sustainable Infrastructure? Evidence from Construction Companies' Reports' Content Analysis

Silvia Gordano, Daniel Torchia, Laura Corazza, and Dario Cottafava

1 Introduction

Infrastructure is the backbone of society and economy around the world. It plays a crucial role in driving countries' immediate economic growth—by means of creating jobs, generating earnings, and boosting spending—and longer-term wealth—by increasing accessibility to employment, enhancing education opportunities through better connectivity, and increasing equality through access to critical utilities (KPMG, 2020). It has been proven that, over a timeline of 20 years, there is an additional US$3.7 injected into the economy for every US$1 invested in infrastructure (Business Roundtable, 2019). This is why, in the aftermath of the COVID-19 pandemic, governments have placed infrastructure

S. Gordano (✉) • D. Torchia • L. Corazza • D. Cottafava
Department of Management, Università degli Studi di Torino, Turin, Italy
e-mail: silvia.gordano@unito.it; daniel.torchia@unito.it; laura.corazza@unito.it; dario.cottafava@unito.it

D. Vrontis et al. (eds.), *Business for Sustainability, Volume I*, Palgrave Studies in Cross-disciplinary Business Research, In Association with EuroMed Academy of Business, https://doi.org/10.1007/978-3-031-37361-9_9

development on top of their agenda. The significance of digital connectivity and infrastructure resilience to natural disasters has also become more apparent during the COVID-19 breakdown.

Although infrastructure may generate huge positive impacts on society and economies, its negative externalities are widely recognised by civil society (Corazza et al., 2022a). The integration of sustainability in infrastructure development is undoubtedly a core issue and key challenge in the construction industry. Discussions around this issue are not only relevant for the global size of construction industry—US$1.75 trillion for the world's top 200 constructors in 2020 (Construction Europe, 2021)—but especially for the large-scale effects on society and the environment that construction activities have, ranging from smaller endeavours to mega or giga-projects (Gellert & Lynch, 2003). As society needs change, calling for energy transition and solutions to fight climate change, infrastructure needs to initiate and stimulate it. For instance, considering that around seventy percent of the world's carbon emissions result from infrastructure construction and use (KPMG, 2022), infrastructure built in current times will likely determine the world's ability to meet the 2050 Net Zero targets outlined by the Paris Agreement. Therefore, infrastructure has the power to strongly contribute to delivering socio-economic benefits (Chan et al., 2022), as well as environmental ones (OECD, 2019), for future generations.

The concept of sustainable infrastructure (SI) is at the heart of the United Nations' Sustainable Development Goal (SDG) 9—*Industry, Innovation and Infrastructure*, which promotes the transition towards sustainable industrialisation. In particular, targets related to SDG 9 include, among others, the development of quality, reliable, sustainable, and resilient infrastructure to support economic development and human well-being (target 9.1). Moreover, it must also consider the upgrading of infrastructure to make it sustainable, with an increased resource-use efficiency and a greater adoption of green technologies and processes (target 9.4).

Given the centrality of infrastructure for societies, it is rather unsurprising that SDG 9 is one of the best examples to show the interconnection among SDGs (Nilsson et al., 2017). It likely connects with SDG 6 (*Clean water and sanitation*), 7 (*Affordable and clean energy*), 8 (*Decent work and economic growth*), 11 (*Sustainable cities and communities*), 12 (*Responsible consumption and production*), 13 (*Climate action*), 14 (*Life below water*), and 15 (*Life on land*). Infrastructure, by relating to transport, energy, water, and telecommunications (Thacker et al., 2019), has a direct or indirect influence on most targets included in the SDGs, therefore playing a crucial role in the advancement of sustainable development, which justifies the necessity to properly identify what it is meant by sustainable infrastructure.

However, how this concept should be defined, and consequently assessed, has sparked debate over time. SI incorporates a multitude of interconnected dimensions, is long-term by nature, and involves numerous risks and stakeholders (Ferrer et al., 2018). The multifaceted concept of SI is reflected in the variety of sustainability assessment frameworks developed by professional bodies and authorities (for instance, CEEQUAL, NYSDOT, Greenroads, ISI, ISCA), as well as across relevant studies throughout the infrastructure sustainability literature (Sahely et al., 2005, Dasgupta & Tam, 2005; Ugwu & Haupt, 2007; Shen et al., 2011; Chan et al., 2022), to measure infrastructural projects' performance.

Drawing from different conceptualisations and related assessment methods proposed in theory and practice (Thomé et al., 2016; Chan et al., 2022), this chapter aims to explore how the concept of SI is conceived by companies operating in the construction industry. In order to capture the meaning that companies attach to the concept of SI, a content analysis on the latest-available non-financial disclosures published by the top 10 European construction companies is conducted.

The chapter aims to advance the ongoing debate on sustainable infrastructure (e.g., Berardi, 2013; Chan et al., 2022; Corazza et al., 2022a), which is a new and ever-evolving field (Ferrer et al., 2018). Specifically, we add to the academic literature on the topic and to existing professional assessment frameworks, a company-centred perspective. This helps in understanding how conceptualisations provided by scholars and professionals are interpreted by companies and expressed in their corporate disclosures, in order to contribute to their mutual shaping.

The chapter is structured as follows. First, we discuss the concept of sustainable infrastructure by briefly reviewing relevant literature and assessment frameworks developed by professional bodies and scholars. We then detail the methodology adopted in the study. Finally, we present and discuss our research findings.

2 Literature Review

2.1 Sustainable Infrastructure

Infrastructure encloses a set of engineered facilities, utilities, and systems (Ferrer et al., 2018). These complex engineering systems involve high uncertainties, risks, and profound and lasting impacts on the economy, environment, and society (Zeng et al., 2015). Such complexity is reflected in the high rates of project failure, in terms of cost overrun and time delays (Flyvbjerg, 2014). Zeng et al. (2015), after reviewing relevant literature on the theme, cluster infrastructure complexity into technical, organisational, and environmental. The discourse on infrastructure has traditionally developed around themes of physical infrastructure and its socio-technical aspects (Ferrer et al., 2018). Organisational complexity can be linked to the differentiation and interdependency of organisations involved (Baccarini, 1996): infrastructural projects are a place where different levels of governance are intertwined, from supranational institutions to national, regional, and local governments (Ferrer et al., 2018). The environmental component of complexity has instead been associated with elements such as trust, availability of resources and skills, political influence, level of competition, strategic pressure, interference with existing sites and weather conditions (Bosch-Rekveldt et al., 2011). Zeng et al. (2015) underline that especially the organisational and environmental elements of infrastructure complexity, being strictly linked to considerable social responsibility challenges, clearly reveal the urgent need of sustainability management in infrastructure.

The sustainability concept, by encapsulating engineering, environmental, economic, and social sciences (El-Diraby & Osman, 2011), is multidisciplinary, and still maintains openness to adaptation to different social and ecological contexts (Trigo et al., 2022). In the literature, it commonly goes hand in hand with the concept of sustainable development, so that the two terms are often used interchangeably. The origin of these concepts can be traced back to the 1980s from a publication entitled 'Our Common Future', also known as the 'Brundtland Report', which defines sustainable development as "meeting the needs and aspirations of the present generation without compromising the ability of future generations to meet their needs" (Brundtland, 1987, p. 292). The concept mainly rests on three dimensions, that is, economic development, environmental protection, and social equity, as stated at the UN Rio Summit for 'Environment and Development', in 1992. When it comes to reconciling business' profit-oriented goals with the principles of sustainable development, the concept of the 'triple bottom line' (TBL), or three-P (People, Planet, and Profit), becomes relevant. Under the TBL approach, integrating sustainability in business organisations is about balancing a company's social, environmental, and economic impacts (Elkington, 1994).

Traditionally time, cost and quality compliances, commonly referred to as the 'iron triangle', have been accepted as the most widely used criteria for measuring construction project performance (Atkinson, 1999). However, over time, the validity of the iron triangle has been questioned throughout the academic and industry literature on project management, due to its efficiency-based focus, which neglects business-oriented results and customer satisfaction (Garrett, 2008). Besides the attempts made to introduce additional constraints to the traditional model (PMI, 2009), the integration of the notion of sustainability in project management has gained attention (Grevelman & Kluiwstra, 2010; Silvius & Schipper, 2011; Rahat et al., 2022). As a consequence, scholars and practitioners have started referring to sustainable project management, which can be defined as "the management of project-orientated change in policies, assets or organizations, with consideration of the economic, social, and environmental impact of the project, its result, and its effect, for now and for future generations" (Silvius et al., 2009).

The role of infrastructure in advancing sustainable development was recognised in the 1980s; however, the discussion appeared to be mostly limited to the sphere of environmental stewardship. Related to this, Berardi (2013) argues that the notion of 'sustainable building' has often suffered from a conceptual misconception that (almost) solely relates to energy efficiency, wrongly leading to an interchangeable use of sustainable building, green building, and even high-performance building. The scholar advocates the need to move towards a strong and eco-systemic view of sustainability for buildings. This implies that all the dimensions of sustainability, and how they are interrelated, must be considered, going beyond the mere environmental approach, by looking at the building as a live system that flows dynamically with nature (Reed, 2007).

Over time, the sustainable infrastructure field has gradually broadened its scope from green infrastructure (GI) to the TBL of sustainability (Thomé et al., 2016). This is testified by the definition provided by the Inter-American Development Bank (2018), which refers to SI as "infrastructure projects that are planned, designed, constructed, operated, and decommissioned in a manner to ensure *economic* and *financial*, *social*, *environmental* (including climate resilience), and *institutional* sustainability over the entire life cycle of the project" (p. 11, emphasis added). By adopting this position, it clearly emerges that referring to sustainable infrastructure entails considering the broad range of environmental, social, and economic impacts generated and the multitude of stakeholders directly and indirectly involved, throughout the whole project lifecycle.

The evolution of the concept is further emphasised by review works recently carried out (Thomé et al., 2016; Ferrer et al., 2018). For instance, Thomé et al. (2016) highlight that studies conducted on the topic progressively shifted from early concerns related to materials for the greening of buildings, resource efficiency, and storm water runoff, to a broader integration of economic and social aspects of environmental sustainability. These include replacement of construction materials, refinements of GI assessment tools, and adaptation of assessment tools to urban settings in the developing world.

Nonetheless, the field of sustainable infrastructure is relatively new and ever-growing (Thomé et al., 2016). Furthermore, given the wide range of issues that should be encompassed within sustainable infrastructure, it is not surprising that a significant body of research is developing around tools and assessment methods to support project teams in managing and delivering sustainable construction.

2.2 Sustainable Infrastructure Assessment Methods

Moving away from traditional monetisation-based methods used to evaluate infrastructure projects, in the last decade a number of new methods and assessment tools have been proposed to assess the sustainability of infrastructure projects (Mostafa & El-Gohary, 2014). Among the most popular sustainability assessment frameworks, it is worthy to mention the Building Research Establishment Environmental Assessment Method (BREEAM) (formerly CEEQUAL), Green Leadership in Transportation Environmental Sustainability (GreenLITES), Greenroads, Envision, and the IS rating scheme. For instance, BREEAM was launched by the UK Building Research Establishment (BRE) in 1990. It comprises sustainability issues related to energy, health and well-being, transport, water, materials, waste, land use and ecology, and pollution. The Envision framework, which is the result of a successful collaboration between the Institute for Sustainable Infrastructure (ISI) and the Zofnass Program for Sustainable Infrastructure at the Harvard University Graduate School of Design, is adopted in North America and applied to more than 100 infrastructure projects, collectively accounting for more than US$106 billion in infrastructure development. It includes 64 sustainability and resiliency criteria, divided into five major categories (i.e., quality of life, leadership, resource allocation, the natural world, and climate and resilience). Yet, the IS rating scheme, developed by the Infrastructure Sustainability Council of Australia and used in Australia and New Zealand, is made up of 15 major components, categorised into six themes—management and governance; using resources; emission, pollution and waste; ecology; people and place; and innovation—to assess the sustainability of infrastructure projects.

Review works of these rating systems reveal that that existing ones are imbalanced in relation to the relevance dedicated to the three pillars of the TBL, with an emphasis placed on environmental credits compared to economic and social aspects (Shaw et al., 2012; Surbeck & Hilger, 2014). To overcome such limitations, a wide array of assessment methods has been also proposed by scholars across the literature. For instance, Diaz-Sarachaga et al. (2017) develop a Sustainable Infrastructure Rating

System (SIRSDEC) aimed at balancing the relevance of the three pillars of sustainability in developing countries. Liu et al. (2021) propose a metric system consisting of 4 measurement dimensions—the TBL with an additional managerial pillar—15 criteria and 50 metrics required for life-cycle SI evaluation. Yet, some authors provide SDG-related measures for assessing infrastructure (Delanka-Pedige et al., 2021), while others focus on evaluating the socio-economic impact of megaprojects (Corazza et al., 2022b).

Against this background, Chan et al. (2022) review the major existing frameworks elaborated by professional bodies and proposed in the academic literature, in order to develop a comprehensive assessment framework for SI. Starting from the reviewing work, they additionally collect data from professionals, sustainability experts and project managers, and conduct a confirmatory factor analysis to find out the components and subcomponents mostly associated with the evaluation of SI.

In our analysis, we leverage Chan et al. (2022)'s framework, as one of the most comprehensive and updated SI assessment frameworks to discover if different components of sustainable infrastructure emerged from our analysis of corporate disclosures.

3 Methodology

3.1 Research Method and Sample Selection

Our research goal is to investigate the underlying ideas that companies associate with the concept of SI. To this aim, we conduct a content analysis of corporate reports. Corporate narrative's contents and characteristics have been proven to be effective for detecting how the discourse around social issues, such as environmentalism, sustainable development, and corporate social responsibility (CSR), is constructed and reflected in organisational messages and disclosures (Buhr & Reiter 2006; Tregidga & Milne 2006; Laine 2009; O'Connor & Shumate 2010; Beauchamp & O'Connor 2012).

The nature of our content analysis is both deductive and inductive. It is deductive since the research starts from models and definitions of sustainable infrastructure provided in theory and practice, and we subsequently look at how the concept plays out in corporate narratives. Specifically, we draw upon Chan et al.'s assessment framework (2022) to analyse the components and subcomponents associated with the notion of sustainable infrastructure. At the same time, the inductive element highlights the nature of the data, as information on sustainable infrastructure can be gained, which not only applies to the manifest content but mostly to latent contents, resulting from the interpretation of the texts (Graneheim & Lundman, 2004).

The study focuses on companies operating in the construction industry. To select our sample, we leverage the 2021 CE100 list of European Contractors, compiled by Construction Europe, in which construction companies are ranked by revenues. In particular, we concentrate on the top 10 companies in the list. For each company, we analyse all the up-to-date disclosures on sustainability-related topics available on the company website. Companies' literature includes mostly sustainability reports, annual reports, integrated reports, as well as other more specific documents, such as climate strategy, sustainability plan, and so on.

3.2 Data Collection and Analysis

To carry out our analysis, we first screen sustainability-related information provided by companies in the documents published on their website by entering a search query based on the following keywords: '*sustainable infrastructure*', '*sustainable construction*', '*sustainable building*', and '*resilient building*'. This keyword-based search allows us to limit information reported throughout the whole document to information specifically related to the notion of sustainable infrastructure. We do not include terms such as 'green infrastructure' or 'green building' to avoid restricting the conceptualisation of SI to environmental issues. Additionally, we look for text paragraphs where the SDG 9 is explicitly referred to, by conducting both a terminology and visual search. Subsequently, we extract information located in the same paragraphs where the identified keywords/icons are mentioned/represented. Even though a company does not specifically provide a definition of sustainable infrastructure or building, its reported targets and/or relevant actions put in place can be seen as implicit statements, from which interpretation of the concept can be reasonably derived. Thus, all relevant information is manually coded. Specifically, the coding procedure aims to identify the following key aspects related to SI, as emerged from the literature:

1. the project lifecycle phase(s) addressed (OECD, 2019);
2. the components (i.e., sustainability issues/topics) and sub-components (i.e., sustainability sub-topics) related to SI (Chan et al., 2022);
3. the metrics employed to assess SI.

After the coding procedure, quantitative and qualitative analyses are accomplished, to both objectively present facts from the text in the form of frequencies and facilitate the interpretation of the analysed data.

4 Findings and Discussion

Nine companies out of ten show some information associated with the terms identified (see Methodology section), whilst for one of them the keyword-based search does not return any result. For such companies, key aspects related to SI are presented in Table 9.1 and discussed in more detail in the following.

4.1 Project Lifecycle Phase

Almost all SI-related information analysed applies to the *design* and *execution* lifecycle phases of projects, thus indicating that environmental, social, and economic positive/negative impacts related to the project are viewed as crucial elements to be considered since the genesis (i.e., planning) of the building/ infrastructural project, as well as during the following construction and operation stages. Only one company in the sample refers to the final lifecycle phase of infrastructure, that is, the dismantling

Table 9.1 Aspects related to sustainable infrastructure

Sustainable Infrastructure					
Project life-cycle phases	Sustainability dimensions	Components	Subcomponents	Example of related actions	Assessment metrics
– DESIGN (9) – CONSTRUCTION (9) – DISMANTLING (1)	ENVIRONMENTAL	Energy (9)*	GHG emissions control (8)	Reduction of greenhouse gas emissions (Scope 1, 2, and 3 emissions)	– GRI 305—*Emissions* (2) – GRI 302—*Energy* (2) – GRI 306—*Effluents and waste* (1) – Emissions avoided (in millions of tons of CO_2 equivalent) by implementing environmental solutions (1) – Building energy intensity (Sector Disclosure Construction and Real Estate) (1) – Building's energy and carbon balance (1) – Sales in projects/number of projects with sustainable certifications (e.g., ISO 14001, LEED) (4) – Number and percentage of construction projects with sustainable solutions in bidding processes and/or during preconstruction processes (1) – R&D+i investments in eco-projects (1) – Percentage of revenue according to EU Taxonomy alignment methodology (1)
			Energy use (9)	Upgrading of sites to reach positive-energy status, improvement of energy efficiency in buildings, delivery of construction materials using waterways	
			Renewable energy (5)	Design and construction of buildings self-sufficient in 100% renewable energies	
		Materials (5)	Materials reuse (4)	Reuse of excavated material in the same infrastructure or in another production cycle	
			Materials recycling (2)	Offering to customers the use of recycled construction materials	
			Innovative materials (2)	Development of new projects and materials that increase the resilience of infrastructure	
			Material quality control (1)	Use of material products with environmental credentials	
			Material intensity (1)	Reduction of construction materials, monitoring of materials lifecycle impacts	
			Local materials (1)	Use of local materials on a site-specific basis	
		Water (3)	*Stormwater* management (2)	*Implementation of grey- and rain-water* recovery systems	
			Water use (1)	Reducing water consumption in operations	
		Waste (2)	Construction and operational waste (2)	Use of prefabricated modules to facilitate low waste construction, reuse of treated marine sediment to avoid marine dumping	
			Divert from landfill (1)	Recycling of removed trees to reduce waste disposal	
		Biodiversity** (3)	Protection/ **restoration** of biodiversity (3)	Excavation practices that make use of specific additives to meet environmental protection requirements, while also adapting to the geotechnical and hydrogeological complexities of the construction area	

(continued)

Table 9.1 (continued)

Sustainable Infrastructure					
Project life-cycle phases	Sustainability dimensions	Components	Subcomponents	Example of related actions	Assessment metrics
			Ecological connectivity (1)	Avoid negative impacts on habitats, wildlife corridors, and sediment transport	
	SOCIAL	**Impact on local community** (3)	Noise control (2)	Use of mass battery storage systems to reduce noise	– Social value calculated using the national social value measurement framework (1)
			Traffic issues (2)	Reduction of traffic congestion	
		Community engagement (3)	Skill development opportunities (2)	Investment in future talent through apprenticeship schemes and work placement opportunities	
			Level of engagement (1)	Seminars and newsletters dedicated to environmental issues to raise awareness of the entire supply chain, site visits for groups of students	
			Quality relationship (1)	Work in short local loops	
			Future visions (1)	Involvement in associations and industry initiatives, support for academic projects/ collaboration with universities	
		Innovation (3)	**Design for change** (2)	Development of eco-districts, building reversibility, launch of start-ups and creation of spin-offs	
			Innovation sharing (2)	Deployment of technologies to support customers in energy transition and reduction of carbon footprint	
	ECONOMIC	Project management (2)	Procurement and supply chain governance (1)	Supplier pre-qualification questionnaires related to the implementation of a sustainability policy, monitoring of the sustainability performance monitoring of suppliers	– GRI 201—*economic performance* (1) – GRI 203—*indirect economic impacts* (1)
			Type of contract (1)	Project coverage by comprehensive performance contracts	
			Environmental management (1)	Use of software solutions to manage the environmental performance of buildings	

*Numbers into parenthesis indicate frequency of mentioning

**Components and subcomponents marked in bold indicate where a more suitable coding label is attributed by the authors compared to Chan et al. (2022)'s framework and disposal phase. This is consistent with the notion that project processes are dynamic, non-linear, and involve progressively decreasing levels of risk and uncertainty through time (Winch, 2001). Indeed, decisions and behaviours related to the early phases are highly risky and have profound and irreversible impacts (Ma et al., 2017). Additionally, recent research highlights a substantial lack of tools, practices, and standards addressing the ultimate lifecycle stages in the assessment frameworks panorama (Corazza et al., 2022a). Nevertheless, this is essential for embracing a long-term perspective and implementing circular economy practices, which can help restoring land and natural ecosystems.

4.2 Components and Subcomponents of SI

As Table 9.1 illustrates, components are grouped according to the three dimensions of sustainability (i.e., environmental, social, and economic). In the environmental pillar, the component 'Energy' records the highest relative importance, appearing in all corporate disclosures. This testifies that the attribute 'sustainable' is largely anchored to the project's capability of reducing negative impacts stemming from greenhouse gas (GHG) emissions and positively contributing to climate neutrality. Unsurprisingly, SI-related information is often provided in corporate disclosure sections related to environmental issues and climate change actions. These findings can be mainly motivated by the strong impact exerted by the construction sector in terms of energy consumption and GHG emissions, which account for 38% of total global energy-related CO_2 emissions (United Nations Environment Programme, 2020). Traditionally, energy-related criteria represent the most influencing measurement for assessing the sustainability of a building (Berardi, 2012), so that the terms 'sustainable buildings' and 'energy-efficient buildings' have been often used interchangeably (Berardi, 2013). This aspect is likely to be perceived as even more relevant in the light of the EU classification system—the so-called EU Taxonomy—publicly presented in March 2020. Indeed, the purpose of the EU Taxonomy is to translate the EU's climate and environmental objectives into criteria for specific economic activities. The analysis also shows that most subcomponents concern the efficient use of energy and the reduction of electrical and petroleum consumption, while fewer companies mention investing in renewable energy sources. The component 'Materials' is also recurrent. The analysis supports that planning and operating a sustainable infrastructure calls for devoting attention to materials employed. Previous studies indeed reveal that issues tied to materials are prominent in almost all existing assessment frameworks (Chan et al., 2022) and are highlighted by recent research works as a core matter in sustainable infrastructure development (Thomé et al., 2016). In particular, companies show a great focus on reducing the impact of their material usage by reusing and also recycling them. While reusing entails keeping materials out of the waste stream by passing materials used in the same infrastructure or in another production cycle with little or no processing, recycling involves collecting, segregating, processing, and manufacturing materials into new products. Some companies also report about the usage of certified and innovative low-carbon building materials, that is, low-energy-embodied materials. By contrast, using local materials appears not to be a prevailing option for construction companies. Indeed, this practice may lead to higher costs and delays in building projects (Hayles & Kooloos, 2005). Topics related to 'Water' are quite often connected to the notion of SI as well. Particularly, water management is usually mentioned in reference to water use reduction and stormwater management (for instance, rainwater recovery and reuse and flood prevention systems implementation). Furthermore, 'Biodiversity' goals, in terms of ecosystem protection and biodiversity restoration, appear to be attributed to the function of SI. These SI attributes clearly evoke the notion of 'green' infrastructure promoted by the European Union (EU) as infrastructure planned and designed "to ensure that natural areas remain connected together, to restore the health of ecosystems and allow species to thrive across their entire natural habitat so that nature keeps on delivering its many benefits to us" (European Commission, 2022). Under this perspective, infrastructure must become an integral part of spatial planning and territorial development. Moving forward, within the social pillar, components related to community, specifically 'Impact on local community' and 'Community engagement', find space. Intangible impacts of infrastructure have been highlighted as a white spot in many existing assessment frameworks (Chan et al., 2022), where the focus on environmental components largely outweighs social sustainability. However, the companies analysed appear to link, to some extent, the concept of SI to social responsibilities and efforts. Indeed, the conceptualisation of SI looks to be related, on the one hand, to the capability of limiting, as much as possible, negative effects falling over local communities (noise and dust control, traffic congestion avoidance, etc), and on the other hand, to the involvement in community development actions aimed at empowering them for their own and each other's wellbeing. The latter may include initiatives such as information-sharing endeavours, seminars, and workshops on sustainability issues to raise awareness along the supply chain, educational events dedicated to youngsters, apprenticeship and work placement opportunities. In some cases, SI is also linked to innovation, in terms of ground-breaking project design and sharing of innovation to improve people's life. By contrast, the concept is rarely associated with waste management (for instance, construction and operational waste reduction). Consistently with the paucity of consideration concerning the dismantling phase of infrastructural projects, no company refers to waste management in demolition. Concerning the economic dimension, in line with prior research (Marcelino-Sádaba et al., 2015; Chan et al., 2022), our findings support that project management is hardly considered in connection with SI, therefore suggesting that project management practice needs to enlarge its horizon, departing from the 'iron triangle' to fully incorporate sustainable development principles.

4.3 Assessment Metrics

Data collected on metrics employed by companies to measure SI-related aspects reveal that most companies assess the sustainability of infrastructure by means of environmental criteria. These include, for instance, revenues from projects with environmental certifications (such as, ISO 14001, LEED, etc.), indicators drawn from the Global Reporting Initiative (GRI)—particularly the GRI 302 (*Energy*), GRI 305 (*Emissions*)—sustainable materials (i.e., with an environmental certification) as a percentage of sales, buildings energy balance, R&D expenditures related to eco-projects. These findings testify an overall coherence with the (mis)conception that SI is akin to green infrastructure, being mostly linked to the environmental dimension, while leaving the other dimensions as secondary. The social sphere is considerably less represented, with seldom recalls to the social value of projects, through impact and engagement with the local community, including local contractors and supply chain. The economic dimension is again rather peripheral with sporadic references to the direct and indirect economic project outcomes (GRI 201—*Economic performance*, GRI 203—*Indirect economic impacts*).

5 Conclusions

Infrastructure has the potential to strongly contribute to delivering economic, social, and environmental benefits. However, for the infrastructure sector to stimulate change towards sustainable development, a shift from the traditional paradigm of the 'iron triangle' is required to properly integrate sustainability considerations.

The chapter has aimed to provide novel evidence on how the notion of 'sustainable infrastructure' is conceived and interpreted by companies. The concept of SI has evolved over time and developed towards a comprehensive conceptualisation of sustainability (Berardi, 2013). However, the variety of definitions used to categorise sustainability components and the still prevailing environmental façade of SI in existing assessment frameworks (Chan et al., 2022) call for further investigation and reflection on the concept. While previous studies have mainly considered how the SI notion has evolved in the academic literature (Thomé et al., 2016) and how it should be assessed accordingly (Chan et al., 2022), the way companies interpret and measure it has been largely neglected. In this study, we embrace a company-centred perspective and analyse SI-related contents as disclosed by companies of the construction industry in their corporate reports. This approach complements previous research and contributes towards a better understanding of how existing conceptualisations differ from or converge with companies' interpretation of the concept, thus advancing their mutual shaping. Our findings suggest that, for companies, addressing sustainability in infrastructure projects means devoting strong consideration of sustainability-related issues in the early phases of the project lifecycle (i.e., planning and execution). Very little linkages to the final project stages emerge instead. This is coherent with previous research, which highlights a scarcity of assessment tools related to the deconstruction/demolition phase (Corazza et al., 2022a). Furthermore, the analysis supports that there is not an unequivocal representation of the components of SI. While sharing the view that environmental, or 'green', aspects of sustainability are a fundamental feature for sustainable infrastructure participants to consider (Gupta et al., 2021), differences in the conceptualisation of SI emerge. This is particularly evident when it comes to sustainability aspects less directly linked to the most significant negative environmental impacts stemming from construction activities (e.g., energy consumption, GHG emissions, materials utilisation). To different degrees, initiatives related to the efficient use of water, the prevention of damages caused by natural forces, and the protection and/or restoration of ecosystems, appear to be attached to the concept of SI. This embraces a broader view of SI, which includes a wider range of stakeholders involved and scaled-up actions. At the same time, sustainability in infrastructure is also linked, to a varying extent, on the one hand, to engaging in initiatives for community wealth development and conservation, and on the other hand, to bringing technological advancement and disruptive innovative ideas that can benefit people's life and the industry (Thrassou et al., 2022a, 2022b). In this vein, the notion of SI also encloses social-related issues. Finally, in line with prior research (Chan et al., 2022), the analysis supports that economic considerations (related, for instance, to project management) are rarely associated with SI, as well as waste management, especially in the deconstruction phase.

References

Atkinson, R. (1999). Project management: Cost, time and quality, two best guesses and a phenomenon, it's time to accept other success criteria. *International Journal of Project Management, 17*(6), 337–342.

Baccarini, D. (1996). The concept of project complexity—A review. *International Journal of Project Management, 14*(4), 201–204.

Beauchamp, L. L., & O'Connor, A. (2012). America's most admired companies: A descriptive analysis of CEO corporate social responsibility statements. *Public Relations Review, 38*(3), 494–497.

Berardi, U. (2012). Sustainability assessment in the construction sector: Rating systems and rated buildings. *Sustainable Development, 20*(6), 411–424.

Berardi, U. (2013). Clarifying the new interpretations of the concept of sustainable building. *Sustainable Cities and Society, 8*, 72–78.

Bosch-Rekveldt, M., Jongkind, Y., Mooi, H., Bakker, H., & Verbraeck, A. (2011). Grasping project complexity in large engineering projects: The TOE (Technical, Organizational and Environmental) framework. *International Journal of Project Management, 29*(6), 728–739.

Brundtland, G. H. (1987). Our common future—Call for action. *Environmental Conservation, 14*(4), 291–294.

Buhr, N., & Reiter, S. (2006). *Ideology, the environment and one world view: A discourse analysis of Noranda's environmental and sustainable development reports*. Emerald Group Publishing Limited.

Business Roundtable. (2019). Delivering for America 2019 Report. https://www.businessroundtable.org/delivering-for-america-full-report

Chan, M., Jin, H., van Kan, D., & Vrcelj, Z. (2022). Developing an innovative assessment framework for sustainable infrastructure development. *Journal of Cleaner Production, 368*, 133185.

Construction Europe (2021). News Report: CE100. https://www.construction-europe.com/Files/Download/20210927-112301-CE-09-2021-CE100.pdf

Corazza, L., Cottafava, D., & Torchia, D. (2022a). Toward sustainable infrastructural megaprojects. In W. Leal Fihlo et al. (Eds.), *SDGs in the European region, implementing the UN sustainable development goals—Regional perspectives*. Springer Nature.

Corazza, L., Torchia, D., Cottafava, D., & Tipaldo, G. (2022b). Considering the social and economic implications of infrastructure megaprojects: Theoretical contributions, practical challenges and managerial implications. In R. Kudłak, R. Barkemeyer, L. Preuss, & A. Heikkinen (Eds.), *The impact of corporate social responsibility* (pp. 134–160). Routledge.

Dasgupta, S., & Tam, E. K. (2005). Indicators and framework for assessing sustainable infrastructure. *Canadian Journal of Civil Engineering, 32*(1), 30–44.

Delanka-Pedige, H. M. K., Munasinghe-Arachchige, S. P., Abeysiriwardana-Arachchige, I. S. A., & Nirmalakhandan, N. (2021). Evaluating wastewater treatment infrastructure systems based on UN Sustainable Development Goals and targets. *Journal of Cleaner Production, 298*, 126795.

Diaz-Sarachaga, J. M., Jato-Espino, D., & Castro-Fresno, D. (2017). Methodology for the development of a new Sustainable Infrastructure Rating System for Developing Countries (SIRSDEC). *Environmental Science & Policy, 69*, 65–72.

El-Diraby, T. E., & Osman, H. (2011). A domain ontology for construction concepts in urban infrastructure products. *Automation in Construction, 20*(8), 1120–1132.

Elkington, J. (1994). Towards the sustainable corporation: Win-win-win business strategies for sustainable development. *California Management Review, 36*(2), 90–100.

European Commission. (2022). *The EU strategy on green infrastructure*. https://ec.europa.eu/environment/nature/ecosystems/strategy/index_en.htm

Ferrer, A. L. C., Thomé, A. M. T., & Scavarda, A. J. (2018). Sustainable urban infrastructure: A review. *Resources, Conservation and Recycling, 128*, 360–372.

Flyvbjerg, B. (2014). What you should know about megaprojects and why: An overview. *Project Management Journal, 45*(2), 6–19.

Garrett, D. (2008). *Is the triple constraint the WRONG way to define success*. ILO.

Gellert, P. K., & Lynch, B. D. (2003). Mega-projects as displacements. *International Social Science Journal, 55*(175), 15–25.

Graneheim, U. H., & Lundman, B. (2004). Qualitative content analysis in nursing research: Concepts, procedures and measures to achieve trustworthiness. *Nurse Education Today, 24*(2), 105–112.

Grevelman, L., & Kluiwstra, M. (2010). Sustainability in project management A case study on Enexis. *PM World Today*.

Gupta, H., Kumar, A., & Wasan, P. (2021). Industry 4.0, cleaner production and circular economy: An integrative framework for evaluating ethical and sustainable business performance of manufacturing organizations. *Journal of Cleaner Production, 295*, 126253.

Hayles, C. S., & Kooloos, T. (2005). The challenges and opportunities for sustainable building practices. *Benefits, 2*.

Inter-American Development Bank. (2018). *What is sustainable infrastructure? A framework to guide sustainability across the project cycle*. IADB.

KPMG. (2020). *The sustainable infrastructure opportunity*. https://home.kpmg/xx/en/home/insights/2020/06/covid-19-recovery.html

KPMG. (2022). *Emerging trends in infrastructure 2022*. https://assets.kpmg/content/dam/kpmg/xx/pdf/2022/01/emerging-trends-in-infrastructure-2022.pdf

Laine, M. (2009). Ensuring legitimacy through rhetorical changes? A longitudinal interpretation of the environmental disclosures of a leading Finnish chemical company. *Accounting, Auditing & Accountability Journal, 22*, 1029–1054.

Liu, B., Xue, B., & Chen, X. (2021). Development of a metric system measuring infrastructure sustainability: Empirical studies of Hong Kong. *Journal of Cleaner Production, 278*, 123904.

Ma, H., Zeng, S., Lin, H., Chen, H., & Shi, J. J. (2017). The societal governance of megaproject social responsibility. *International Journal of Project Management, 35*(7), 1365–1377.

Marcelino-Sádaba, S., González-Jaen, L. F., & Pérez-Ezcurdia, A. (2015). Using project management as a way to sustainability. From a comprehensive review to a framework definition. *Journal of Cleaner Production, 99*, 1–16.

Mostafa, M. A., & El-Gohary, N. M. (2014). Stakeholder-sensitive social welfare–oriented benefit analysis for sustainable infrastructure project development. *Journal of Construction Engineering and Management, 140*(9), 04014038.

Nilsson, M., Griggs, D., Visbeck, M., Riegler, C., & McCollum, D. (2017). Introduction: A Framework for Understanding SDG Interactions. *A guide to SDG interactions: From science to implementation. International Council for Science (ICSU).*

O'Connor, A., & Shumate, M. (2010). An economic industry and institutional level of analysis of corporate social responsibility communication. *Management Communication Quarterly, 24*(4), 529–551.

OECD. (2019). Sustainable Infrastructure for Low-Carbon Development in Central Asia and the Caucasus: Hotspot Analysis and Needs Assessment. In *Green Finance and Investment*. OECD Publishing.

PMI. (2009). *A guide to the project management body of knowledge: PMBOK guide* (4th ed.). Project Management Institute.

Rahat, R., Ferrer, V., Pradhananga, P., & ElZomor, M. (2022). Developing an effective front-end planning framework for sustainable infrastructure projects. *International Journal of Construction Management*, 1–18.

Reed, B. (2007). Shifting from 'sustainability' to regeneration. *Building Research & Information, 35*(6), 674–680.

Sahely, H. R., Kennedy, C. A., & Adams, B. J. (2005). Developing sustainability criteria for urban infrastructure systems. *Canadian Journal of Civil Engineering, 32*(1), 72–85.

Shaw, G., Kenny, J., Kumar, A., & Hood, D. (2012). Sustainable infrastructure operations: A review of assessment schemes and decision support. In

Proceedings of the 25th Australian Road Research Board Conference (pp. 1–18). Australian Road Research Board (ARRB).

Shen, L., Wu, Y., & Zhang, X. (2011). Key assessment indicators for the sustainability of infrastructure projects. *Journal of Construction Engineering and Management, 137*(6), 441–451.

Silvius, A. J. G., Brink, J., & van den, Köhler, A. (2009, June). Views on sustainable project management. In K. Kähköhnen, A. S. Kazi, & M. Rekola (Eds.), *Human Side of Projects in Modern Business, eds.* IPMA Scientific Research Paper Series.

Silvius, G. A. J., & Schipper, R. (2011). Taking responsibility: The integration of Sustainability and Project Management. *PM World Today* 13.

Surbeck, C. Q., & Hilger, H. (2014). Social sustainability and important indicators in infrastructure. In *World Environmental and Water Resources Congress 2014*, 2078–2093.

Thacker, S., Adshead, D., Fay, M., Hallegatte, S., Harvey, M., Meller, H., et al. (2019). Infrastructure for sustainable development. *Nature Sustainability, 2*(4), 324–331.

Thomé, A. M. T., Ceryno, P. S., Scavarda, A., & Remmen, A. (2016). Sustainable infrastructure: A review and a research agenda. *Journal of Environmental Management, 184*, 143–156.

Thrassou, A., Vrontis, D., Efthymiou, L., & Uzunboylu, N. (2022a). An overview of business advancement through technology: Markets and marketing in transition. In A. Thrassou, D. Vrontis, L. Efthymiou, Y. Weber, S. M. R. Shams, & E. Tsoukatos (Eds.), *Business Advancement through Technology Volume I. Palgrave Studies in Cross-disciplinary Business Research, in Association with EuroMed Academy of Business.* Palgrave Macmillan. https://doi.org/10.1007/978-3-031-07769-2_1

Thrassou, A., Vrontis, D., Efthymiou, L., & Uzunboylu, N. (2022b). An overview of business advancement through technology: The changing landscape of work and employment. In A. Thrassou, D. Vrontis, L. Efthymiou, Y. Weber, S. M. R. Shams, & E. Tsoukatos (Eds.), *Business Advancement through Technology Volume II. Palgrave Studies in Cross-disciplinary Business Research, in Association with EuroMed Academy of Business.* Palgrave Macmillan. https://doi.org/10.1007/978-3-031-07765-4_1

Tregidga, H., & Milne, M. J. (2006). From sustainable management to sustainable development: A longitudinal analysis of a leading New Zealand environmental reporter. *Business Strategy and the Environment, 15*(4), 219–241.

Trigo, A., Marta-Costa, A., & Fragoso, R. (2022). Sustainability assessment: A tool to build resilience in the face of future crisis. In *Business Under Crisis, Volume III* (pp. 47–86). Palgrave Macmillan.

Ugwu, O. O., & Haupt, T. C. (2007). Key performance indicators and assessment methods for infrastructure sustainability—a South African construction industry perspective. *Building and Environment, 42*(2), 665–680.

United Nations Environment Programme. (2020). *2020 Global status report for buildings and construction: Towards a zero-emission, efficient and resilient buildings and construction sector.*

Winch, G. M. (2001). Governing the project process: a conceptual framework. *Construction Management and Economics, 19*(8), 799–808.

Zeng, S. X., Ma, H. Y., Lin, H., Zeng, R. C., & Tam, V. W. (2015). Social responsibility of major infrastructure projects in China. *International Journal of Project Management, 33*(3), 537–548.

10

Weak Sustainable Development Trajectories and Evolving Organisational Physiologies: Empirical Evidence from Greece

Dimos Chatzinikolaou and Charis Vlados

1 Introduction

This chapter's aim is threefold. First, we will examine the physiological transformation of firms located in a regional business ecosystem that is less robust in terms of sustainable development. Second, we will investigate whether the apparent "dominance" of monad-centric physiology—relatively instinctive strategic decisions, somewhat sporadic technological choices, and management based extensively on day-to-day practice—is related to the underperformance of regions with similar dynamics and prospects. Third, we will derive general theoretical guidelines for helping

The original version of the chapter has been revised. A correction to this chapter can be found at https://doi.org/10.1007/978-3-031-37361-9_13

D. Chatzinikolaou
Department of Economics, Democritus University of Thrace, Komotini, Greece
e-mail: dimchatz@econ.duth.gr

D. Vrontis et al. (eds.), *Business for Sustainability, Volume I*, Palgrave Studies in Cross-disciplinary Business Research, In Association with EuroMed Academy of Business, https://doi.org/10.1007/978-3-031-37361-9_10

these socioeconomic systems evolve, setting the stage for considering meso–micro policies to reinforce these weak (less developed and competitive) organisations.

This research seems to fill a gap in the literature on empowering entrepreneurship and strategy-making in less-developed regions. The relevant literature tends to distinguish firms according to their size, looking mainly at the dynamic characteristics of small- and medium-sized enterprises. Thus, it overlooks, to some extent, the organic developmental problems highlighted by the organisational physiology approach (cf. Belyaeva & Lopatkova, 2020; Karagouni, 2018; Lampadarios & Kyriakidou, 2020; Migliaccio & Rossetti, 2020). Instead, this chapter synthesises different surveys we have implemented in some less developed companies, which we have approached from a biological perspective. Thus, it seems that this research fills a relative gap in the literature by attempting to discern the deeper evolving causes of their comparative underdevelopment—such a study seems necessary given that beneath seemingly identical quantities can lie significant differences in qualitative dimensions (e.g., Montanari & Kocollari, 2020).

The remainder of the chapter is structured as follows. Section 2 reviews relevant literature and introduces the conceptual framework. Next, Section 3 captures and analyses the methodology for approaching these research objectives. Section 4 presents (a) secondary macro–meso socioeconomic data concerning a less developed Greek region (Eastern Macedonia–Thrace) and (b) results of field research examining the physiology of specific organisations in this business ecosystem. The concluding Sect. 5 discusses and critically integrates the results of this empirical investigation. It also presents research limitations, prospects for enriching the findings, and policy directions.

C. Vlados (✉)
Department of Economics, Democritus University of Thrace,
Komotini, Greece

School of Business, University of Nicosia, Nicosia, Cyprus

School of Social Sciences, Business & Organisation, Administration,
Hellenic Open University, Patras, Greece
e-mail: cvlados@econ.duth.gr

2 Literature Review

> We cannot define a caterpillar and then use the same definition for a butterfly [Edith Penrose, "The theory of the growth of the firm," a book published in 1959.]

Marshall (1890), although a forerunner of neoclassical economics, was one of the first to relate evolutionary–Darwinian biology to economics, understanding that *natura non facit saltum*. In modern evolutionary economics, biological metaphors are a *conditio sine qua non* for a dialectical–evolutionary view of the firm (Nelson et al., 2018). In the evolutionary theory of economics and political economy, the firm responds proactively to changes in the external environment (Nelson & Winter, 1982). This actor is at the heart of socioeconomic dynamics, adapting according to the skills and dynamic capabilities it articulates over time (Hodgson & Knudsen, 2004; Teece et al., 1997). Also, some approaches conceptualise the evolution of these entrepreneurial organisations in biological and ecosystem terms (e.g., Foster, 1997; Witt, 2006). According to Vlados (2004), firms resemble biological species with distinct organisational physiologies due to unique internal Stra.Tech.Man (Strategy–Technology–Management) compositions. The author suggests that (a) organisational strategy is about where we are and why we desire a direction toward the targeted destination, (b) technology is about how and why we create, diffuse, and reproduce expertise, and (c) management is about how and why we manage resources in particular ways (Vlados, 2004). Evolutionary organisational physiology—in terms of Stra.Tech.Man—is path-dependent, as distinct past choices of strategy, technology, and management determine their future development (e.g., Chatzinikolaou & Vlados, 2019).

Organisational physiology captures a micro actor's evolution and sustainability prospects, meaning its ability to address current pressing problems by considering future profound transformations of the newly emerging global economy (e.g., Onyama, 2021; Vargas-Hernández & Orozco Quijano, 2022). This physiological approach leads to a typology of different entrepreneurship structures. In Vlados' (2004) view, there are three main types of entrepreneurial physiology: monad-centred, massive, and flexible. Business monad-centredness refers primarily to instinctive strategic decisions, sporadic technological choices, and management based solely on day-to-day practice. Business massiveness means strategy based mainly on mechanistic-oriented performance measurement methods, linear technology, and highly specialised, narrowly focused management. Business flexibility corresponds to an evolutionary-historical strategy, increasingly networked technology, and management constantly tending toward participatory forms. Based on this approach, the Greek entrepreneurial ecosystem appears to be home primarily to monad-centred firms, which are at the root of Greece's chronic competitiveness lags (Vlados et al., 2021).

In this study, we empirically test some of the relevant aspects of the Stra.Tech.Man approach. Figure 10.1 illustrates the synthesising theoretical background we introduce based on this perspective.

Evolutionary economics studies socioeconomic systems as interactions of macro–meso–micro determinants (e.g., Dopfer et al., 2004). The new globalisation that emerges today unifies the macrosocial and macroeconomic levels, structurally transforming all actors and spatial systems (Chatzinikolaou & Vlados, 2022b). In particular, the new globalisation marks the critical transition in the global economy that began to unfold

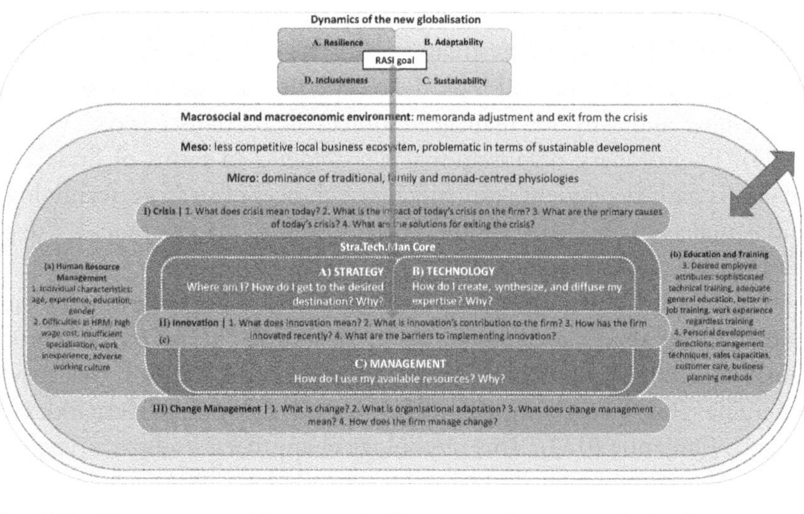

Fig. 10.1 The conceptual framework. (Source: Authors' own design)

around 2008—although incubated earlier through the structural maturation of the previous regime (globalisation). The financial crisis of 2008, the pandemic of 2019–2020 that hastened the fourth industrial revolution, and the Russian invasion in Ukraine of 2022 that expedited the ongoing energy transition are milestones of the emerging new globalisation (Chatzinikolaou & Vlados, 2022b). Also, since we will be studying a Greek region, we mention that the macroenvironment in Greece has been rapidly adjusted in recent years. Greek governments signed successive memoranda of understanding with the International Monetary Fund and relevant European institutions as loan agreements that contributed to the gradual exit from the internal structural crisis (e.g., Andrikopoulos & Nastopoulos, 2015).

Concerning today's emerging new globalisation, the relevant literature mainly distinguishes low-performance scenarios for the near future (e.g., Bhattacharya et al., 2017; Killian, 2021). In other research we are currently conducting on innovation and change management for the new globalisation, we have evidence that the RASI synthesis (Resilience–Adaptability–Sustainability–Inclusiveness) should be the long-term goal of all actors as the international community appears to be increasingly sensitive to these issues (e.g., World Economic Forum, 2018).

Regarding the Stra.Tech.Man organisational core, we suggest this as the primary diagnostic mechanism—it is the epicentre that generates innovation in different physiological types of firms (monad-centred, massive, or flexible). In this conceptual framework that we introduce, the achievement of RASI goals structurally reshapes global development prospects and the sustainability of local–regional business ecosystems, which include interdependent firms (Moore, 1993; Rinkinen & Harmaakorpi, 2018). The Greek economy is seemingly dominated by traditional, family-centred, and monad-centred physiologies, leading local business ecosystems to problems of competitiveness and sustainable growth. In the conceptual scheme we introduce, socioeconomic organisations can achieve their overall RASI goals through three-level syntheses:

A. Crisis–Innovation–Change Management. The organisation must understand (a) that crises are evolutionarily inevitable and irreversible, (b) that innovations are providing solutions to old or new problems to exit from crises, and (c) that effective change management is a prerequisite for innovation but also for the continuous assimilation of the transformations that these innovations bring (see also Chatzinikolaou & Vlados, 2022a).

B. Strategy–Technology–Management. The organisation must understand its core philosophies and processes—in terms of Stra.Tech.Man organisational physiology—enhancing its competitive strengths and innovation potential (see also Vlados & Chatzinikolaou, 2019a, 2020).
C. Human Resource Management (HRM)–Education and Training–Innovation. The organisation must achieve the organic synthesis of HRM with the Stra.Tech.Man core by emphasising continuous in-business and extra-business training of stakeholders to innovate (see also Vlados & Chatzinikolaou, 2020).

3 Methods

This study integrates one qualitative and three mixed surveys in Eastern Macedonia–Thrace. The inductive and empirically grounded research in these studies aimed to interpret specific behaviours of individuals in this area by interviewing them in their business setting and creating interactional conditions (Corbin & Strauss, 2015; Neergaard & Ulhøi, 2007). We followed a variant of Lindlof and Taylor's (2002) qualitative analysis, designing different interview schedules, sometimes accompanied by psychometric scales and open-ended questions, turning the survey into a mixed-methods approach. According to Lindlof and Taylor (2002, p. 195), the interview schedule "is one way to increase the reliability and credibility of data." Table 10.1 shows the number of firms in the sample, divided according to the number of employees.

The sample consists of 230 cases and includes mainly micro and small enterprises (1–10 and 11–50 employees) in the services sector. We picked primarily less competitive companies through our knowledge from years of living and research in this area—conventional sampling that turned purposive subsequently (McCrae & Purssell, 2016). Like Yitshaki and Kropp (2016), we assigned undergraduates of the local university to meet with the managers or owners of the firms and ask them specific questions

Table 10.1 The sample

Empirical scope	Type	1–10	11–50	20–250	50–250	>251	Sector
Crisis–Innovation–Change Management	Qualitative	38	17				Services
Strategy–Technology–Management	Mixed			45[a]		4	Mainly services
Strategy Perception and Implementation	Mixed	44[b]	10				Services
HRM–Education and Training–Innovation	Mixed	45	25		2		Retail

[a]Most of them employ 20–30 people
[b]Primarily 1 to 5 workers

and sound record all answers. We also instructed the interviewers to ask for further reactions when the respondent's understanding seemed insufficient to cover the "why" behind each question (a laddering-type approach, Corbridge et al., 1994). We designed these *in vivo* studies according to the qualitative research principles of Corbin and Strauss (2015), who contend that emergence and interaction are more important than what is already known.

The four sets of interviews were conducted between 2017 and 2019. The "Crisis–Innovation–Change Management" triangle was the research base that posed the questions related to these respective dimensions, as Fig. 10.1 shows (see also Chatzinikolaou & Vlados, 2022a). The "Strategy–Technology–Management" physiology questionnaire explored extended forms of the Stra.Tech.Man core (see also Vlados & Chatzinikolaou, 2019a). The empirical study concerning the physiological exploration of strategy examined dimensions of perception, planning, and implementation—in greater depth than the Stra.Tech.Man framework and for one of its three aspects (see also Vlados & Chatzinikolaou, 2019b). This examination of strategic perception and implementation contrasted fundamental contributions to the literature (e.g., Hamel & Prahalad, 1989; Mintzberg, 1987; Peters & Waterman, 1982; Porter, 1980, 1990). Finally, the triangle "HRM–Education and Training–Innovation" was the theoretical background for the empirical examination of problems concerning the companies' human resources and why their evolution is linked to organisational physiology (see also Vlados & Chatzinikolaou, 2020).

All surveys aimed at comparing—in the form of self-evaluation, as a variant of action research (e.g., Ross et al., 1998; Winter, 1982)—the past situation with the current perception of a given aspect or problem. Section 3 first presents relevant macro, meso, and micro evidence on the Region of Eastern Macedonia–Thrace (REMTh) and then analyses the findings of these studies in terms of organisational physiology. Section 4 interprets these results, approaching the issue from a critical perspective and based on "thick description" principles that can illuminate causes underlying qualitative research results. Ryle (2009) introduced this approach to distinguish the difference between observations of surface behaviours (thin) and contextual conditions that lead to the occurrence of these interactions (thick). According to Ponterotto (2006), a researcher uses this approach to subjectively explain why certain human behaviours of the studied cases occur during data collection. This approach utilises ethnographic and other relevant historical dimensions to interpret the experience. Finally, raw data from these four studies are available upon request in spreadsheets. All information remains confidential, as we promised our respondents during the interviews.

4 Results

4.1 The Business Ecosystem of the REMTh

This area constitutes one of the 13 NUTS 2 regions in Greece, a country with structural competitiveness problems worsened by the decade-long socioeconomic crisis (e.g., Andrikopoulos & Nastopoulos, 2015). Greek firms appear to be less competitive than their Western European counterparts, and these comparative weaknesses have significantly exacerbated the Greek economy's prolonged fiscal and structural crisis (e.g., Giotopoulos et al., 2017). According to the latest Global Entrepreneurship Monitor (2022), confidence in new ventures is still low despite the recent high performance of the Greek economy—this fact illustrates competitiveness deficiencies. GDP per capita decreased by 22% in the REMTh between 2010 and 2019, while in the Greek economy by 12% (see www.

statistics.gr). This unfavourable development mainly occurred because the REMTh is a border region whose productive fabric is based primarily on agricultural activities. Figure 10.2 illustrates this comparative lag of the REMTh, showing its position among the NUTS 2 areas of the EU.

The REMTh performs above average only in Agriculture, Forestry, and Fishing. The private services sector (G–J, K–N)—which mainly concerns

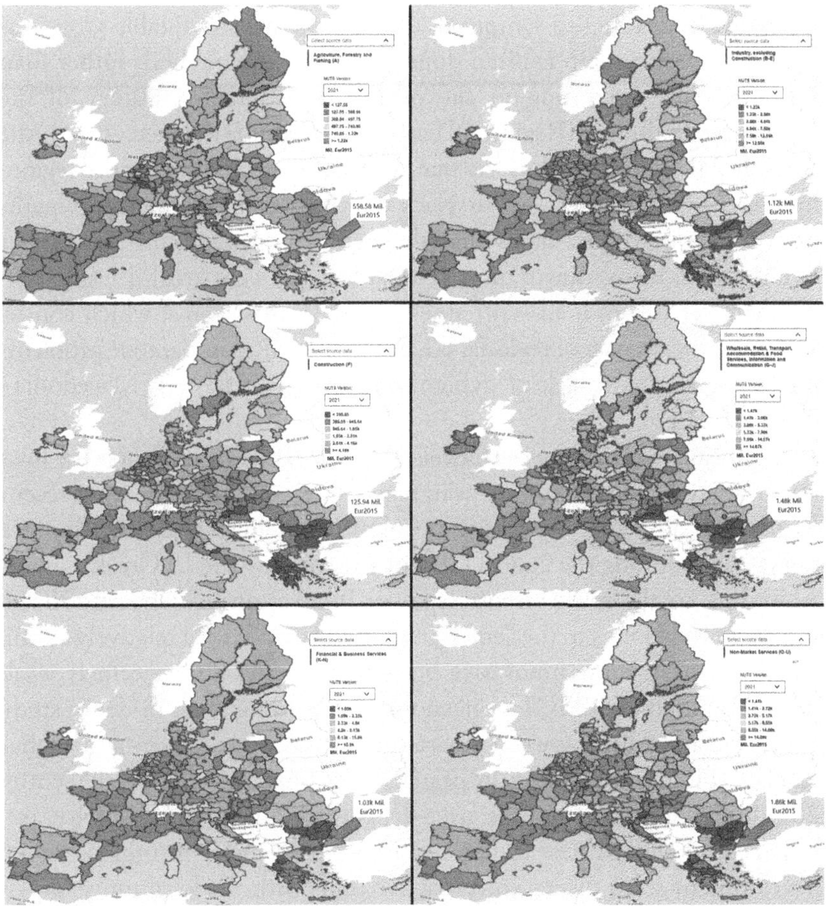

Fig. 10.2 Gross value added of NACE 2 sectors (comparison with EU, constant 2015 prices in EUR). Own elaboration, based on the following: EU Urban Data Platform Plus, https://urban.jrc.ec.europa.eu

the sample considered in the next section—performs poorly. Gross value added is also at the lowest relative levels in manufacturing and construction. Simultaneously, non-private services perform slightly better due to relatively larger budgets in defence and education (cf. Boden et al., 2015). The Agriculture, Forestry, and Fishing sector is proportionally more specialised than the other industries even though it records a lower amount of gross value added.

This discrepancy is the main structural problem of competitiveness in the REMTh, leading to symptoms of less dynamic sustainable growth as local entrepreneurship is often done by traditional methods rather than systematically. According to the official development strategy of the Managing Authority (Region of Eastern Macedonia–Thrace, 2014), the agricultural sector, which is the main field of specialisation in the region, has low competitiveness due to a lack of modern entrepreneurship methods. The same report notes that the manufacturing sector has similar structural problems due to most companies' relatively small size and family character (see monad-centredness). Also, tourist firms, which constitute a significant part of regional GDP, face chronic comparative problems of introversion and lack of dynamism (Region of Eastern Macedonia–Thrace, 2014).

As a result, innovation performance in the REMTh is among the lowest compared to all other European regions. According to the most recent Regional Competitiveness Index (Annoni & Dijkstra, 2019), the area ranks 265th among the 268 EU28 and 12th among the 13 Greek regions. According to the most recent Regional Innovation Scoreboard (2021), the REMTh belongs to the "emerging innovators," with a relatively strong performance in some innovative business processes and extremely weak in the employment of ICT professionals. According to an in-depth study on the relationship between smart-specialisation structures and higher education in the REMTh (European Commission: Joint Research Centre, 2021), the local economy is over-dependent on low-productivity and low-technology business functions. These deficiencies in organisational development seem to prevent proactive links with the local university—which provides education in a wide range of disciplines.

Boden (2017) presents in-depth guidelines for regional specialisation in the REMTh, which emerged through field surveys and focus-group sessions with stakeholders (Foray, 2014). The author suggests that the Managing Authority should invest more vigorously in helping the internationalisation of local firms, focusing on specific market outlets. Boden (2017) also urges regional quadruple-helix actors in the REMTh to formulate strategies based on value chains from existing innovation infrastructures and capabilities instead of focusing on potential comparative disadvantages of the region.

4.2 The Physiological Evolution of Less Competitive Firms in the REMTh

Therefore, based on the business morphology of the REMTh, we expect to find robust evidence of monad-centredness in most firms operating in the secondary or tertiary sector. In the following analysis, we present findings of relevant field studies that converge toward this direction. Below, we list the results of questionnaires on how small entrepreneurs perceive different composite crisis, innovation, and change management dimensions, focusing on conclusions emerging from these findings (see also Chatzinikolaou and Vlados 2022a).

I. Crisis: For these small entrepreneurs, a structural upheaval seems to mean—almost entirely—something that arises mainly as an external conjunctural change that causes reduced revenues and demand due to increased taxation, excessive borrowing, and intensified competition. In the perception of these individuals, the national government seems to be mainly responsible and should reduce tax rates, increase subsidies, and strengthen social welfare mechanisms.
II. Innovation: When asked about dimensions of innovative progress, these small entrepreneurs perceive an extraordinary improvement—mainly because of luck and inspiration. They argue that this organisational improvement does not seem directly related to their day-to-day operations. To a significant extent, these individuals do not appear competent in describing how they have innovated recently—they consider their low innovativeness almost exclusively due to unfavourable conditions in the external business environment. In the percep-

tion of these small entrepreneurs, ineffective government policies are the perpetuating cause of these obstacles, proposing as a solution the facilitation by banks of loans with lower lending rates and the further diffusion of European business support programmes.

III. Change management: The prevailing perception is that "everything remains unchanged in the background" for these small entrepreneurs. They perceive change management—for the most part—as an immediate and short-term response to external adverse fluctuations. These individuals show that they adapt mainly by demonstrating remarkable resilience—they seem willing to limit their ambitions and the firm's profitability to survive. They also exhibit a relative lack of understanding and implementation of systematic change management processes.

These small entrepreneurs in the service sector of the REMTh seem to perceive the crises as mainly quasi-external phenomena that the national government can cure with sectoral protection, lower taxation, and enhanced aggregate demand. In terms of innovation, these organisations appear to have distinct shortcomings leading to lower profitability and competitiveness. They also do not seem to implement—as much and systematically—change management methodologies, which are imperative for overcoming crises.

We present below-identified inefficiencies of small entrepreneurs in different compositional dimensions of strategy, technology, and management (see also Vlados & Chatzinikolaou, 2019a).

A. Strategy: These less competitive organisations mostly exhibit limited vertical integration dynamics and negligible sectoral diversification. Also, the firm's geographic expansion is mainly local, leading to difficulties in finding suppliers and financial resources with a broader geographic reach. The information technology integration strategy and the overall production process are also mainly local. Finally, these small entrepreneurs appear to a large extent not to develop the human resources of their enterprises strategically.

B. Technology: We find a relative lack of systematisation due to comparative deficiencies in the overall technological perspective of the organisation. We also see comparatively limited investment in facilities and general modernisation. These small entrepreneurs seem to use new technology to a relatively small extent to improve productivity, resulting in neither creating nor exploiting niches of high-value-added knowledge. They also show limited technological superiority over competitors, as the range of specialised products is usually small. The product core also appears to lack specialisation, a trend reflected in information technology's comparatively diminished use and development (Thrassou et al., 2022a, 2022b).

C. Management: These small entrepreneurs seem to face comparative difficulties in developing a modern management philosophy—systematisation is limited, mainly due to the family nature of the enterprises. Thus, we find relatively little investment in managerial skills and limited use of modern and advanced forms of leadership. These comparative shortcomings are also evident from the relative absence of formal human resource development processes, corporate social responsibility mechanisms, and total quality management approaches. Overall, outward entrepreneurial orientation through managerial innovations in these organisations appears limited.

By distributing questionnaires with psychometric scales to these small entrepreneurs, we saw that they rated these different "Strategy–Technology–Management" dimensions higher in the present than in the past—the paradox is that we identified comparative inadequacies from our in-depth qualitative review of the cases. Overall, we found an effort of strategic refocusing, technological modernisation, and systematisation of management, which does not seem to be successful for the required innovative transition in organisational physiology and structure.

We present below how small entrepreneurs perceive and implement more specific strategic concepts compared to the strategy-technology-management synthesising approach we field-tested in the previous survey (see also Vlados & Chatzinikolaou, 2019b).

i. These companies show relative inadequacy in establishing and monitoring a principal strategic goal.

ii. Their general conception of strategy does not appear to be much oriented toward flexibility in dealing with change.
iii. We find an almost universal absence of a written mission statement.
iv. To a large extent, the strategy does not consider all the stakeholders in structuring the vision and mission.
v. Most of these organisations do not seem to exploit extra-sectoral trends to make strategic choices—see PEST synthesis (exploring political, economic, social, and technological factors).
vi. These firms do not monitor—as much and systematically—the external environment using Porter's (1980) five forces analysis.
vii. These firms do not seem to reinforce—to a significant extent—their competitiveness through strategic interaction with the local external environment.
viii. They do not appear to be doing much strategic benchmarking by comparing successful practices within and outside their field of activity.
ix. They do not appear to typically implement an internal audit strategy through systematic monitoring and evaluation of comparative strengths.
x. These firms do not extensively use Mintzberg's (1987) 5P approach to strategy (plan, ploy, pattern, position, or perspective).
xi. To a large extent, they do not seem to proactively build core competencies and strategic intent by changing the game rules.
xii. Their strategic elaboration seems, in many cases, insufficient in creating a synthesising evolving mission–vision–philosophy triangle.
xiii. Strategic planning does not extensively appear to create comparative advantages in the firm's day-to-day practice.
xiv. Strategic decisions primarily involve the owner without group consultation.
xv. The generic strategy seems to be based mainly on the saleability of a product rather than on broader social dimensions.
xvi. These firms show relative inadequacy in diffusing organisational excellence practices throughout business processes (cf. Peters & Waterman, 1982).

By distributing questionnaires with psychometric scales to these small entrepreneurs, we saw that they rated these specific strategic dimensions higher in the present compared to the past—the paradox is that we identified comparative inadequacies from our in-depth qualitative review of the cases. As in the field research on the Strategy–Technology–Management triangle, these small entrepreneurs claimed to be trending towards a more systematic implementation of their business strategy—yet they did not seem to justify this rapid progress adequately. By examining 16 critical strategic questions, these firms seemingly have not recently innovatively transformed their organisational physiology.

Regarding the last step of these complementary surveys on the physiological characteristics of specific organisations, we present below the results of questionnaires on how small entrepreneurs perceive different compositional dimensions of HRM, education–training, and innovation (see also Vlados & Chatzinikolaou, 2020).

(a) Human Resource Management: These individuals have relatively ambiguous perceptions of the personal characteristics of employees. On the one hand, they seem interested in staff experience and training. On the other hand, they claim, to some extent, that nothing has changed in how they manage their people and that they do not apply specific relevant selection criteria. They also show ambiguous perceptions—to a significant degree—of the difficulties they face in HRM. On the one hand, they are concerned about high salary costs, insufficient staff expertise, and work inexperience. On the other hand, they largely fail to clarify why these problems are essential for their businesses, stating—in a quasi-static way—that they require minimal skills from their staff.

(b) Education and Training: Equally fluctuating are their perceptions of education and training processes. On the one hand, they show eagerness to employ people with high skills and relevant work experience. On the other hand, they appear to underutilise their staff's higher education and training, requiring them to perform low-skilled tasks. Thus, although they seem to be sensitive toward the personal development of their employees, they do not seem to take much initiative—formal or informal.

(c) Innovation: The perceptions of these small entrepreneurs are also, to some extent, contradictory on innovation issues. For example, most

> small entrepreneurs say that their value on innovation increases over time and that there is—in essence—no innovative progress in small retail firms like theirs. Therefore, to a significant extent, we find a relative absence of a link between innovation, HRM, and education–training in the perceptions of these small entrepreneurs.

By distributing questionnaires with psychometric scales to these individuals, we saw that they rated all the compositional dimensions of HRM, education–training, and innovation higher in the present compared to the past—the paradox is that we identified comparative inadequacies from the in-depth qualitative review of the cases. As in the previous surveys, these small entrepreneurs claimed that they have recently tended toward the systematisation of their HRM, education–training, and innovation processes. However, the findings point to a different picture.

In the previous section, we showed that innovation performance in the REMTh—particularly concerning service sector firms—is among the lowest compared to the EU. Our findings seemingly confirm that the relative dominance of monad-centredness in firms can lead the entire business ecosystem to comparative underdevelopment (see competitiveness deficits). We also see yet another paradox. The physiological transformation of these firms—in recent years, according to the self-assessments we studied—shows that it simultaneously involves elements of massification and monad-centredness. On the one hand, these firms appear to desire a transformation mainly toward increased massiveness. On the other hand, they remain relatively captive to their existing competitiveness potential. The findings of these field studies revealed discrepancies regarding this desire, and the next section discusses in depth why this is the case.

5 Critical Discussion and Conclusions

In this study, we presented the results of different questionnaires that preliminarily diagnosed the organisational physiology of specific firms. After this synthesis, it appears that the conclusions of each survey are enriched as the findings complement each other. We saw that most small entrepreneurs in a less developed region exhibited a relatively poor perception of the Crisis–Innovation–Change Management triangle compared to contemporary business development theory. Regarding the Stra. Tech.Man physiology of these firms, we also found a gap in the perception of these small entrepreneurs compared to organisational development theory. Most of them also seemed to perceive the triangle of HRM–Education and Training–Innovation in a somewhat fragmented way, as they did not seem able to elaborate in depth on the conceptual and practical prerequisites of this evolutionary link. Therefore, we conclude that the organisational physiology approach enables us to delve into problems of competitiveness and sustainability in less developed business ecosystems, helping to analyse dimensions of resilience in the new globalisation that go deeper than the mere size of the firm. Improving an entrepreneurial ecosystem seems to depend on the physiological strengthening of locally established firms. In the following section, we delve into this insight.

5.1 The Organisational Physiology as a Diagnostic Approach and Policy Implications

These preliminary physiological diagnoses are an "x-ray" of the REMTh, highlighting specific problems of organisational underdevelopment and future evolutionary prospects. Based on a thick description, we can examine some of our qualitative findings from a different—more profound—perspective. During data collection, the respondents seemed to embellish their answers to some extent, fearing possible negative criticism from the local community, which is the primary clientele. Many small entrepreneurs also gave responses limited in scope and depth when the interviewers sometimes asked for clarification during the interview. One explanation for this behaviour is based on the relative lack of knowledge that the small entrepreneurs had about the issues under consideration. We also note again that we had an earlier heightened sense of the competitiveness problems that the REMTh seems to be facing, which allowed us to quickly understand which firms were less and more competitive. In support of this hypothesis, several of these less-dynamic firms under consideration appear to be inactive today. Based on the initial objectives, we conclude the following:

First, we see a desire for systematisation with solid evidence of monad-centredness in the physiological transformation of these firms. This contradiction starts from the monad-centric physiological core (in Stra.Tech. Man terms). The perceptions of these small entrepreneurs seem to confirm that monad-centric firms implement their strategy mainly on instinct, often make technological decisions sporadically, and manage organisational resources primarily based on their day-to-day experience. *Prima facie*, we find a relative absence of fundamental business organisation knowledge in these small entrepreneurs. Another explanation is their relatively limited growth ambitions—to some extent, they seem to disbelieve that entrepreneurship means the aspiration to create a "private kingdom" (cf. Schumpeter, 1934). Concerning their physiological transformation, another finding during data collection is that most respondents showed a relative "teacher-like disposition" toward the interviewers (who were mostly younger). One explanation for this behaviour is the introversion that characterises these firms, which led these small entrepreneurs to seek relative concealment of their weaknesses, trying to "go on the offensive" as they felt criticised. Therefore, we conclude that these less competitive firms transformed for the worse—in terms of physiology—during the Greek crisis.[1]

Second, the research that first introduced the Stra.Tech.Man physiology seems to be reaffirmed (see Vlados, 2004), as it argued that most Greek firms are monad-centred, leading the entire socioeconomic system to a problematic adaptation to globalisation. These four field surveys we conducted in the REMTh show an apparent dominance of monad-centric entrepreneurship forms, especially in low-value-added sectors (cf. Fig. 10.2). They also reflect the challenges of adapting to the new globalisation; the achievement of RASI objectives seems increasingly distant for these enterprises, making the REMTh—*lato sensu*—relatively weak regarding its sustainable development trajectory.

Third, as it seems, the small entrepreneurs of such weak firms (in organisational dynamics) tend to invent external enemies to cover up their competitive shortcomings. They do not seem to analyse in depth their internal weaknesses (due to introversion), exhausting themselves on the external threats that are reasonably multiplying for them. Hence, traditional—mainly neoclassical or neo-Keynesian-oriented—macro–meso policies for the horizontal reinforcement of spatial entities are becoming increasingly ineffective nowadays (cf. Chatzinikolaou et al., 2021; Nelson et al., 2018). Since physiological differences are subtle and complex, approaches that see homogeneous firms in specific sectors appear increasingly myopic (cf. Gomes & Gubareva, 2021). Ostensibly, entrepreneurship support policies today should focus on providing business development tools—not simply stimulating demand with cheap or "free money"—to help these organisations hybridise into more flexible forms of Stra.Tech.Man physiology.

If there are enough sick people, the state must ensure that hospitals are built. Similarly, in economies with many less competitive firms, policymakers should ensure that they provide mechanisms to strengthen their physiology that is, resources for hiring professional consultants or providing in-house advice (e.g., Adam-Smith & McGeever, 1995). We contend that the Institutes for Local Development and Innovation—a mechanism for intervention and policy articulation introduced by Chatzinikolaou and Vlados (2021) but not yet implemented on the ground—is a step in the right direction. As Chatzinikolaou and Vlados (2021) argue, the aim of this proposed entrepreneurship support institution in regional entrepreneurial ecosystems could be to interconnect actors that can foster entrepreneurship and that are uncoordinated in a region, providing "Stra.Tech.Man business clinic" services. This institution could be a mechanism to strengthen less competitive organisations in the REMTh, as the diagnosis of physiology presented in this chapter could be a form of service provision. Such an intervention at the meso–micro level could monitor its development environment and take initiatives to coordinate relevant actors. It could also offer free advice through grants or own interventions (essentially being a "business clinic") and publish region-wide development results periodically (e.g., annually).

5.2 Limitations and Prospects

Inevitably, the present chapter is subject to some limitations that must be mentioned but are nonetheless potential prospects for future research. The physiological transformation we have studied concerns developments that preceded the COVID-19 pandemic and the Russian invasion that is currently changing the global energy and geo-economic map. Therefore, we believe an update of the research could shed light on new aspects. It also did not consider the apparent high performance of the Greek economy after its crisis and the increasingly important role that the REMTh is nowadays acquiring due to the strategic importance of the region's ports for the Western alliance and the US. Also, the findings are inevitably limited to the REMTh. Future research could explore the physiological transformation of other areas—possibly more (or less) developed European–Greek regions. Such a re-approach would probably make the findings more reliable. Finally, a form of pilot support for some enterprises in the form of free consultancy could serve as a springboard to see whether a policy for supporting them with such tools would make sense as it would strengthen their physiology. However, most of the less capable entrepreneurs—in terms of integrating their businesses into a sustainable growth spiral of the region—said that they do not wish to cooperate further with our team, which makes their empowerment an intractable problem.

Note

1. Nevertheless, there were some exceptional cases of companies that deserve mention. We merely examined the apparent trends for most firms, focusing on less dynamic micro-businesses in the tertiary sector. However, by distributing the same questionnaires to more dynamic exporting firms (some employing more than 250 employees; cf. SEVE, 2018), we saw the distance between less and more developed firms in the REMTh. We also observed that even massive or flexible firms could have monad-centred elements.

References

Adam-Smith, D., & McGeever, M. (1995). Training and Enterprise Councils and small- and medium-sized enterprises: Not meeting needs or just not meeting the customer? *Journal of Small Business and Enterprise Development, 2*(3), 149–157. https://doi.org/10.1108/eb020957

Andrikopoulos, A., & Nastopoulos, C. (2015). *Κρίση και ρεαλισμός [Crisis and realism]. Propobos.* Publications.

Annoni, P., & Dijkstra, L. (2019). *The EU regional competitiveness index 2019.* Publications Office of the European Union.

Belyaeva, Z., & Lopatkova, Y. (2020). The impact of digitalization and sustainable development goals in SMEs' strategy: A multi-country European study. In A. Thrassou, D. Vrontis, Y. Weber, S. M. R. Shams, & E. Tsoukatos (Eds.), *The changing role of SMEs in global business: Volume II: contextual evolution across markets, disciplines and sectors* (pp. 15–38). Springer International Publishing. https://doi.org/10.1007/978-3-030-45835-5_2

Bhattacharya, A., Khanna, D., Schweizer, C., & Bijapurkar, A. (2017, April 25). The new globalization: Going beyond the rhetoric. *BCG Henderson Institute.* https://www.bcg.com/en-gr/publications/2017/new-globalization-going-beyond-rhetoric.aspx

Boden, M. (2017). RIS3 Implementation in Lagging Regions: Lessons from Eastern Macedonia and Thrace. *European Structural & Investment Funds Journal, 5*(1), 77–83.

Boden, M., dos Santos, P., Haegeman, K., Marinelli, E., & Valero, S. (2015). *European parliament preparatory action: Actual and desired state of the economic potential in regions outside the Greek capital Athens* (EUR 27570). Publications Office of the European Union. https://doi.org/10.2791/34670

Chatzinikolaou, D., Demertzis, M., & Vlados, C. (2021). European entrepreneurship reinforcement policies in macro, meso, and micro terms for the post-COVID-19 era. *Review of European Studies, 13*(2), 39–56. https://doi.org/10.5539/res.v13n2p39

Chatzinikolaou, D., & Vlados, C. (2019). Evolutionary economics and the Stra.Tech.Man approach of the firm into globalization dynamics. *Business, Management and Economics Research, 5*(10), 146–160. https://doi.org/10.32861/bmer.510.146.160

Chatzinikolaou, D., & Vlados, Ch. (2022a). Crisis, innovation and change management: A blind spot for micro-firms? *Journal of Entrepreneurship in Emerging Economies.* https://www.emerald.com/insight/content/doi/10.1108/JEEE-07-2022-0210/full/html

Chatzinikolaou, D., & Vlados, C. (2022b). The world system's mutational crisis and the emergence of the new globalization. In B. Lamotte (Ed.), *Économie sociale et crises du XXIe siècle* (pp. 163–192). L'Harmattan.

Corbin, J. M., & Strauss, A. L. (2015). *Basics of qualitative research: Techniques and procedures for developing grounded theory*. Sage.

Corbridge, C., Rugg, G., Major, N. P., Shadbolt, N. R., & Burton, A. M. (1994). Laddering: Technique and tool use in knowledge acquisition. *Knowledge Acquisition, 6*(3), 315–341. https://doi.org/10.1006/knac.1994.1016

Dopfer, K., Foster, J., & Potts, J. (2004). Micro-meso-macro. *Journal of Evolutionary Economics, 14*(3), 263–279. https://doi.org/10.1007/s00191-004-0193-0

European Commission: Joint Research Centre. (2021). *Higher education for smart specialisation: The case of Eastern Macedonia and Thrace*. Publications Office. https://data.europa.eu/doi/10.2760/612671

Foray, D. (2014). From smart specialisation to smart specialisation policy. *European Journal of Innovation Management, 17*(4), 492–507. https://doi.org/10.1108/EJIM-09-2014-0096

Foster, J. (1997). The analytical foundations of evolutionary economics: From biological analogy to economic self-organization. *Structural Change and Economic Dynamics, 8*(4), 427–451. https://doi.org/10.1016/S0954-349X(97)00002-7

Giotopoulos, I., Kontolaimou, A., & Tsakanikas, A. (2017). Antecedents of growth-oriented entrepreneurship before and during the Greek economic crisis. *Journal of Small Business and Enterprise Development, 24*(3), 528–544. https://doi.org/10.1108/JSBED-01-2017-0003

Global Entrepreneurship Monitor. (2022). *Global entrepreneurship monitor 2021/2022 Global report: Opportunity amid disruption*. GEM.

Gomes, O., & Gubareva, M. (2021). Complex systems in economics and where to find them. *Journal of Systems Science and Complexity, 34*(1), 314–338. https://doi.org/10.1007/s11424-020-9149-1

Hamel, G., & Prahalad, C. K. (1989). Strategic intent. *Harvard Business Review, 67*(3), 63–76.

Hodgson, G., & Knudsen, T. (2004). The firm as an interactor: Firms as vehicles for habits and routines. *Journal of Evolutionary Economics, 14*(3), 281–307. https://doi.org/10.1007/s00191-004-0192-1

Karagouni, G. (2018). The role of Dynamic Entrepreneurial Capabilities and innovation in intergenerational succession of family firms. In D. Vrontis, Y. Weber, A. Thrassou, S. M. R. Shams, & E. Tsoukatos (Eds.), *Innovation and capacity building: Cross-disciplinary management theories for practical applications* (pp. 31–54). Springer International Publishing. https://doi.org/10.1007/978-3-319-90945-5_3

Killian, L. J. (2021). Taming the dark side of the new globalization. In S. H. Park, M. A. Gonzalez-Perez, & D. E. Floriani (Eds.), *The Palgrave handbook of corporate sustainability in the digital era* (pp. 355–376). Springer International Publishing. https://doi.org/10.1007/978-3-030-42412-1_18

Lampadarios, E., & Kyriakidou, N. (2020). Critical success factors for SMEs in the UK chemical distribution industry: The 'Brexit' Effect. In A. Thrassou, D. Vrontis, Y. Weber, S. M. R. Shams, & E. Tsoukatos (Eds.), *The changing role of SMEs in global business: Volume I: paradigms of opportunities and challenges* (pp. 155–177). Springer International Publishing. https://doi.org/10.1007/978-3-030-45831-7_8

Lindlof, T. R., & Taylor, B. C. (2002). *Qualitative communication research methods* (2nd ed.). Sage Publications.

Marshall, A. (1890). *Principles of economics*. Macmillan.

McCrae, N., & Purssell, E. (2016). Is it really theoretical? A review of sampling in grounded theory studies in nursing journals. *Journal of Advanced Nursing, 72*(10), 2284–2293. https://doi.org/10.1111/jan.12986

Migliaccio, G., & Rossetti, L. U. (2020). Italian furniture sector SMEs: Sustainability and commercial ethics. In A. Thrassou, D. Vrontis, Y. Weber, S. M. R. Shams, & E. Tsoukatos (Eds.), *The changing role of SMEs in global business: Volume II: Contextual evolution across markets, disciplines and sectors* (pp. 225–259). Springer International Publishing. https://doi.org/10.1007/978-3-030-45835-5_11

Mintzberg, H. (1987). The strategy concept I: Five Ps for strategy. *California Management Review, 30*(1), 11–24. https://doi.org/10.2307/41165263

Montanari, S., & Kocollari, U. (2020). Defining the SME: A multi-perspective investigation. In A. Thrassou, D. Vrontis, Y. Weber, S. M. R. Shams, & E. Tsoukatos (Eds.), *The changing role of SMEs in global business: Volume II: Contextual evolution across markets, disciplines and sectors* (pp. 61–82). Springer International Publishing. https://doi.org/10.1007/978-3-030-45835-5_4

Moore, J. (1993). Predators and prey: A new ecology of competition. *Harvard Business Review, 71*(3), 75–86.

Neergaard, H., & Ulhøi, J. P. (Eds.). (2007). *Handbook of qualitative research methods in entrepreneurship*. Edward Elgar.

Nelson, R., Dosi, G., Helfat, C., Winter, S., Pyka, A., Saviotti, P., Lee, K., Malerba, F., & Dopfer, K. (2018). *Modern evolutionary economics: An overview*. Cambridge University Press.

Nelson, R., & Winter, S. (1982). *An evolutionary theory of economic change*. The Belknap Press of Harvard University Press.

Onyama, D. N. (2021). *Profitability, productivity, and sustainability: Organizational behavior and strategic alignment*. Routledge.

Peters, T. J., & Waterman, R. H. (1982). *In search of excellence: Lessons from America's best-run companies*. Harper & Row.

Ponterotto, J. (2006). Brief note on the origins, evolution, and meaning of the qualitative research concept thick description. *The Qualitative Report, 11*(3), 538–549. https://doi.org/10.46743/2160-3715/2006.1666

Porter, M. (1980). *Competitive strategy: Techniques for analyzing industries and competitors*. Free Press.

Porter, M. (1990). *The competitive advantage of nations*. Free Press.

Region of Eastern Macedonia–Thrace. (2014). *Το Επιχειρησιακό Πρόγραμμα «Ανατολική Μακεδονία και Θράκη» 2014–2020 [The Operational Programme "Eastern Macedonia and Thrace" 2014–2020]*. https://www.eydamth.gr/index.php/extras/to-programma

Regional Innovation Scoreboard. (2021). *Regional innovation scoreboard 2021: Regional profile of Greece*. https://research-and-innovation.ec.europa.eu/statistics/performance-indicators/regional-innovation-scoreboard_en

Rinkinen, S., & Harmaakorpi, V. (2018). The business ecosystem concept in innovation policy context: Building a conceptual framework. *Innovation: The European Journal of Social Science Research, 31*(3), 333–349. https://doi.org/10.1080/13511610.2017.1300089

Ross, J. A., Rolheiser, C., & Hogaboam-Gray, A. (1998). Skills training versus action research in-service: Impact on student attitudes to self-evaluation. *Teaching and Teacher Education, 14*(5), 463–477. https://doi.org/10.1016/S0742-051X(97)00054-1

Ryle, G. (2009). The thinking of thoughts: What is 'Le Penseur'doing? In *Collected Essays 1929–1968* (pp. 516–532). Routledge.

Schumpeter, J. (1934). *The theory of economic development: An inquiry into profits, capital, credit, interest, and the business cycle* (R. Opie, Trans.; Reprint Edition: New Brunswick, N.J, Transaction Books, 1983, Social science classics series). Harvard University Press.

SEVE. (2018). *Χαρτογράφηση της εξαγωγικής δραστηριότητας της Ελλάδας ανά περιφέρεια [Mapping the export activity of Greece per region]*. Greek

Exporters Association. https://www.seve.gr/wp-content/uploads/2019/12/ΠΕΡΙΦΕΡΕΙΑΚΑ_2014-2018_Short-Version.pdf

Teece, D. J., Pisano, G., & Shuen, A. (1997). Dynamic capabilities and strategic management. *Strategic Management Journal, 18*(7), 509–533. https://doi.org/10.1002/(SICI)1097-0266(199708)18:7<509::AID-SMJ882>3.0.CO;2-Z

Thrassou, A., Vrontis, D., Efthymiou, L., & Uzunboylu, N. (2022a). An overview of business advancement through technology: Markets and marketing in transition. In A. Thrassou, D. Vrontis, L. Efthymiou, Y. Weber, S. M. R. Shams, & E. Tsoukatos (Eds.), *Business advancement through technology volume I* (Palgrave Studies in Cross-disciplinary Business Research, in Association with EuroMed Academy of Business). Palgrave Macmillan. https://doi.org/10.1007/978-3-031-07769-2_1

Thrassou, A., Vrontis, D., Efthymiou, L., & Uzunboylu, N. (2022b). An overview of business advancement through technology: the changing landscape of work and Employment. In A. Thrassou, D. Vrontis, L. Efthymiou, Y. Weber, S. M. R. Shams, & E. Tsoukatos (Eds.), *Business advancement through technology volume II* (Palgrave Studies in Cross-disciplinary Business Research, in Association with EuroMed Academy of Business). Palgrave Macmillan. https://doi.org/10.1007/978-3-031-07765-4_1

Vargas-Hernández, J. G., & Orozco Quijano, E. P. (2022). Business under crisis: Strategic organizational sustainability—a contextual transformation. In D. Vrontis, A. Thrassou, Y. Weber, S. M. R. Shams, E. Tsoukatos, & L. Efthymiou (Eds.), *Business under crisis, volume III: Avenues for innovation, entrepreneurship and sustainability* (pp. 19–45). Springer International Publishing. https://doi.org/10.1007/978-3-030-76583-5_2

Vlados, Ch. (2004). *La dynamique du triangle stratégie, technologie et management: L'insertion des entreprises grecques dans la globalisation [The dynamics of the triangle of strategy, technology and management: The insertion of Greek enterprises into globalisation]* [Thèse de doctorat de Sciences Économiques, Université de Paris X-Nanterre]. http://www.theses.fr/2004PA100022

Vlados, C., & Chatzinikolaou, D. (2019a). Business ecosystems policy in Stra.Tech.Man terms: The case of the Eastern Macedonia and Thrace region. *Journal of Entrepreneurship, Management and Innovation, 15*(3), 163–197. https://doi.org/10.7341/20191536

Vlados, C., & Chatzinikolaou, D. (2019b). Strategy perception and implementation on less developed business ecosystems micro and small enterprises: The service sector of Eastern Macedonia and Thrace. *Business Management and Strategy, 10*(2), 27–63. https://doi.org/10.5296/bms.v10i2.15008

Vlados, C., & Chatzinikolaou, D. (2020). Stra.Tech.Man innovation, HRM and perception of educational needs in underdeveloped business ecosystems: The case of retail sector firms in Eastern Macedonia and Thrace. *International Journal of Human Resource Studies, 10*(2), 330–354. https://doi.org/10.5296/ijhrs.v10i2.17139

Vlados, C., Koronis, E., & Chatzinikolaou, D. (2021). Entrepreneurship and crisis in Greece from a neo-Schumpeterian perspective: A suggestion to stimulate the development process at the local level. *Research in World Economy, 12*(2), 1–16. https://doi.org/10.5430/rwe.v12n2p1

Winter, R. (1982). "Dilemma Analysis": A contribution to methodology for action research. *Cambridge Journal of Education, 12*(3), 161–174. https://doi.org/10.1080/0305764820120303

Witt, U. (2006). Evolutionary concepts in economics and biology. *Journal of Evolutionary Economics, 16*(5), 473–476. https://doi.org/10.1007/s00191-006-0034-4

World Economic Forum. (2018). *Agile governance: Reimagining policy-making in the Fourth Industrial Revolution* [White Paper]. https://www.weforum.org/whitepapers/agile-governance-reimagining-policy-making-in-the-fourth-industrial-revolution/

Yitshaki, R., & Kropp, F. (2016). Motivations and opportunity recognition of social entrepreneurs. *Journal of Small Business Management, 54*(2), 546–565. https://doi.org/10.1111/jsbm.12157

11

Sustainability for Healthcare Organisations and Systems: Cultivating Strategy and Governance Processes for a Better Future

Lior Naamati-Schneider and Fiorella Pia Salvatore

1 Introduction

Healthcare systems and organisations face enormous and complex challenges because of the changing ecosystem surrounding them, including economic, demographic, and technological changes (Benjamin, 2010; Frist, 2014; WHO, 2016, 2017). The continuing demand for health services is a product of the increase in life expectancy that has accompanied the ageing of the population and an increase in the rate of chronic diseases. This demand is reflected in the growing development of services

L. Naamati-Schneider (✉)
Health Systems Management Department, Hadassah Academic College Jerusalem, Jerusalem, Israel
e-mail: Liorna@hac.ac.il

F. P. Salvatore
Department of Economics, Università di Foggia, Foggia, Italy
e-mail: fiorellapia.salvatore@unifg.it

D. Vrontis et al. (eds.), *Business for Sustainability, Volume I*, Palgrave Studies in Cross-disciplinary Business Research, In Association with EuroMed Academy of Business, https://doi.org/10.1007/978-3-031-37361-9_11

and technologies in healthcare fields, but it is not accompanied by growth in financial resources (Schmid et al., 2010).

These changes in the complex ecosystem of healthcare organisations create a turbulent, challenging, and competitive environment with which the organisations and their leaders must contend in order to survive (Denis & van Gestel, 2015; Ginter, 2018). The gap between growing healthcare spending and the limited funding for healthcare organisations and systems is undoubtedly one of the most challenging problems facing healthcare today and threatening its future sustainability. The constantly increasing gap between the development-spurred demand and budgetary constraints must be bridged, and healthcare systems must adapt and change in order to survive. These needs have driven healthcare organisations to change their managerial, organisational, and economic behaviour (Bin-Nun & Ofer, 2006; Boehm, 1998; McKee & Healy, 2002; Naamati-Schneider, 2021; Schmid et al., 2010).

Furthermore, healthcare organisations have always been committed to identifying sustainable organisational and managerial solutions that enable them to respond successfully to the pressures to which they are subjected. The current health emergency, linked to the spread of the COVID-19 pandemic, has significantly increased the pressure on various healthcare entities and, in particular, on some healthcare organisations, such as hospitals, to substantially reorganise their activities and services (Elarabi & Johari, 2014; Zangrandi et al., 2020). Given the complexity of the activities that characterise healthcare organisations and the current scenario of profound change, it is essential to reset corporate governance processes and strategic processes in order to respond effectively to these pressures and generate a positive impact on the performance of healthcare organisations (Zangrandi et al., 2020).

The COVID-19 pandemic accelerated processes of change worldwide, especially in the medical field, because of the need to provide high-quality healthcare services under conditions of severe stress, lack of familiarity with the illness, patient overload, and staff shortages. At the same time, healthcare organisations experienced a substantial decrease in cash flow caused by a drastic decline in other patient services and a reduction in the number of elective surgeries and other medical activities (Argenziano et al., 2020; Naamati-Schneider & Zaks, 2022). These factors have contributed to the development of telemedicine services by applying information and communications technologies (ICT) to healthcare services. This application of ICT has aroused great interest among healthcare managers, who aim to use new and renewed methods for providing healthcare services (Salvatore & Fanelli, 2021a, 2021b).

In general, the context of profound instability that currently characterises the economic, social, and even healthcare systems has severely damaged the organisations' reputations as well as their structure by forcing them to produce an immediate and creative variety of medical, managerial, and financial solutions to address the damage caused by the crisis (Bar, 2020; Ron & Weiss, 2020). This ongoing health crisis, together with other types of problems, such as economic crises, has put a strain on healthcare organisations around the world (Bozorgmehr et al., 2020).

In Agenda 2030, signed in 2015 (United Nations, 2016) and made up of 17 sustainable development goals, goal No. 3, 'good health and well-being', aims to improve the unified vision of the health system, incorporating an integrated and sustainable business approach in healthcare organisations. The provision of local healthcare services, the implementation of technologies to increase the sustainability of regional health supply chains by facilitating the transition toward a circular economy, a more marked propensity for interconnection with other health industry chains, and adaptation in terms of accountability to new and renewed accounting systems, represent the main challenges with which top management in healthcare organisations must contend.

Indeed, these challenges, together with the technological renewal resulting from the fourth industrial revolution, must make businesses and their stakeholders ready to face and implement new changes in their organisational structures (Tjahjono et al., 2017).

Gruchmann et al. (2019) assert that the individual can be indifferent to sustainable business practices when these are not properly communicated. In this regard, to remove the information asymmetry, Corporate Social Responsibility (CSR) can be of support. CSR can act as a connector between the entities' social responsibility goals and the application of these sustainable practices and technologies in healthcare organisations (Hah & Freeman, 2011). Healthcare organisations have already applied CSR by encouraging the concrete application of sustainable practices and allowing for greater accessibility, providing what can be seen as a 'universalisation of opportunities' (Asante Antwi et al., 2021). In this sense, healthcare organisations that voluntarily adopt CSR contribute positively to society (Torugsa et al., 2012).

Many healthcare organisations have adopted practices derived from the principles of ethical respect and sustainability, and this is a reason for great pride. However, there is a need to scale them up, bring them to the community's attention, and disseminate them as widely as possible (Cruz & Boehe, 2010). Therefore, the social responsibility of healthcare organisations is also promoted by their commitment to achieving global sustainable goals. These goals make it possible to benefit the common good. Sustainable practices, which are included in CSR, ultimately facilitate recognising healthcare organisations' link with their social responsibilities. Given this background, the main focus is on the rationalisation of healthcare spending and the need to constantly aim for efficiency without compromising the quality of the healthcare system. In this sense, the healthcare organisations' peculiarities, the managerial approach to achieving good performance, and management control enable informed choices while respecting specific levels of effectiveness and efficiency (Lunkes et al., 2018). This may be achieved by adopting methods and behaviours that preserve the planet's resources, the natural environment, and ecosystems and allow them to renew themselves. Today's sustainability approach increasingly guides human activity, even in the economic realm.

In this chapter, we present and map change processes in a particular healthcare organisation, the hospital, based on a literature review of the topic and in-depth interviews with medical staff. First, we will review the concept of sustainability and the way it affects health systems and healthcare organisations; we will also address this by reviewing relevant recent literature. Further, we will present the themes that were obtained in the analysis. Deepening and expanding knowledge of this topic may help decision-makers in the field make system-wide decisions related to managing the system, adopting efficient managerial tools, avoiding resistance to change, and making it more efficient and sustainable. This will enable the laying of the foundations for change and, therefore, for the structural improvement of the healthcare organisation as a whole.

2 Nurturing Sustainability: Impact on Health Systems and Healthcare Organizations

'Sustainability' refers to a kind of development and human activity that meets the current needs of humankind but does not harm future generations' ability to meet their own needs. It can be used to guide decisions at the global, national, and individual levels (Berg, 2019). Sustainability is commonly described in terms of three pillars: environmental, economic, and social (Purvis et al., 2019). The *Three Pillars of Sustainability* Model first appeared in the Treaty of Amsterdam in 1997, elaborated by the European Commission (Council of the European Union, 1997). In this model, the concept of sustainability includes the environment and is also related to economic development and social organisations (Kash et al., 2014). Therefore, even in healthcare organisations, sustainable development lays its foundations on environmental, social, and economic pillars (Infante et al., 2013).

More specifically, from an environmental point of view, the efficient and effective development of the constitutive characteristics and the lasting economic functionality of healthcare organisations, as well as a good and careful design of the structures and business processes, enables the reduction of travel and thus pollution, limits the emergence of new healthcare facilities, and reduces medical waste (Dullet et al., 2017; Vidal-Alaball et al., 2019).

From a social point of view, healthcare organisations must increasingly allow patients to have a more comfortable healthcare experience and facilitate their involvement in decision-making processes by generating a sort of corporate social reporting. This will increase the feeling of general well-being experienced within the healthcare organisation (Leoni et al., 2021).

Finally, concerning economic sustainability, the development of both the constitutive characteristics of healthcare organisations and the systems used to carry out company assessments represent tools capable of generating income, work, and greater efficiency of services. In terms of income, it creates new job opportunities for developing and implementing new technologies in the organisation (Lai & Stacchezzini, 2021; Lombrano & Iacuzzi, 2020). In terms of performance efficiency, the new tools for assessing corporate financing will enable more careful management of resources and general savings for healthcare organisations (Salvioni & Gennari, 2016).

Sustainable management and its activities are aimed at improving the patient's quality of life, positively affecting physicians' and healthcare managers' perceptions of the sustainability concept (Rich et al., 2018). In other words, the sustainability concept has contributed to a re-evaluation of the links between economic growth and the environment (Cavicchi & Vagnoni, 2017).

Strategic governance is an essential business function that enables healthcare managers to improve the analysis of internal and external environmental factors from a sustainable perspective. In the healthcare context, strategic governance planning consists of a basket of aims, indications, and updates of business scenarios to specify the main operations performed by healthcare organisations (Ginter et al., 2018; Rodríguez-Labajos et al., 2018). However, strategic governance planning can also be seen as the point at which the company's arrangement for achieving its aims begins (Clarke et al., 2014).

Moreover, healthcare sustainability can also be seen as the ability to use technology to enable the health system to do much more with existing resources or with the addition of practical resources. Therefore, this challenge has driven the system to seek various creative solutions while adopting managerial solutions, new accounting models, and business behavioural patterns to survive and increase sustainable health outcomes. As part of these solutions, healthcare organisations have adopted digital transformation processes, among other solutions, to build back better (Braithwaite et al., 2016). This goal is achieved by looking toward the future and identifying intermediate targets, rather than returning to the same patterns that created threats and prevented resilience to such crises as COVID-19 (Khan et al., 2020; Raghavan et al., 2021). In the economic sense of COVID-19, for example, being 'built back better' means investing in a sustainable economy that strengthens the environment and the climate and does not harm them. For health systems and organisations to become sustainable, they must adapt to the ever-changing challenges and complex turbulent environment surrounding them

(Braithwaite et al., 2018). Given the similarity in need for enhancing the workforce, providing efficient development, and ensuring that clinicians keep up-to-date with technological changes (Thrassou et al., 2022a, 2022b), coupled with budgetary limitations, the question of how to provide financially viable, efficient, accessible, and affordable healthcare for all is relevant for all healthcare systems and challenges every country (Braithwaite et al., 2018).

Delivering affordable, cost-effective outcomes over time requires multiple adaptive approaches, coordinated action, and numerous stakeholders (Chambers et al., 2013; Fineberg & Lecture, 2012). To be sustainable, their resources need to meet their objectives. Therefore, policymakers and healthcare managers should achieve sustainable goals by implementing improvements, interventions, and change strategies (Braithwaite et al., 2018).

3 Research Design and Methods

This chapter presents a preliminary study that combines a literature review based on strategic changes in Israel's healthcare system in the last decade and a categorical qualitative pilot study based on open-ended, in-depth interviews with managers and doctors within the health system, in order to construct a grounded theory (Shkedi, 2011; Shleski & Alpert, 2007; Tsabar Ben Yehoshua, 2016). The analysis of the interviews affords a broad view of the processes of change that the healthcare market is undergoing. This qualitative approach was chosen because it allows participants to respond in their own words and offer their perspectives on how the organisations are coping with the process of change described above. Adaptability and sustainability require strategic change at all levels of the organisations (Naamati-Schneider, 2020, 2021). Therefore, managers and clinicians are subject to complex situations and many environmental factors, as well as internal factors—that is, the staff—whose character and worldviews are crucial in bringing about change. Their perceptions and attitudes are integral parts of the organisation's complex reality, culture, and environmental influences that form the background for change (Samuel, 2012).

4 Findings

There is a widespread consensus that healthcare systems and their organisations consistently implement strategic, managerial, and renewed accounting and marketing processes to adapt to the surrounding ecosystem and its demands. The analysis of the data in this study reveals that most of the professionals working within the system agree that to be a part of this process, they must embrace change and focus on sustainability, especially after facing the pandemic crisis.

Healthcare managers and professionals working in healthcare organisations represent the main actors in obtaining sustainable performance. They play a decisive role in supporting the achievement of high corporate standards as they engage in clinical and other activities (Fanelli et al., 2019). Many of them have managerial positions that assume high levels of organisational responsibility. Consequently, the traditional practices of human resource management, characterised by a strong bureaucratisation of processes, must be questioned to facilitate management models aimed at supporting and enhancing professionals in their managerial roles while being attentive to sustainability practices (Brown, 2004).

The professionals usually refer to 'sustainability' as a substitute for the term 'efficiency'. For them, 'sustainable health' mainly means the aspiration to use technology to enable the health system to do much more with existing resources or with additional practical resources. Therefore, in this context, there are several main categories related to digital transformation as a systemic change that brings with it outstanding efficiency and effectiveness. The categories are digital transformation for sustainability, digital services tools, patient empowerment through digital transformation, and challenges and barriers to the processes.

4.1 Digital Transformation

Digital transformation is one of the characteristics of the twenty-first century, forcing the world to adapt to frequent technological changes in many fields, including the healthcare sector (Marques & Ferreira, 2020; Schwab, 2017). In healthcare organisations, the implementation of digital transformation involves managerial practices and accounting models. It also involves organisational and strategic changes to improve medical and organisational performance according to the sustainable perspective and to promote high-quality, efficient, and accessible healthcare services. In addition, the changes include the various uses of technological developments to provide significant business value to clients (patients) and organisations (Naamati-Schneider, 2022, 2023).

Digital transformation includes using high-tech products and technologies in the healthcare world, information and communication technologies (ICT), and innovative solutions for many health-related activities. Among these solutions are the use of artificial intelligence; the use of big data for research, treatment, and improvement of the organisation's managerial process; sharing of information between health organisations to create a treatment continuum; personalised medicine; implementation of robotics in treatment and surgery; the use of digital tools and apps for diagnosis and treatment; and development of distance services (Marques & Ferreira, 2020; Salvatore & Fanelli, 2021b). In addition, healthcare professionals point out that adopting these processes helps healthcare organisations improve their reputation and gain a competitive edge in their highly competitive environment (Matt et al., 2015; Naamati-Schneider, 2020).

The digital transformation has enabled healthcare organisations to expand their activities, retain clientele throughout the pandemic, and even generate income. The transformation involved partnering with start-up and biotech companies and technologies that made immediate solutions possible to such problems as providing telemedicine, distance data analysis, distance monitoring of patients, touchless technology treatment, robotics, and innovative respiratory devices. Thus, the current crisis intensified the digital revolution and the business processes of healthcare organisations. In this sense, digital change may partially solve sustainability challenges by providing high-quality and readily available medical services even under challenging conditions.

Digital transformation in healthcare is emerging as a sustainable way to support the capacity building of healthcare services (Salvatore & Fanelli, 2021a, 2021b). It is well known that all investments in sustainable digital transformation reduce the expenditure of the organisation's resources and, at the same time, increase the sustainability of the health system (Cavicchi et al., 2019). The regular use of digital technology, in fact, has allowed the dematerialisation of some services; for example, the collection of patient data through electronic medical records. To ensure that the combination of digital transformation strategies within the assets of healthcare organisations is a sustainable action, it is necessary to identify a process that facilitates the inclusion of social factors within the supply chain of digital technologies (Faggini et al., 2019; Polese et al., 2018). Thus, the greater the skills that local healthcare organisations have, the more programs for using digital applications are effectively used on the territory. This correlation is made up of variables that impact each other, developing the sustainability of the entire healthcare system in which the organisations are located (Lai & Stacchezzini, 2021).

However, up to now, there is enormous diversity in the scope of embracing and implementing strategies for change and adaptation in the healthcare system and organisations worldwide because the processes are introduced only partially, primarily because of the difficulties involved and because of opposition by staff, managers, and clients (Naamati-Schneider, 2020, 2021). According to the analysis, digital transformation gained momentum following the outbreak of the COVID-19 pandemic in 2020 because the constraints of social distancing meant that the system and the staff needed to implement immediate changes for diagnosis and treatment (Confortes, 2020a; Peek et al., 2020).

4.2 Digital Customer Services Tools

Digital transformation in healthcare customer services is one of the themes that arose from the analysis. Telemedicine and treating patients by means of digital tools are also emerging as sustainable ways of supporting capacity building of healthcare services in developing countries.

In times of crisis, such as the COVID-19 pandemic, the adoption of telehealth digital care has been one of the main tools for coping with the constraints of social distancing (Confortes, 2020a; Peek et al., 2020). Digital tools for distance diagnosis and treatment, such as robotics for identification and the use of telemedicine for communication and medical treatment, have become essential tools for organisations to survive in crises and beyond (Confortes, 2020b; Naamati-Schneider, 2020; Naamati-Schneider & Zaks, 2022).

According to the professionals interviewed in this study, it is commonly assumed that investing in these digital tools for health services is a step toward making the organisation more sustainable, and this view is apparent in the literature review as well. According to AlJaberi et al. (2020) and Cavicchi et al. (2019), all telemedicine investments reduce the disease burden while growing the healthcare system's sustainability as a whole. In many cases, to achieve and develop digital services tools, the health system needs to collaborate with, and rely on, the high-tech and biotech industries. Healthcare systems and organisations have become a more integrated ecosystem that includes biopharma, MedTech, and digital health and healthcare in a single bio-convergent industry (Israel's Life Sciences Industry IATI Report, 2019; Naamati Schneider & Zaks, 2020).

Similarly, using the resources of telemedicine for health services, such as patient data collection by creating online archives, requires using the resources of other authorities and organisations, such as HMOs, and collaborations between them. However, to guarantee the sustainable effectiveness of the integration between telemedicine strategies and healthcare systems and organisations, a collaborative technique is needed to identify the best practices and evidence-based trials and to include social factors in the supply of telemedicine services (Salvatore & Fanelli, 2021a, 2021b).

4.3 Patient Empowerment through Digital Transformation

The professionals point out that digital tools will be an excellent way to strengthen and empower patients. Viewing their medical information and becoming active in the therapeutic and administrative processes make patients part of the treatment. They can follow the management of their treatment, make appointments, and manage their medical file, thus becoming the centre of the treatment. Centring the patient has been recognised by medical practitioners in recent years as building trust and improving the therapist–patient relationship and the patient's response to the proposed treatment (Naamati-Schneider, 2020). This optimises the treatment process and enables good cooperation between therapist and patient, thus improving and facilitating sustainable health processes.

4.4 Challenges and Barriers to the Processes

These processes of moving toward a more sustainable healthcare system force the organisation and its employees to adopt new technologies; complex organisational and managerial strategic changes are essential. However, the professionals point out many difficulties they face in the processes. Some point out that although the system is supposed to become more efficient and provide services more equitably to the population, individuals differ in their ability to take advantage of these changes.

The professionals raise the issue of opposition to adopting the change processes, both on the part of the population and the part of the employees and staff. There are also differences within the same organisation at different levels of management. This indicates a difficulty in implementing strategic change processes, as observed in previous studies Naamati-Schneider, 2020, 2022.

The professionals highlight challenges in implementing new systems with the staff, difficulties in protecting patient information and confidentiality, fear of losing data, complex storage systems, the need for backups, and cyber-attacks as significant obstacles in implementing digital changes.

5 Discussion and Conclusions

Among the many changes in healthcare systems and healthcare organisations that have occurred over the past decade around the world, we can point to digital transformation as a critical process in several areas, including not only medical areas, such as healthcare services, diagnostics, treatment research, and therapeutic paths, but also managerial areas, such as organisational models, governance developments, constitutive business characteristics, and economic functionalities. All these change processes have been thought to improve the quality and effectiveness of healthcare

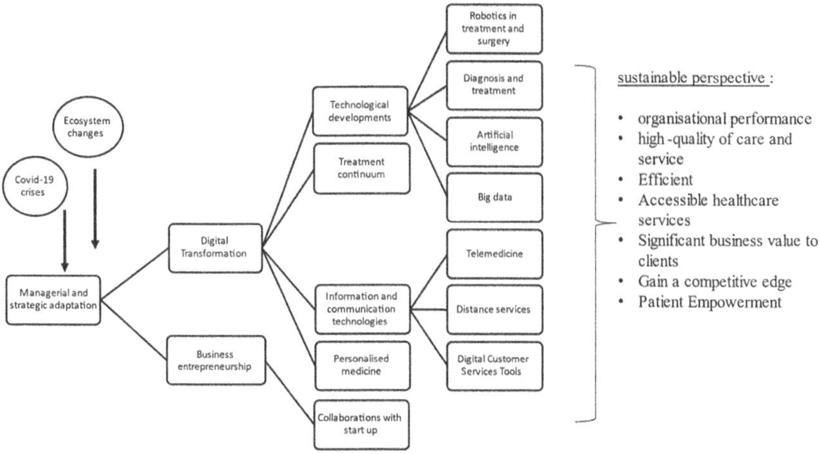

Fig. 11.1 Ecosystem changes and their implications on the sustainability of health systems organisations

services and treatment, to make treatment safer and enhance follow-up, and to improve the sustainability approach of healthcare professionals and managers and the strategies implemented by healthcare organisations, thus improving the system's sustainability. However, we have yet to learn the total cost and change in mortality in the wake of the use of digital technologies in health care (Keasberry et al., 2017) (Fig. 11.1).

The strong trend in national digital health policies (Global Observatory for eHealth, 2022) highlights the commitment many healthcare organisations are making to the use of digital technologies to promote Sustainable Development Goals, support universal health coverage, and ensure the future of healthcare. Improving the accessibility and quality of healthcare is the principal interest of health systems and the strategies envisaged by healthcare organisations worldwide. As previously mentioned, the three pillars on which the sustainability concept is based (environmental, social, and economic) also support the development of essential public healthcare functions, such as the definition of integrated health service groups, corporate healthcare policies, and multi-sectoral actions designed for patients and communities.

Digital technologies are essential resources for delivering health services, and their diffusion is growing rapidly. Indeed, in recent years, digital technology has been integrated in various areas that encourage primary care and essential health functions to protect public health. In this context, prevalent uses of digital technologies include seeking medical knowledge resources, promoting clinical support, measuring the quality of care provided, calculating the spread of infectious diseases, and monitoring supplies of drugs and vaccines.

From a community perspective, managers of healthcare organisations that incorporate digital technologies need more and more in-depth knowledge and resources to ensure that the technologies they adopt actually meet their needs and can be developed, managed, and used effectively. However, today there is enormous diversity in the extent to which healthcare systems and organisations worldwide embrace and implement strategies for change and adaptation because the processes are only partial, primarily due to difficulties and opposition by some staff managers and patients (Naamati-Schneider, 2020, 2022).

This pilot study shows that the digital transformation processes that were accelerated by the COVID-19 pandemic have become an integral part of the healthcare market's adaptation to its constantly changing, dynamic, and competitive environment. These changes are a part of the solution to the existing gap between growing healthcare spending and the limited funding for healthcare systems (Naamati-Schneider, 2020, 2021; Naamati-Schneider & Zaks, 2022). This is a global problem because health systems must contend with balancing the budget and the uncompromising demand for innovation, quality, and safety (Ricciardi et al., 2019). Embracing digital transformation is a step toward more sustainable, strong, and efficient healthcare systems and organisations, because it can be used for the benefit of the patients, the medical staff and managers, and the organisation as a whole (Denis & van Gestel, 2015).

The findings of this exploratory study align with earlier findings that map the main areas of change and point to the need for a broad study and deepening of knowledge regarding the implementation of digital transformation processes and their ramifications for healthcare organisations, managers, doctors, and patients (van der Zande et al., 2018).

Digital processes can have effects at personal, organisational, and systemic levels; therefore, these processes must be carried out within the framework of an organised change while addressing barriers, difficulties, and opposition to the process. The potential inherent in these processes is broader than the optimisation of a specific medical case, as it is an opportunity for making an inclusive change in the system. This change will optimise many services and can lead, for example, to the shortening of queues, shortening of wait times in the emergency room, reduction of hospitalisations and the duration of hospitalisation, conversion to home hospitalisations, and reduction of the workload. The change can also lead to a fundamental change in health promotion in the population while empowering the patient, making medical information accessible, increasing public health literacy, changing the population's health behaviour, and promoting quality, effective, and accessible medicine for all.

The changes will also have far-reaching consequences for the system's future, as they will enable the redesign of the supply chain of medical services to balance the needs of the system and its resources. Other consequences will also affect healthcare organisations of the future. Given the changes needed to be implemented today to use new digital technologies sustainably, healthcare organisations will increasingly be seen as essential for a modern healthcare system, in which social and economic barriers should not affect the ability to guarantee equity in the provision of sustainable care services.

Harnessing the potential of digital technologies for healthcare requires cross-sector collaboration and strategic governance planning (Romiti et al., 2022). Healthcare managers will have to develop assessment tools capable of estimating the benefits (and risks) these technologies could bring to the financing and budgets of healthcare organisations, and they must study business strategies that can enable the effective integration of promising technologies. In this way, innovative management approaches can be introduced to guarantee the realisation of benefits while avoiding any damage.

Highlighting this topic may help make system-wide decisions and adopt efficient managerial tools in order to avoid resistance to change. This will enable the laying of the foundations for change and, therefore, for the structural improvement of the healthcare organisation worldwide, ensuring a more sustainable and affordable healthcare system for the benefit of both the patient and the healthcare workers.

References

AlJaberi, O. A., Hussain, M., & Drake, P. R. A. (2020). Framework for measuring sustainability in healthcare systems. *International Journal of Healthcare Management, 13*, 276–285.

Argenziano, M., Fischkoff, K., & Smith, C. R. (2020). Surgery scheduling in a crisis. *New England Journal of Medicine*. https://doi.org/10.1056/NEJMc2017424

Asante Antwi, H., Zhou, L., Xu, X., & Mustafa, T. (2021). Beyond COVID-19 pandemic: an integrative review of global health crisis influencing the evolution and practice of corporate social responsibility. *Healthcare, 9* (4), 453. Multidisciplinary Digital Publishing Institute.

Bar, A. (2020, July 4). The positive side of the Coronavirus—A digital leap forward: People have discovered the internet's capabilities. https://www.bizportal.co.il/general/news/article/781921 (Hebrew)

Benjamin, R. M. (2010). Multiple chronic conditions: a public health challenge. *Public Health Reports, 125*, 626–627.

Berg, C. (2019). *Sustainable action: Overcoming the barriers* (1st ed.). Routledge. https://doi.org/10.4324/9780429060786

Bin-Nun, G., & Ofer, G. (2006). Ten Years of the National Health Law: 1995–2005. *The National Institute for Health Policy Research* (Hebrew).

Boehm, A. (1998). *Marketing in human services*. Tcherikover (Hebrew)

Bozorgmehr, K., Saint, K., Kaasch, A., Stuckler, D., & Kentikelenis, A. (2020). COVID and the convergence of three crises in Europe. *Lancet Public Health, 5*, e247–e248.

Braithwaite, J., Matsuyama, Y., & Mannion, R. (2016). How to do better health reform: a snapshot of change and improvement initiatives in the health systems of 30 countries. *International Journal for Quality in Health Care, 28*, 843–846.

Braithwaite, J., Testa, L., & Lamprell, G. (2017). Built to last? The sustainability of health system improvements, interventions and change strategies: a study protocol for a systematic review. *BMJ Open, 7*, e018568. https://doi.org/10.1136/bmjopen-2017-018568

Braithwaite, J., Mannion, R., Matsuyama, Y., Shekelle, P. G., Whittaker, S., Al-Adawi, S., Ludlow, K., James, W., Ting, H. P., Herkes, J., McPherson, E., Churruca, K., Lamprell, G., Ellis, L. A., Boyling, C., Warwick, M., Pomare, C., Nicklin, W., & Hughes, C. F. (2018). The future of health systems to 2030: a roadmap for global progress and sustainability. *International Journal for Quality in Health Care, 30*(10), 823–831. https://doi.org/10.1093/intqhc/mzy242

Brown, K. (2004). Human resource management in the public sector. *Public management review, 6*(3), 303–309. https://doi.org/10.1080/1471903042000256501

Cavicchi, C., Oppi, C., & Vagnoni, E. (2019). On the feasibility of integrated reporting in healthcare: A context analysis starting from a management commentary. *Journal of Management and Governance, 23*, 345–371.

Cavicchi, C., & Vagnoni, E. (2017). Does intellectual capital promote the shift of healthcare organisations toward sustainable development? Evidence from Italy. *Journal of Cleaner Production, 153*, 275–286.

Chambers, D. A., Glasgow, R. E., & Stange, K. C. (2013). The dynamic sustainability framework: addressing the paradox of sustainment amid ongoing change. *Implement Science, 8*, 117.

Clarke, C. L., Keyes, S. E., Wilkinson, H., Alexjuk, J., Wilcockson, J., Robinson, L., Corner, L., & Cattan, M. (2014). Organisational space for partnership and sustainability: lessons from the implementation of the National Dementia Strategy for England. *Health and Social Care in the Community, 22*(6), 634–645.

Confortes, Y. (2020a, April 1). How the Coronavirus reshaped health by means of technology. *Anashim ve-mahshevim.* https://www.pc.co.il/featured/313802/ (Hebrew)

Confortes, Y. (2020b, May 25). Digital health after the Coronavirus: Lessons drawn and future challenges. *Anashim ve-mahshevim.* https://www.pc.co.il/featured/316320/ (Hebrew)

Council of the European Union. (1997). Treaty of Amsterdam (97/C 340/01). *Official Journal of the European Communities.* Retrieved November 21, 2022, from http://eur-lex.europa.eu/legal-content/EN/ALL/?uri=OJ:C:1997:340:TOC

Cruz, L. B., & Boehe, D. M. (2010). How do leading retail MNCs leverage CSR globally? Insights from Brazil. *Journal of Business Ethics, 91*, 243–263.

Denis, J. L., & van Gestel, N. (2015). Leadership and innovation in healthcare governance. In E. Kuhlmann, R. H. Blank, I. L. Bourgeault, & C. Wendt (Eds.), *The Palgrave international handbook of healthcare policy and governance* (pp. 425–440). Palgrave Macmillan. https://doi.org/10.1057/9781137384935_26

Dullet, N. W., Geraghty, E. M., Kaufman, T., Kissee, J. L., King, J., Dharmar, M., Smith, A. C., & Marcin, J. P. (2017). Impact of a university-based outpatient telemedicine program on time savings, travel costs, and environmental pollutants. *Value Health, 20*, 542–546.

Elarabi, H. M., & Johari, F. (2014). The impact of human resources management on healthcare quality. *Asian journal of management sciences & education, 3*(1), 13–22. https://doi.org/10.5539/ass.v10n8p55

Faggini, M., Cosimato, S., Nota, F. D., & Nota, G. (2019). Pursuing sustainability for healthcare through digital platforms. *Sustainability, 11*, 165.

Fanelli, S., Lanza, G., Zangrandi, A., & Enna, E. (2019). Innovare nei metodi di gestione nelle aziende sanitarie pubbliche: quali variabili di successo? *Azienda Pubblica, 3*(2019), 237–254.

Fineberg HV, Lecture S. (2012)A successful and sustainable health system how to get there from here. The New England Journal of Medicine 366:1020–1027.

Frist, W. H. (2014). Connected health and the rise of the patient-consumer. *Health Affairs, 33*, 191–193.

Ginter, P. M. (2018). *The strategic management of health care organizations*. John Wiley & Sons.

Ginter, P. M., Duncan, W. J., & Swayne, L. E. (2018). *The strategic management of health care organisations*. John Wiley & Sons.

Global Observatory for eHealth. (2022). Directory of eHealth policies. World Health Organisation. Retrieved November 10, 2022, from http://www.who.int/goe/policies/en/.

Gruchmann, T., Schmidt, I., Lubjuhn, S., Seuring, S., & Bouman, M. (2019). Informing logistics social responsibility from a consumer-choice-centered perspective. *The International Journal of Logistics Management, 30*, 96–116.

Hah, K., & Freeman, S. (2011). Multinational enterprise subsidiaries and their CSR: A conceptual framework of the management of CSR in smaller emerging. *Journal of Business Ethics, 98*, 281–295.

Infante, C. E. D. C., Mendonça, F. M., & Michele, P. (2013). Triple bottom line analysis of oil and gas industry with multicriteria decision making. *Journal of Cleaner Production, 52*, 289–300.

Israel's Life Sciences Industry IATI Report. (2019). https://www.iati.co.il/files/files/IATI%20Israeli%20Life%20Sciences%20Industry%202019%20Report.pdf

Kash, B. A., Spaulding, A., Gamm, L. D., & Johnson, C. E. (2014). Healthcare strategic management and the resource based view. *Journal of Strategy and Management, 7*(3), 251–264.

Keasberry, J., Scott, I. A., Sullivan, C., Staib, A., & Ashby, R. (2017). Going digital: A narrative overview of the clinical and organisational impacts of eHealth technologies in hospital practice. *Australian Health Review, 41*(6), 646–664. https://doi.org/10.1071/AH16233

Khan, N., Jones, D., Grice, A., Alderson, S., Bradley, S., Carder, P., & Neal, R. (2020). A brave new world: the new normal for general practice after the COVID-19 pandemic. *BJGP Open, 4*(3). https://doi.org/10.3399/bjgpopen20X101103

Lai, A., & Stacchezzini, R. (2021). Organisational and professional challenges amid the evolution of sustainability reporting: A theoretical framework and an agenda for future research. *Meditari Accountancy Research, 29*, 405–429.

Leoni, G., Lai, A., Stacchezzini, R., Steccolini, I., Brammer, S., Linnenluecke, M., & Demirag, I. (2021). Accounting, management, and accountability in times of crisis: Lessons from the COVID-19 pandemic. *Accounting, Auditing & Accountability Journal, 34*, 1305–1319.

Lombrano, A., & Iacuzzi, S. (2020). Comparing health system performance. *Economia Aziendale Online, 11*, 175–189.

Lunkes, R. J., Naranjo-Gil, D., & Lopez-Valeiras, E. (2018). Management control systems and clinical experience of managers in public hospitals. *International Journal of Environmental Research and Public Health, 15*(4), 776.

Marques, I. C. P., & Ferreira, J. J. M. (2020). Digital transformation in the area of health: Systematic review of 45 years of evolution. *Health and Technology, 10*(3), 575–586.

Matt, C., Hess, T., & Benlian, A. (2015). Digital transformation strategies. *Business & Information Systems Engineering, 57*(5), 339–343. https://doi.org/10.1007/s12599-015-0401-5

McKee, M., & Healy, J. (2002). *Hospitals in a changing Europe* (European Observatory on Health Care Systems Series). Open University Press. http://www.euro.who.int/en/about-us/partners/observatory/publications/studies/hospitals-in-a-changing-europe-2002

Naamati-Schneider, L. (2020). Strategic management as adaptation to changes in the ecosystems of public hospitals in Israel. *Israel Journal of Health Policy Research, 9*(1), 1–11.

Naamati-Schneider, L. (2021). Public-private: unequal competition Israeli public hospitals vs the private health-care system following government reforms. *International Journal of Organizational Analysis, 29*(6), 1381–1394.

Naamati-Schneider, L. (2022). Intraorganization conflicts of interest in hospitals adapting to a changing ecosystem. *Journal of Health Organization and Management, 36*(3), 265–278.

Naamati-Schneider, L. (2023). The effect of digitazation on service orientation and service perception among Israeli healthcare professionals: A qulitative study. *Digital Health, 9*. https://doi.org/10.1177/20552076231191892

Naamati-Schneider, L., & Zaks, O. (2022). Public hospitals in crisis: Managerial and strategic adaptation. In D. Vrontis, A. Thrassou, Y. Weber, S. M. R. Shams, E. Tsoukatos, & L. Efthymiou (Eds.), *Business under crisis, volume II. Palgrave Studies in Cross-disciplinary Business Research, in Association with EuroMed Academy of Business*. Palgrave Macmillan. https://doi.org/10.1007/978-3-030-76575-0_3

Peek, N., Sujan, M., & Scott, P. (2020). Digital health and care in pandemic times: Impact of COVID-19. *BMJ Health & Care Informatics, 27*(1). https://doi.org/10.1136/bmjhci-2020-100166

Polese, F., Carrubbo, L., Caputo, F., & Sarno, D. (2018). Managing healthcare service ecosystems: Abstracting a sustainability-based view from hospitalization at home (HaH) practices. *Sustainability, 10*, 3951.

Purvis, B., Mao, Y., & Robinson, D. (2019). Three pillars of sustainability: in search of conceptual origins. *Sustain Sciene, 14*, 681–695. https://doi.org/10.1007/s11625-018-0627-5

Raghavan, A., Demircioglu, M. A., & Orazgaliyev, S. (2021). COVID-19 and the new normal of organisations and employees: an overview. *Sustainability, 13*(21), 11942.

Ricciardi, W., Pita Barros, P., Bourek, A., Brouwer, W., Kelsey, T., Lehtonen, L., & Expert Panel on Effective Ways of Investing in Health (EXPH). (2019). How to govern the digital transformation of health services. *European Journal of Public Health, 29*(s3), 7–12. https://doi.org/10.1093/eurpub/ckz165

Rich, C., Singleton, J. K., & Wadhwa, S. S. (2018). *Sustainability for healthcare management: A leadership imperative*. Routledge.

Rodríguez-Labajos, L., Thomson, C., & O'Brien, G. (2018). Performance measurement for the strategic management of health-care estates. *Journal of Facilities Management, 16*, 217–232.

Romiti, A., Del Vecchio, M., Milani, C., & Sartor, G. (2022). Italian healthcare organisations facing new dimensions: changes in governance structure. *Journal of Management and Governance, 27*, 1–29.

Ron, R., & Weiss, R. (2020). The ramifications of reducing elective activity in hospitals during the Coronavirus crisis: Insights and conclusions. *Harefua, 159*(7), 475–476. (Hebrew).

Salvatore, F. P., & Fanelli, S. (2021a). Indicators and criteria for efficiency and quality in public hospitals: A performance evaluation model. *Global Business and Economics Review, 25*(3/4), 212–230.

Salvatore, F. P., & Fanelli, S. (2021b). The healthcare organisation in COVID-19 Age: An evaluation framework for the performance of a telemonitoring model. *Sustainability, 13*, 12765.

Salvioni, D., & Gennari, F. (2016). Corporate governance, ownership, and sustainability. *Corporate Ownership and Control, 13*, 606–614.

Samuel, Y. (2012). *Organisations: Introduction to the theory of the organisation*. Kinneret, Zmora-Bitan (Hebrew).

Schmid, A., Cacace, M., Götze, R., & Rothgang, H. (2010). Explaining health care system change: problem pressure and the emergence of "hybrid" health care systems. *Journal of Health, Politics, Policy, and Law., 35*(4), 455–486. https://doi.org/10.1215/03616878-2010-013

Schwab, K. (2017). *The fourth industrial revolution*. Currency.

Shasha, S. M. (1999). Incorporation of hospitals—whither? *Social Security, 54*, 50–130. (Hebrew).

Shkedi, A. (2011). *The meaning behind the words: Methodologies in qualitative research—in practice*. Ramot, Tel Aviv University (Hebrew).

Shleski, S., & Alpert, B. (2007). *Paths in writing qualitative research: From deconstruction of the reality to construction of the text*. Mofet Institute (Hebrew).

Thorpe, K. E., Ogden, L. L., & Galactionova, K. (2010). Chronic conditions account for the rise in Medicare spending from 1987 to 2006. *Health Affairs, 29*, 718–724.

Thrassou, A., Vrontis, D., Efthymiou, L., & Uzunboylu, N. (2022a). An overview of business advancement through technology: Markets and marketing in transition. In A. Thrassou, D. Vrontis, L. Efthymiou, Y. Weber, S. M. R. Shams, & E. Tsoukatos (Eds.), *Business Advancement through technology volume I* (Palgrave Studies in Cross-disciplinary Business Research, in Association with EuroMed Academy of Business). Palgrave Macmillan. https://doi.org/10.1007/978-3-031-07769-2_1

Thrassou, A., Vrontis, D., Efthymiou, L., & Uzunboylu, N. (2022b). An overview of business advancement through technology: The changing landscape of work and employment. In A. Thrassou, D. Vrontis, L. Efthymiou, Y. Weber, S. M. R. Shams, & E. Tsoukatos (Eds.), *Business advancement through technology volume II* (Palgrave Studies in Cross-disciplinary Business Research, in Association with EuroMed Academy of Business). Palgrave Macmillan. https://doi.org/10.1007/978-3-031-07765-4_1

Tjahjono, B., Esplugues, C., Ares, E., & Pelaez, G. (2017). What does industry 4.0 mean to supply chain? *Procedia Manufacturing, 13*, 1175–1182.

Torugsa, A., O'Donohue, W., & Hecker, R. (2012). Capabilities, proactive CSR and financial performance in SMEs: Empirical evidence from an Australian manufacturing industry sector. *Journal of Business Ethics, 109*, 483–500.

Tsabar Ben Yehoshua, N. (2016). *Traditions and streams in qualitative research: Strategic approaches and advanced tools*. Mofet Institute (Hebrew)

United Nations—Sustainable Development Goals. (2016). Retrieved November 19, 2022, from https://www.un.org/sustainabledevelopment/sustainable-development-goals/

van der Zande, M. M., Gorter, R. C., Bruers, J. J., Aartman, I. H., & Wismeijer, D. (2018). Dentists' opinions on using digital technologies in dental practice. *Community Dentistry and Oral Epidemiology, 46*(2), 143–153. https://doi.org/10.1111/cdoe.12345

Vidal-Alaball, J., Franch-Parella, J., Lopez Seguí, F., Garcia Cuyàs, F., & Mendioroz Peña, J. (2019). Impact of a Telemedicine program on the reduction in the emission of atmospheric pollutants and journeys by road. *International Journal of Environmental Research and Public Health, 16*, 4366.

World Health Organisation. (2016). Global observatory for eHealth. Global diffusion of eHealth: making universal health coverage achievable. World Health Organisation, Geneva. Retrieved November 10, 2022, from http://apps.who.int/iris/bitstream/10665/252529/1/9789241511780-eng.pdf?ua=1

World Health Organisation. (2017). Universal health coverage. Retrieved June, 2022, from https://www.who.int/newsroom/fact-sheets/detail/universal-health-coverage-(uhc)

Zaks, O. (2020). *Mergers and acquisitions in the dynamic reality of high-tech in Israel: Success or failure*. Tzameret. Zimmerman, M. A., & Zeitz.

Zangrandi, A., Fanelli, S., Donelli, C. C., & Elefanti, M. (2020). *Crisis managment: la gestione di un ospedale durante una pandemia*. EGEA.

12

Cause-Related Marketing and Philanthropy at Times of Crisis and Increasing Digitisation

Marlen Demetriou, Leonidas Efthymiou, and Avros Morphitis

1 Introduction

Increasing competition has led companies to seek competitive advantage through philanthropic activities (Delanoy, 2020). Such activities offer double benefits. On the one hand, they create solutions to various problems and value to the broader society. On the other hand, they improve a company's image, reputation and performance and enhance its relationship with customers. Philanthropic activities are part of Corporate Social Responsibility (CSR), which entails that companies go beyond their legal obligations and take into consideration dimensions that concern economic, social and ecological sensitivities. Lately, studies support that the three dimensions should be a legal requirement for corporations' CSR

M. Demetriou • L. Efthymiou (✉) • A. Morphitis
Department of Management, School of Business, University of Nicosia, Nicosia, Cyprus
e-mail: demetriou.m@unic.ac.cy; efthymiou.l@unic.ac.cy; avros.morphitis@aucy.ac.cy

D. Vrontis et al. (eds.), *Business for Sustainability, Volume I*, Palgrave Studies in Cross-disciplinary Business Research, In Association with EuroMed Academy of Business, https://doi.org/10.1007/978-3-031-37361-9_12

(Bachir, 2021). Moreover, CSR is more effective when it is part of a continuous effort, aiming to build long-lasting relationships and social alliances of mutual benefit (Garel & Petit-Romec, 2021). Short-term CSR initiatives fail to develop long-term loyalty since there are neither convincing nor accepted by customers and society. Within this context, a useful tool for building long-lasting relationships is the so-called Cause-Related Marketing (CRM) (Thomas et al., 2020).

Within this framework, the current chapter examines the impact of economic and health crises on Corporate Social Responsibility and Cause-Related Marketing programmes. To do so, it explores the nature of a long-term social partnership between a retailer, Lidl Cyprus and a non-for-profit charity, the Cyprus Anti-Cancer Society. The impact of this social partnership on the retailer's reputation and brand image is also explored, along with the role of technology in supporting philanthropy in times of crisis.

The analysis draws on repeated interviews with the president and key managers in Lidl Cyprus and the Cyprus Anti-Cancer Society. Aiming to explore the impact of economic as well as health crises on CSR and CRM programmes, the study adopted a longitudinal design, which enables examination of the current phenomena over a long period of time. The same participants, including the President of the Board, the Communication and PR manager of the Cyprus Anti-Cancer Society and the Team Manager of Communications at Lidl Cyprus, have been interviewed repeatedly over a period of seven years (between February 2015 and June 2022).

The chapter is organised as follows: the next section introduces the reader to the local context through a review of critical events. It also offers a brief background analysis of the Cyprus Anti-Cancer Society and Lidl Cyprus. Afterwards, the analysis presents the theoretical grounds of the study. In Sect. 3, the analysis discusses the study's research design and methods, prior to presenting the findings in Sect. 4. Then, Sect. 5 presents a summary of the analysis, along with a number of recommendations.

1.1 The Local Context

In March 2013, Cyprus was insolvent due to excessive fiscal spending that led to a large government deficit (Batiz-Lazo & Efthymiou, 2016). At the same time, two major Cypriot banks that were holders of Greek bonds recorded remarkable losses and defaulted following the restructuring of Greek government debt. On 16 March 2013, to avoid a bank run, the Cyprus government decided to shut down the entire banking system. For 13 consecutive days, banks had their doors closed, all accounts remained frozen, capital controls were imposed and people could withdraw only small amounts from Automated Teller Machines (ATMs). Eventually, a one-off bail-in was imposed on its major banks, with a 6.75% levy on deposits (Efthymiou & Michael, 2016). In other words, depositors and investors lost their money without their consent.

For many years after the bail-in, the Cypriot economy and society were crippled by the crisis. People lost their jobs, the unemployment rate rose to 14.3%, the number of homeless people increased rapidly, and poverty was widespread among the so-called middle class. Families were unable to pay their rents and bills, whereas, from March 2013 to January 2018 the Non-Performing Loans Ratio was almost 50% (CEIC, 2022). Some families were forced to stop their children from studying while others had no access to healthcare. Businesses faced limited liquidity, fewer investment opportunities, and bankruptcies (Efthymiou & Michael, 2016), whereas, Cyprus' credit rating was reduced to junk status by international credit rating agencies.

Before Cyprus and its citizens were given the opportunity to recover from the financial crisis, COVID-19 arrived to cripple the economy further. The Cypriot economy is predominantly supported by the Tourism and Hospitality sectors, which contribute almost 20% to the national Gross Domestic Product (GDP). 'Prior to the COVID-19 outbreak in early 2020, tourist arrivals were steadily growing at a record-breaking pace', whereas, more luxury, high-end, boutique, marina and casino hotels were being built throughout the island (Efthymiou et al., 2020, p. 294). However, the lockdowns, travel restrictions, limitations of movement, travel bans and other mandatory measures imposed as part of

COVID-19 had a direct impact on Tourism, which in turn hit transportation, storage, wholesale and retail sectors, as well as food manufacturing, financial services and more. According to PWC (2020), the economic downturn in 2020 was similar or greater to the 2013 economic recession.

Then, the Russo-Ukrainian war in February 2022, along with the sanctions implemented by Europe and other parts of the world, extended the economic downturn even further. With the ban on Russian flights, the 800,000 Russian tourists that used to visit Cyprus each year, were reduced to zero, with an estimated loss of 600 million euros (Hadjicostis, 2022). Once again, the negative impact spread to other sectors, including transportation, retail, banks and more.

The three critical events (bail-in levy, COVID-19 and Ukrainian war), hit the Cypriot economy successively. In less than a decade, the Cypriot economy had to deal with unprecedented challenges, with little space for adaptation. Crisis became habitual and repetitive (Vrontis et al., 2022a, 2022b), leaving a wound on businesses, employment and the society as a whole (Thrassou, Efthymiou, et al., 2022; Thrassou, Uzunboylu, et al., 2022). Within this turbulent and unstable ecosystem, the current chapter explores the response of corporations to social partnerships, including CSR and CRM. But prior to that, the analysis offers a brief background review of the 'Cyprus Anti-Cancer Society' and 'Lidl Cyprus'. It is worth mentioning that the current chapter adds to existing studies in the area of cancer control and philanthropy (e.g. Legg et al., 2022).

1.2 The Cyprus Anti-Cancer Society and Lidl Cyprus

The Cyprus Anti-Cancer Society (established in 1971) is a registered non-profit charity organisation that offers free palliative care to all cancer patients in Cyprus. The aim of the society is also to support the patients' families and caregivers and inform the wider public about cancer prevention, diagnosis, treatment and relief. The Anti-Cancer Society has two palliative care centres, one in Nicosia and one in Limassol. The centre in Nicosia is the only hospice in Cyprus, which provides a wide range of palliative services, including pain control and other symptoms deriving from the illness or its treatment, psychosocial support and physiotherapy.

The centre in Limassol has been built and equipped in line with European standards and quickly became a point of support for cancer patients in the western part of Cyprus. It offers palliative care and other supportive treatments such as transfusions and hydrations.

At the same time, the Anti-Cancer Society provides homecare services to cancer patients who choose to remain at home. The service employs nurses, psychologists, social workers and physiotherapists who work with the patient's oncologist and count on the support of the doctors of the anti-cancer society. This team of professionals work together to ensure comprehensive care, tailored to the needs of each individual patient. The patients are usually referred to the service by their treating physician. However, the patients or their families can seek help at society's offices in different parts of the island. The patients can also borrow relevant equipment from the centres, such as special medical beds, wheelchairs, oxygen delivery systems and more. All services and equipment are provided **free** to all residents in Cyprus. The cost of those services is covered by corporate donations, individual donations, charity activities and governmental support. However, following the financial bail-in, which involved a deposit levy in March 2013, most donors were unable to continue supporting the cause.

Moreover, one of the companies that has been a long-term supporter of the Anti-Cancer Society is Lidl Cyprus. Lidl Cyprus is a multinational corporation that entered the local market in 2010 and since then has opened 18 stores. It employs more than 600 people. It invests in a Sustainable Development Strategy, which incorporates specific values and responsible business practices along the following five areas: Products, Environment, Employees, Society and External Partners. Based on this philosophy, Lidl Cyprus has a Social Alliance with the Cyprus Anti-Cancer Society (CAS). The impact of Lidl's decision to support the Anti-Cancer Society on the corporation's reputation and brand image is examined in this chapter along with the impact of those programs on the survival of the Anti-Cancer Society.

2 Literature Review

Strategic Philanthropy, Cause-Related Marketing and Corporate Social Responsibility

Delanoy (2020) holds that global competition has led companies to seek competitive advantage through philanthropic activities to benefit and create value for society and the business's performance. Some companies have connected their philanthropic activities to business strategy, calling it strategic philanthropy (Van Cranenburgh & Arenas, 2014). In this context, corporate philanthropy is seen as a strategic investment that offers many advantages to society and helps to better position the company. Companies that adopt strategic philanthropy as an investment try to incorporate it in a more multi-stakeholder dimension strategy, also known as Corporate Social Responsibility (CSR).

While some companies view CSR as an expansion of the corporate strategy and a means to acquire marketing power, management still has the challenge of being more serious in understanding how CSR programs impact different communities. As Salam and Bajaba (2022, p. 1188) suggest, marketing often fails to consider a target market's social needs 'while ignoring society at large'. The authors propose that marketing should be applied responsibly, so firms can improve their reputation while promoting sustainable living. Moreover, Bachir (2021) holds that corporations are legally required to take CSR initiatives where the mechanisms are left to their choice within the three dimensions of sustainability, namely environmental, economic and services. In a similar vein, Aparna et al. (2022) explain how corporate social responsibility (CSR) is mandatory in certain countries and sectors, such as the Indian hotel sector. Such initiatives may be functional, which address specific human resource needs, supply chain, market activity and corporate, where companies focus on development, corporate governance or environmental protection (He & Harris, 2020).

Moreover, cause-related marketing (CRM) refers to a program where the company commits to donating an amount dependent on meeting a threshold of sales over a certain period. The CRM campaign may be related to a product or company with the interest of benefiting non-governmental organisations or another partner with legitimacy in the selected cause or experience in financial management. CRM is employed as a way of involving a company's customers in the company's CSR initiatives. For example, in India, TV stations invite customers to participate in commercials to educate the disenfranchised in the community by advertising a product where the proceeds are directed towards the cause. Bhatti et al. (2022) argue that companies view CRM as a win-win situation since they increase customer loyalty and improve the company's brand image. The initiatives taken are often examined based on the company's core values, vision, mission, or the immediate challenges in its social environment or at the time. According to Gil-Gomez et al. (2020), some of the benefits of CRM are attracting new customers, access to niche market segments, increasing product sales, and creating a positive brand image. Today, it seems that customers are no longer satisfied with just receiving the product or service since they expect to generate value beyond the quality in the area of CSR. Gradually, CSR has become an expected business practice in the broader society (Amin-Chaudhry, 2016).

The motivating factors of CRM concern retaining high-value employees, protecting environmental resources, building brand trust and loyalty, controlling costs to optimise efficiency, and establishing better relationships with investors, partners, and government agencies (Bhatti et al., 2022). However, involvement in CRM proves to be a challenge to companies during economic recessions, and their legitimacy in the concern for causes is put to the test by the stakeholders. Companies that withdraw their financial support for these companies suffer negative brand perceptions. Notably, businesses must meet their qualitative and quantitative metrics without suffering failure or losses associated with the core focus on CRM practices (Kacprzak et al., 2021).

A company's higher officials, such as the CEO, are responsible for aligning the corporation's interests with those of the stakeholders in economic, non-economic, and mixed measures of success. The success of CRM campaigns is tethered to the compatibility between the company and the sustainability of the cause (Bhatti et al., 2022). The sales team's performance reflects high compatibility between the company and the selected cause. The prevalence of technology in communication has lowered the costs of CRM, leading to more effective coordination of such initiatives (Kacprzak et al., 2021). This ease has also led to the development of communities that influence the company's success and ability to influence company initiatives.

CSR in the Era of COVID-19

The COVID-19 pandemic raised concerns in business supply chains and an economic downturn that limited business normal operations and people's earnings and lifestyles, along with the known health risks. Bachir (2021) argues that due to the harsh economic and social conditions, the CRM expectations of prominent brands and the opportunity to acquire new customers have been perceived by some brands as suitable areas of CSR. Local communities and customers appreciate the support and welcome initiative by large brands that were more often focused on mitigating the effects of the crisis and establishing support mechanisms for these communities. According to He and Harris (2020), companies have been tested for their legitimacy in their CRM initiatives. Notably, due to the social distress caused by the pandemic, some retailers have taken advantage of the circumstances to profiteer from these circumstances. Such cases led the Competition and Markets Authority of the UK to set up a task force to investigate companies profiteering from the pandemic by inflating prices or distorting the supply chain to manipulate the prices as desired. The crisis tested companies for their commitment to ethical business conduct and CSR.

Due to the financial strain caused by the obstruction of business, some companies have sought short-term strategies that benefit the firm rather than a long-term investment in their CSR initiatives. Some businesses were not hesitant to engage in unethical business conduct during this crisis and simultaneously participated in measures taken to fight the virus (He & Harris, 2020). These measures were taken to accomplish some organisational objectives and stakeholders' accountability. The marketing activities and ideas have been influenced by more exacerbation of social inequalities, such as poverty, and informed the company's interest in social and economic issues affecting the socially disenfranchised. Certainly, the pandemic presented an array of opportunities for CSR activities, more so for companies that could render help and assistance to ameliorate the impact of the pandemic (Demetriou, 2021). For example, companies in both the US and UK rendered their facilities for manufacturing masks and hand sanitisers among some of the necessary products to reduce the rate of the virus' spread.

Other areas of CSR were in the organisation of services. For example, some retail chains established specific times for 'at risk' individuals, such as the elderly, for shopping. Firms that were genuine and authentic in their CSR initiatives established a stronger brand image and customer loyalty (Delanoy, 2020). Such loyalty is likely to create longer customer lifecycles that greatly incentivise companies to participate in CSR agendas of their interest. The marketing activities and ideas have been influenced by more exacerbation of social inequalities, such as poverty, and informed the company's interest in social and economic issues affecting the social disenfranchised (He & Harris, 2020). Notably, the COVID-19 has led ethical and leading brands to acknowledge the benefits of meaningful customer relations, satisfaction, and loyalty.

CSR in the Digital Era

The diffusion of technology and prevalence of digitisation (Batiz-Lazo et al., 2022) offers CSR the data required to inform their CSR initiatives and identify the communities in need. Further, the digital has expanded the scope of CSR for businesses beyond their immediate society (Delanoy, 2020). As part of building a sustainable business, corporations are required to address the prevalent challenges in their environment. The company's impact on its physical or social environment is not only implemented in CSR initiatives but also in the values that guide business in the supply chain and public relations. According to Gayathri (2019), pervasive measures have been taken to use social media platforms, such as Twitter, Facebook and YouTube, for activities conducted by a company globally. Demetriou (2021) argues that companies have the room to cater to customer relations and need to realise holistic feedback gathering to prevent one approach to performing analysis. Consequently, the CSR initiatives in the digital era have been collaborative among companies rather than the individual. Due to public participation and access to information about initiatives, companies could participate in national and global initiatives in CSR.

For example, small to global companies used the company websites to educate the public on the prevention and safety measures to protect themselves from contracting COVID-19. The digital platform's core contribution to the practice of CSR has been facilitating communication that has created space for co-innovation, co-learning, and collaborative decision-making and implementation (Gayathri, 2019). The development of these platforms has not only increased the reach of CSR activities to the people in need and expanded their scope to address issues that affect communities that are disenfranchised, or that may not be primary consumers of products from companies that have the unique ability to offer assistance at marginal costs to such communities. The current chapter, aims at exploring the potential use of technology and digitisation as part of CSR and CRM by Lidl Cyprus and the Cyprus Anti-Cancer Society.

3 Research Design

By examining the collaboration of Lidl Cyprus and Cyprus Anti-Cancer Society (CAS), the current chapter seeks to understand the nature of long-lasting social alliances at times of crisis. A major question is whether corporations are able and willing to continue their CSR and CRM programs during pandemics, economic downturns and other critical events. Also, the chapter evaluates the impact of the social partnership on Lidl's brand image and reputation as well as the survival of the Cyprus Anti-Cancer Society.

To address these objectives, Qualitative Longitudinal Research emerged as a useful tool, since it allows one to examine a phenomenon over a greater time span and length (Holland et al., 2006). The purpose of long fieldwork, over a period of seven years, is to enable an examination of different critical events, along with possible changes in social alliances. It enabled to analyse the CRM activities of Lidl Cyprus, all the way from the post bail-in period (in 2013), the outbreak of COVID-19 in 2019, and the economic downturn due to the Russo-Ukrainian war in 2022.

For the purposes of the study, several semi-structured interviews were conducted between February 2015 and June 2022. The interviews enabled a deeper investigation of various viewpoints, motivations and drivers. It was important to examine the motive of Lidl when they decided to form a social partnership with the Cyprus Anti-Cancer Society, just after the crisis in 2013, along with the effectiveness of the strategy during the last nine years (2013–2022). The participants included the CSR manager of Lidl Cyprus, and on behalf of the Cyprus Anti-Cancer Society: the President of the Board and the PR and Communication Officer. All the participants were firmly related to the topic under investigation, and the most appropriate persons to answer our questions. Access to participants was not difficult to attain, since the first author in this chapter has participated repeatedly in CSR activities with both organisations and has had personal links with their management for a number of years.

4 Findings

During the interviews with Lidl's management, it was clear that a long-lasting social partnership is beneficial for both the retailer and the charity. As Lidl's manager said, 'Our mission is to take an active and essential role in society and support our fellow human beings. Without CAS, we wouldn't be able to achieve our mission'. Also, the manager explained their plan, which is to actively formulate processes and mobilise society towards acting for and participating in the common good. 'This is even more important than simply donating money or goods to CAS', she added.

Lidl's alliance with CAS lasted firmly through critical events for almost a decade: 'We have been part of this alliance for 9 years and we always act with a sense of responsibility and empathy for a good cause'. At the same time, Lidl is very proud because CAS characterises 'Lidl Cyprus as a valuable ally in the effort to alleviate the pain of our fellow human beings suffering from cancer and to support their loved ones'.

When asked about the value of Cause-Related Marketing in comparison to any other form of Corporate Philanthropy, the manager pointed to the long-term and sustainable nature of CRM: 'CRM builds long-lasting, strong and fruitful bonds with not only the charity we support but with all other stakeholders'. She also added that the socio-economic study of the company includes measurable results in the form of indicators. As presented in Table 12.1, the results reveal a positive impact of this CRM strategy on Lidl's brand image and the positive perception of its stakeholders, including employees, customers, suppliers and the broader society in Cyprus. Such findings resonate with previous studies in the field, which support that CRM offers long-lasting win-win situations (Delanoy, 2020) since it increases customer loyalty and improves a company's brand image (Bhatti et al., 2022).

Moreover, the interviewee concluded that the corporation started this social partnership during a very difficult period for the survival of CAS, just after the bail-in that shocked the Cypriot economy and society in 2013. The levy of depositors' money had a tremendous negative impact on Cypriots. However, the social partnership with CAS continued with innovative and profitable projects. Soon after, COVID-19 arrived to worsen the economy even further. According to the interviewee, at that point, Lidl Cyprus decided to intensify its contribution to the CAS even further. The corporation participated in the 'Adopt-a-Room' programme at the 'Arodaphnousa' Palliative Care Center. 'That was an extra amount of 100,000 Euro', the manager said, and added: 'At the same time, we organized and covered all expenses of a special Music Event at a Local TV

Table 12.1 Summary of findings

CRM is beneficial for both the corporation and the charity
Some corporations, plan their CRM activities carefully, going beyond simple donations
Long-term CRM activities have a very positive impact on corporations
A decade-long partnership lasted through several critical events
Crises events strengthened, rather than weakening this particular partnership
Long-term CRM is linked to sustainability, metrics/ measurable indicators
CRM influences positively a brand image, stakeholders' perception, and society
Corporations that are part of long-term CRM, are often willing to participate in additional/ extra activities
If profit organizations do not get actively involved at times of crises, charity organization may seize to exist

Channel which helped CAS to raise an additional amount of 40,000 Euro'. As presented in Table 12.1, these findings reveal that corporations participating in long-term CRM events are often willing to participate in additional activities.

Likewise, since CAS' existence was challenged by continuous financial constraints, as a result of the poor economic landscape and then COVID-19, Lidl decided to continue covering all expenses for the Nutritional Program of the hospice. As the manager said, 'We will stand by the side of CAS during such critical events, since everyone at Lidl Cyprus believes in the cause, we trust our partners and we want CAS to continue offering its valuable services to all cancer patients and their families for free'.

Another round of interviews took place after the outbreak of the Russo-Ukrainian war in February 2022. After the lockdowns, limitations of movement and other mandatory measures imposed as part of COVID-19, now Cypriots (along with most people around the world) had to deal with weaker economic growth, sky-rocketing inflation, very high prices and damaged supply chains. Once again, the partnership between Lidl Cyprus and CAS remained strong. Interestingly, Lidl's Cause-Related Marketing has intensified even further during such critical events. Instead of being discouraged, the crisis has made Lidl's manager intensify their CRM and philanthropy activities even further (Table 12.1).

The findings collected at Lidl were triangulated with the findings collected at CAS. The researchers had several fruitful interviews with the president of the Cyprus Anti-Cancer Society to better understand the nature and impact of the social partnership with Lidl.

The President of CAS outlined the value of the contribution, which was initiated during the critical economic events of 2013. According to the interviewee, CAS faced extreme economic problems during the financial crisis in 2013. Most corporations stopped their financial support since their accounts had to go through levy. Ordinary Cypriots, who were supporting fund raising activities, ended up being unemployed or with considerable salary cuts. But CAS had to keep up with its promises and responsibilities. 'We had to continue offering our services to cancer patients across Cyprus for free', he said, and added: 'Thanks to initiatives such as that of Lidl, the Bank of Cyprus and a few more valuable social partners, we managed to survive those difficult times'. Since then, the social partnership with Lidl continues with the same enthusiasm and creativity.

When additional crises were added to the existing financial difficulties, namely the pandemic of COVID-19 and then the war in Ukraine, the social partnership continued uninterrupted. As the president said: '[t]he COVID-19 pandemic has affected us all. Nevertheless, we had to continue serving thousands of cancer patients across Cyprus by adapting our free services to the new actualities. Once more Lidl, as a loyal partner, supported our organization with additional initiatives'. In one of the interviews, the president concluded in the following way: 'Lidl stood by our side since 2013 and helped us deal with the challenges with hope and optimism. We now know that we have strong, long-lasting alliances to support our cause'. In another interview, the president concluded with a similar statement: 'Lidl Cyprus is one of our most valuable allies, and we are grateful to have it by our side'. Such findings reconfirm the importance of long-lasting relationships when CRM is used over a period of time. It also proves that social partnerships are likely to last, and even intensify at times of crisis.

During an interview with the Communications and PR Manager of CAS, an attempt has been made to identify the nature of the social partnership from a Marketing point of view. The manager was very enthusiastic while explaining in detail the nature of CAS' collaboration with Lidl Cyprus and provided a list of activities of the CRM campaign:

1. Lidl Cyprus donates a percentage of the selling price of a product every Christmas. Through this action, the company calls on the Cypriot public to support the work of the Cyprus Anti-Cancer Society by purchasing a certain product. This year, Lidl offered €15 with each purchase of selected wooden toys.
2. They are the main sponsors of the 'Dinner of Love', which is a fundraising dinner held at the Presidential Palace. Due to the COVID-19 restrictions, the event was cancelled this year. At this point, it is important to underline the support of technology since Lidl decided to double its sponsorship budget and held a telethon through TV, which

brought more than double donations for CAS compared to the traditional fundraising dinner.
3. The Lidl Food Academy hosted various fundraising events, including fashion shows, tea parties and other charity activities. Also, during Christmas, volunteers use the facilities of the Lidl Food Academy to prepare homemade desserts that are sold at CAS' Christmas event.
4. On a random basis, Lidl has been providing 'special treats', such as ice cream or candy, for patients and families at the 'Arodafnousa' Hospice.

'From a marketing point of view', the manager explained, 'as this relationship grows, we came to realize that Lidl has been creating a good "social-responsibility" image, which represents its corporate values'. The manager also added that '[e]very action receives a good amount of publicity (ATL and BTL). This has a direct impact on CAS' patients, families, volunteers and personnel, who become great communicators of the Lidl's brand and CSR'. Also, the manager mentioned that during the last 9 years, Lidl provided to CAS donations (both monetary and products) of more than €460,000. Also, as mentioned earlier, since 2015, Lidl Cyprus covers entirely the nutritional program of Arodafnousa Palliative Care Center, so that patients and families have daily access to tasty and healthy meals. Recognising the society's growing needs and limitations due to COVID-19 and the war in Ukraine, Lidl Cyprus had expanded its support towards CAS, by 'adopting' a room at Arodafnousa and thus covering its operating cost for a year, which amounts to €100.000.

When asked about possible problems arising from the partnership with a profit organisation, the manager responded that such relationships are based on good faith and honesty by both parties. 'Since there is an honest concern about the well-being of people suffering from cancer, this relationship has never faced any unsolved problems'. Also, in line with the literature presented earlier (Kacprzak et al., 2021), the manager of CAS underlined the benefits of forming long-lasting alliances with a profit organisation rather than short-term cooperation. As she said, 'A long-lasting social alliance with Lidl is very beneficial for the Anti-Cancer Society, as we have built a strong relationship with the company and thus, we are able to better communicate our needs to them so they can figure out if they are able to help in any additional way'. She also added:

'our policy is to be respectful towards our donors and not exploit their "kindness"'. In our last interview, the manager reconfirmed existing studies concerning the mutual benefit of CRM. She claimed that 'this long-term partnership benefits the company too, since it is able to build public awareness and connect its brand with a reputable charity like the Cyprus Anti-Cancer Society'.

4.1 The Application of Technology in CRM and CSR

During COVID-19, organising philanthropic activities became incredibly difficult. The lockdowns, limitations of movement and other mandatory measures, meant that most events had to be cancelled, threatening the viability of charity organisations and putting their commitment to charitable giving at risk. Organisations had to work out alternative options. As claimed by the president of CAS, 'despite the difficulties caused by the pandemic, we had to remain by the side of patients with cancer and keep offering our services completely free of charge'. At this point, it seems that technology application and digitisation came to philanthropy's rescue. Technology is what kept charity going.

For example, one of the most popular Greek singers delivered a concert on TV as part of an event called 'the Day of Love'. Traditionally, for the day of love, the Cyprus Anti-Cancer Association organises the 'Dinner of Love' at the country's Presidential Palace—an opportunity for raising support and funds. However, following the imposed social distancing, CAS had to adapt to the new circumstances. With the sponsorship of Lidl Cyprus, the event was brought to the homes of the whole country through TV. During the show, the public (including businesses) could make contributions to the Anti-Cancer Association through text messages.

According to the management of CAS, this event is just one example among many, which became possible due to the application of technology. As presented in Table 12.2, the TV, Internet, teleconferencing mobile phones, SMS, websites, e-banking and other technologies enabled the organisation to hold several events and involved the public in charitable 'giving'. This change had an impact on CAS and its stakeholders. For

Table 12.2 The important role of technology for CRM at times of crisis

Crises such as COVID-19, are reasons for cancelling traditional philanthropic events
Technology came into philanthropy's rescue
Technologies such as the Internet, TV, teleconferencing mobile phones, SMS, websites, cashless transactions and e-banking made charitable activities during COVID-19

instance, digital skills among CAS' staff and volunteers had to be improved, whereas, new software and equipment had to be attained. Such findings are in line with existing studies, supporting that most charities changed how they use digital technology due to the pandemic (King, 2021).

5 Discussion and Practical Implications

Stemming by the findings, it seems that socially responsible companies are likely to adopt and support CRM programmes, even in times of crisis. Lidl Cyprus is one of those companies. Its management shares the view that Cypriot consumers expect profit organisations to play a substantial role in supporting non-profit organisations, especially in periods of economic downturns, poverty and other unprecedented disasters. Such findings resonate with previous studies (e.g. Demetriou, 2021; Amin-Chaudhry, 2016; and Bhattacharya & Sen, 2004), which support that consumers expect corporations to be involved in CSR activities and play an important role in the alleviation of social problems. This view is also aligned with the findings of Nakashima and Ota (2016), who support that CSR contributes to the stability and profitability of businesses during crisis, by transforming their values and image.

Likewise, Lidl's management claimed that their company considers CSR as a great opportunity. Their CRM program has been designed carefully, with a cause of great impact in the Cypriot Society. This strategy resembles Demetriou's (2021), which claims that the chosen cause should offer value to a wide number of stakeholders. Also, Lidl's management believes that their partnership with CAS has facilitated a long-term bonding with their stakeholders. This finding resembles with the observations of Efthymiou et al. (2023), supporting that CRM can be used by companies to establish a distinct brand name and enhance worker motivation. Moreover, stakeholders like to feel they're working for, or doing business with, a socially conscious company, whereas, the potential benefits of CRM include positive public relations, improved customer loyalty and additional market opportunities.

Another very important finding concerns the indicators used by Lidl Cyprus to produce measurable results. The results are included in the company's annual socio-economic report. In other words, the retailer is able to calculate and reconfirm the positive impact of CRM on its brand image—and among its stakeholders—by using metrics and analytics in a systematic and institutionalised manner.

Furthermore, it's not an exaggeration to say that since 2013, CAS' survival is largely chalked up to its partnership with Lidl. Not only because the Cypriot economy was in a terrible condition since 2013, but because three unprecedented crises occurred within a decade—each one succeeding the next. Both representatives of the Anti-Cancer Society emphasised the value of this partnership for the society, both in monetary terms and in building awareness among the society. The social partnership has enabled both Lidl and CAS to benefit substantially, for almost a decade. The mutual benefit of Lidl's CRM program may inspire companies globally to initiate innovative CRM programs during and after the pandemic of COVID-19 and the economic downturn due to the war in Ukraine. CSR-oriented companies around the world must turn challenges into new CRM opportunities, which can benefit the society while enhancing their brand image in a sustainable manner.

Also, during the last decade, technological diffusion and digitisation opened up new dimensions for cause-related marketing. As discussed earlier, the TV, Internet, teleconferencing mobile phones, SMS, websites, social media, e-banking and other technologies and applications enabled CAS to organise several events at times when movement was restricted, social distancing was mandatory and people were locked up in their homes. Charitable 'giving' became possible due to digitisation. By utilising technology, organisations built virtual bridges to reach out to their stakeholders and broader society. Below, we present a graph, representing a model of how the specific social partnership survived through critical events and progressed from traditional CRM to digital philanthropy (Fig. 12.1).

As presented in the graph, social partnerships allow an organisation to partner with a non-profit company that will eventually benefit both. Companies increase sales and marketing share, strengthen brand positioning, enhance corporate image and clout and increase the ability to attract, motivate and retain employees. Non-profit organisations, on the other hand, can see such benefits as increased revenues, enhanced visibility of their causes or messages, connections to a corporation's network of employees, suppliers, distributors and other contacts and a wealth of corporate experience, including marketing expertise and strategy development.

The aim of this particular partnership is a mutually beneficial collaboration between a corporation (Lidl) and a non-profit (CAS) designed to promote the former's sales and the latter's cause. Stakeholders in this partnership are the cancer patients, the board of CAS, the employees and medical staff, suppliers, distributors, employees, banks, volunteers, sponsors, the media and the board of Lidl.

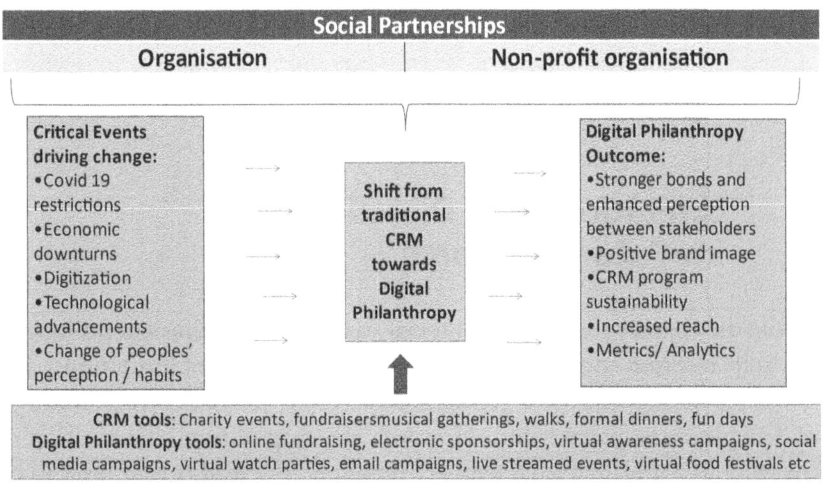

Fig. 12.1 The digital transformation of charity activations in social partnership. (Source: Author's own)

Moreover, the restrictions and opportunities that occurred due to critical events, as presented on the graph, facilitated the replacement of traditional charity events with digital communication tools. Mandatory limitations of physical presence, limited purchasing power, technological advancements and societal changes are some of those changes (Thrassou et al., 2022a, 2022b). Traditional events consist of musical gatherings, walks, formal dinners, fun days and more. Evidently, these events had to be replaced by digital events through online fundraising, electronic sponsorships, virtual awareness campaigns, becoming more active on social media, virtual watch parties, email campaigns, live streamed events, virtual food festivals and other virtual activities. At the same time, the increasing digitisation enabled the retailer to rely on metrics and analytics to measure the impact of its CRM activities. Such processes add to existing studies in the field of nonprofit marketing, which explore the increasing digitisation and its impact on philanthropy (Bernardi & Alhamdan, 2022).

Digitisation and the rapid technological advancements have respectively contributed towards the transformation of CRM activities. Digital philanthropy benefited the social partnerships by reaching even greater crowds and creating a sustainable environment for activities to take place. Accordingly, the adaptation of digital communication tools allowed this partnership not only to overcome the existing economic downturns and change in peoples' habits but also contributed towards a positive brand image.

6 Limitations and Directions for Future Research

While the chapter sheds light on social partnerships at times of prolonged crisis, its research approach and sample have a number of limitations. The sample is limited to two organisations, whereby it draws on the findings of a single social partnership. However, the corporation participating in the study is a multinational retailer. Therefore, the study's findings can be generalised to a certain extent. At the same time, the charity organisation participating in the study represents the voice of key stakeholders, including patients and their families.

Finally, amidst the ongoing digital turn, future research may explore in more depth the digital realm in CRM and CAR as avenues for long-term philanthropy and sustainable development. Also, departing from our findings, future studies may explore in more depth the application of metrics, analytics and indicators as a means of measuring social partnerships within the context of sustainable philanthropy.

References

Amin-Chaudhry, A. (2016). Corporate social responsibility—From a mere concept to an expected business practice. *Social Responsibility Journal, 12*(1), 190–207. https://doi.org/10.1108/SRJ-02-2015-0033

Aparna, K., Amilan, S., & Vimal Raj, L. (2022). Customers' response to mandatory corporate social responsibility in India: An empirical evidence. *Social Responsibility Journal, ahead-of-print*(ahead-of-print). https://doi.org/10.1108/SRJ-04-2021-0174

Bachir, S. (2021). The evolution of customer relationship management in the digital age and its impact on banks. *The Euraseans: Journal on Global Socio-Economic Dynamics*, (3(28)), 50–63. https://doi.org/10.35678/2539-5645.3(28).2021.50-63

Batiz-Lazo, B., & Efthymiou, L. (2016). *The book of payments: Historical and contemporary views on the cashless economy*. Palgrave Macmillan.

Batiz-Lazo, B., Efthymiou, L., & Davies, K. (2022). The spread of artificial intelligence and its impact on employment: Evidence from the banking and accounting sectors. In A. Thrassou, D. Vrontis, L. Efthymiou, Y. Weber, S. M. R. Shams, & E. Tsoukatos (Eds.), *Business advancement through technology, Volume II* (Palgrave Studies in Cross-disciplinary Business Research, In Association with EuroMed Academy of Business). Palgrave Macmillan. https://doi.org/10.1007/978-3-031-07765-4_7

Bernardi, C. L., & Alhamdan, N. (2022). Social media analytics for nonprofit marketing: #Downsyndrome on Twitter and Instagram. *Journal of Philanthropy and Marketing, 27*, e1739. https://doi.org/10.1002/nvsm.1739

Bhattacharya, C. B, & Sen, S. (2004). Doing better at doing good: When, why and how consumers respond to corporate social initiatives. *California Management Review, 47*(Fall), 9–25.

Bhatti, H., Galan-Ladero, M., & Galera-Casquet, C. (2022). Cause-related marketing: A systematic review of the literature. *International Review on Public and Nonprofit Marketing.* https://doi.org/10.1007/s12208-021-00326-y

CEIC. (2022). Cyprus non performing loans ratio. Retrieved July 22, 2022, from https://www.ceicdata.com/en/indicator/cyprus/non-performing-loans-ratio

Delanoy, N. (2020). *Social media and customer engagement: Customer relations in a digital era* (Degree). Walden University.

Demetriou, D. (2021). *SupportCy: A successful Social Responsiveness strategy of the Bank of Cyprus during Covid-19* [Ebook]. Retrieved June 19, 2022, from http://archives.marketing-trends-congress.com/2022/pages/PDF/118.pdf

Efthymiou, L., & Michael, S. (2016). The Cyprus cash crash: A case of collective punishment. In B. Batiz-Lazo & L. Efthymiou (Eds.), *The book of payments: Historical and contemporary views on the cashless economy* (pp. 131–140). Palgrave Macmillan.

Efthymiou, L., Orphanidou, Y., & Panayiotou, G. (2020). Delineating the changing frontstage and backstage segregation in high-end and luxury hotels. *Hospitality & Society, 10*(3), 287–312. https://doi.org/10.1386/hosp_00025_1

Efthymiou, L., Kulshrestha, A., & Kulshrestha, S. (2023). A study on sustainability and ESG in the service sector in India: Benefits, challenges, and future implications. *Administrative Sciences, 13*, 165. https://doi.org/10.3390/admsci13070165

Garel, A., & Petit-Romec, A. (2021). Engaging employees for the long run: Long-term investors and employee-related CSR. *Journal of Business Ethics, 174*, 35–63. https://doi.org/10.1007/s10551-020-04572-8

Gayathri, J. (2019). CSR in the digital era—A access on the CSR communication of companies and identification of services for CSR. *IJITEE, 8*(11). Retrieved June 19, 2022, from https://www.researchgate.net/publication/353209578_CSR_in_the_digital_era

Gil-Gomez, H., Guerola-Navarro, V., Oltra-Badenes, R., & Lozano-Quilis, J. (2020). Customer relationship management: Digital transformation and sustainable business model innovation. *Economic Research-Ekonomska Istraživanja, 33*(1), 2733–2750. https://doi.org/10.1080/1331677x.2019.1676283

Hadjicostis, M. (2022, June 12). Cyprus eyes rebound from loss of Russian, Ukrainian Tourists. Bloomber, European Edition. Retrieved July 24, 2022, from https://www.bloomberg.com/news/articles/2022-06-12/cyprus-eyes-rebound-from-loss-of-russian-ukrainian-tourists

He, H., & Harris, L. (2020). The impact of Covid-19 pandemic on corporate social responsibility and marketing philosophy. *Journal of Business Research, 116*, 176–182. https://doi.org/10.1016/j.jbusres.2020.05.030

Holland, J. Thomson, R., & Henderson, S. (2006). Qualitative longitudinal research: A discussion paper (Families and Social Capital Working Papers). London: London South Bank University.

Kacprzak, M., Milewska, A., Kacprzak, A., & Krol, A. (2021). Corporate social responsibility in the era of the COVID-19 pandemic on the example of companies from Poland, Belgium, and Ukraine. *European Research Studies Journal, XXIV*(3B), 547–562. https://doi.org/10.35808/ersj/2481

King, D. (2021). Respond, recover, reset: The voluntary sector and COVID-19. Retrieved July 27, 2022, from http://cpwop.org.uk/what-we-do/projects-and-publications/covid-19-vcse-organisation-responses/

Legg, M., Hyde, M. K., Chambers, S. K., Ng, S. K., Scuffham, P., Stein, K., & Dunn, J. (2022). Retaining volunteers for the cause: Hope and pride associated with cause-related charity events in cancer control. *Journal of Philanthropy and Marketing, 27*, e1707. https://doi.org/10.1002/nvsm.1707

Nakashima, M., & Ota, S. (2016, December). Association between corporate financial performance and corporate social responsibility in a crisis: Focusing on the March 11 disaster. *Asia-Pacific Management Accounting Journal, 11*(2), 147–167. ISSN 2550-1631. Retrieved May 2, 2021, from http://arionline.uitm.edu.my/ojs/index.php/APMAJ/article/view/475

PWC. (2020, May 13). COVID-19: Impact of the pandemic on the Cyprus economy. Retrieved July 22, 2022, from https://www.pwc.com.cy/en/issues/responding-to-covid-19-helping-our-clients/covid-19-impact-of-the-pandemic-on-the-cyprus-economy.html

Salam, M. A., & Bajaba, S. (2022). Corporate social responsibility during the COVID-19 pandemic: A sequential mediation analysis. *Social Responsibility Journal, 18*(6), 1188–1208. https://doi.org/10.1108/SRJ-03-2021-0118

Thomas, S., Kureshi, S., & Vatavwala, S. (2020). Cause-related marketing research (1988–2016): An academic review and classification. *Journal of Nonprofit & Public Sector Marketing, 32*(5), 488–516. https://doi.org/10.1080/10495142.2019.1606757

Thrassou, A., Efthymiou, L., Vrontis, D., Weber, Y., Shams, S. M. R., & Tsoukatos, E. (2022). Editorial introduction: Crisis in context. In D. Vrontis, A. Thrassou, Y. Weber, S. M. R. Shams, E. Tsoukatos, & L. Efthymiou (Eds.),

Business under crisis, Volume I: Contextual transformations (Palgrave Studies in Cross-disciplinary Business Research, In Association with EuroMed Academy of Business). Palgrave Macmillan. https://doi.org/10.1007/978-3-030-76567-5_1

Thrassou, A., Uzunboylu, N., Efthymiou, L., Vrontis, D., Weber, Y., Shams, S. M. R., & Tsoukatos, E. (2022). Editorial introduction: Business under crises: Organizational adaptations. In D. Vrontis, A. Thrassou, Y. Weber, S. M. R. Shams, E. Tsoukatos, & L. Efthymiou (Eds.), *Business under crisis, Volume II: Organisational adaptations* (Palgrave Studies in Cross-disciplinary Business Research, In Association with EuroMed Academy of Business). Palgrave Macmillan. https://doi.org/10.1007/978-3-030-76575-0_1

Thrassou, A., Vrontis, D., Efthymiou, L., & Uzunboylu, N. (2022a). An overview of business advancement through technology: Markets and marketing in transition. In A. Thrassou, D. Vrontis, L. Efthymiou, Y. Weber, S. M. R. Shams, & E. Tsoukatos (Eds.), *Business advancement through technology, Volume I* (Palgrave Studies in Cross-disciplinary Business Research, In Association with EuroMed Academy of Business). Palgrave Macmillan. https://doi.org/10.1007/978-3-031-07769-2_1

Thrassou, A., Vrontis, D., Efthymiou, L., & Uzunboylu, N. (2022b). An overview of business advancement through technology: The changing landscape of work and employment. In A. Thrassou, D. Vrontis, L. Efthymiou, Y. Weber, S. M. R. Shams, & E. Tsoukatos (Eds.), *Business advancement through technology, Volume II* (Palgrave Studies in Cross-disciplinary Business Research, In Association with EuroMed Academy of Business). Palgrave Macmillan. https://doi.org/10.1007/978-3-031-07765-4_1

Van Cranenburgh, K. C., & Arenas, D. (2014). Strategic and moral dilemmas of corporate philanthropy in developing countries: Heineken in sub-Saharan Africa. *Journal of Business Ethics, 122*(3), 523–536.

Vrontis, D., Thrassou, A., Weber, Y., Riad Shams, S. M., Tsoukatos, E., & Efthymiou, L. (2022a). *Business under crisis, Volume III: Avenues for innovation, entrepreneurship and sustainability*. Palgrave Macmillan. https://doi.org/10.1007/978-3-030-76583-5

Vrontis, D., Thrassou, A., Weber, Y., Riad Shams, S. M., Tsoukatos, E., & Efthymiou, L. (2022b). *Business under crisis, Volume II: Organisational adaptations*. Palgrave Macmillan. https://doi.org/10.1007/978-3-030-76575-0

Correction to: Weak Sustainable Development Trajectories and Evolving Organisational Physiologies: Empirical Evidence from Greece

Dimos Chatzinikolaou and Charis Vlados

Correction to:

Chapter 10 in: D. Vrontis et al. (eds.), *Business for Sustainability, Volume I*, Palgrave Studies in Cross-disciplinary Business Research, In Association with EuroMed Academy of Business, https://doi.org/10.1007/978-3-031-37361-9_10

The original version of this book has been revised. The Chapter 10 author's last name has been corrected to "Dimos Chatzinikolaou".

The updated version of this chapter can be found at
https://doi.org/10.1007/978-3-031-37361-9_10

D. Vrontis et al. (eds.), *Business for Sustainability, Volume I*, Palgrave Studies in Cross-disciplinary Business Research, In Association with EuroMed Academy of Business, https://doi.org/10.1007/978-3-031-37361-9_13

Index

D. Vrontis et al. (eds.), *Business for Sustainability, Volume I*, Palgrave Studies in Cross-disciplinary Business Research, In Association with EuroMed Academy of Business, https://doi.org/10.1007/978-3-031-37361-9

GPSR Compliance

The European Union's (EU) General Product Safety Regulation (GPSR) is a set of rules that requires consumer products to be safe and our obligations to ensure this.

If you have any concerns about our products, you can contact us on ProductSafety@springernature.com

In case Publisher is established outside the EU, the EU authorized representative is:

Springer Nature Customer Service Center GmbH
Europaplatz 3
69115 Heidelberg, Germany

The manufacturer's authorised representative in the EU is Springer
Nature Customer Service Centre GmbH, Europaplatz 3, 69115 Heidelberg,
Germany. If you have any concerns regarding our products, please
contact ProductSafety@springernature.com

Printed and bound by CPI Group (UK) Ltd, Croydon, CR0 4YY
30/09/2026
02225311-0011